IMPLICIT LEARNING AND CONSCIOUSNESS

This controversial and much debated question forms the basis of this collection of essays as the authors discuss whether the measurable changes in behaviour that result from learning can ever remain unconscious. Three issues central to the topic of implicit learning are raised. Firstly, the extent to which learning can be unconscious, and therefore implicit, is considered. Secondly, theories are developed regarding the nature of knowledge acquired in implicit learning situations. Finally, the idea that there are two separable independent processing systems in the brain, for implicit and explicit learning, is considered.

Implicit Learning and Consciousness challenges conventional wisdom and presents the most up-to-date studies to define, quantify and test the predictions of the main models of implicit learning. The chapters include a variety of research from computer modelling, experimental psychology and neural imaging to the clinical data resulting from work with amnesics. The result is a topical book which provides an overview of the debate on implicit learning, and the various philosophical, psychological and neurological frameworks in which it can be placed. It will be of interest to undergraduates, postgraduates and the philosophical, psychological and modelling research community.

Robert M. French comes from a multi-disciplinary background that includes mathematics, translation, computer science and psychology. He is the author of a book on the computer modelling of analogy-making, and numerous publications on topics ranging from foundational issues in cognitive science to specialist areas such as categorisation and learning.

Axel Cleeremans is a cognitive psychologist, teaching at the Université Libre de Bruxelles where he heads the Cognitive Science Research Unit. His research is focused on the relationship between learning and consciousness, and he was the main organiser of the fourth annual meeting of the Association for the Scientific Study of Consciousness in 2000. He is also the author of a book on the mechanisms of implicit learning.

Implicit Learning and Consciousness

An empirical, philosophical and computational consensus in the making

edited by

Robert M. French
Department of Psychology
University of Liège

Axel Cleeremans
Cognitive Science Research Unit
Université Libre de Bruxelles

First published 2002 by Psychology Press
27 Church Road, Hove, East Sussex BN3 2FA

Simultaneously published in the USA and Canada
by Taylor & Francis
29 West 35th Street, New York, NY 10001

Psychology Press in an imprint of the Taylor & Francis Group

British Library Cataloguing in Publication Data
A catalogue record for this book is available from the British
Library

Library of Congress Cataloging-in-Publication Data

French, Robert M. (Robert Matthew), 1951–
    Implicit learning and consciousness : an empirical,
philosophical, and computational consensus in the making /
Robert M. French and Axel Cleeremans.
        p. cm. — (Frontiers of cognitive science)
    Includes bibliographical references and index.
    ISBN 1-84169-201-8
        1. Implicit learning. 2. Consciousness. I. Cleeremans,
    Axel. II. Title. III. Series.
    BF319.5.I45 F74 2002
    153.1'5—dc21
                                        2001048426

ISBN 1-84169-201-8

Typeset in Times by Mayhew Typesetting, Rhayader, Powys
Printed and bound in Great Britain by Biddles Ltd, Guildford and
King's Lynn
Cover design by Terry Foley at Anú Design

Contents

List of contributors

Nick Chater, Department of Psychology, University of Warwick, Coventry, CV4 7AL, UK
E-mail: nick.chater@warwick.ac.uk

Axel Cleeremans, Cognitive Science Research Unit, Université Libre de Bruxelles CP 122, Avenue F.-D. Roosevelt 50, 1050 Bruxelles, Belgium
E-mail: axcleer@ulb.ac.be

Zoltán Dienes, School of Biological Sciences, Experimental Psychology, University of Sussex, Falmer, Brighton BN1 9QG, UK
E-mail: dienes@biols.susx.ac.uk

Robert French, Quantitative Psychology and Cognitive Science, Psychology Department, University of Liège, 4000 Liège, Belgium
E-mail: rfrench@ulg.ac.be

Luis Jiménez, Facultad de Psicología, Universidad de Santiago, 15706 Santiago de Compostela, Spain
E-mail: jimenez@usc.es

Theresa Johnstone, Department of Psychology, University College London, 26 Bedford Way, London WC1E 6BT, UK
E-mail: Theresa.Johnstone@ir.gss.gov.uk

Annette Kinder, Psychology Department, Philipps-Universität, Marburg, Germany
E-mail: Kinder@mailer.uni-marburg.de

Thierry Meulemans, Neuropsychology Unit, University of Liège, 4000 Liège, Belgium
E-mail: thierry.meulemans@ulg.ac.be

Josef Perner, University of Salzburg, Hellbrunnerstrasse 34, A-5020 Salzburg, Austria
E-mail: Josef.Perner@sbg.ac.at

Pierre Perruchet, Universite de Bourgogne, LEAD/CNRS, 6 Boulevard Gabriel, 21000 Dijon, France
E-mail: pierre.perruchet@u-bourgogne.fr

Arthur Reber, Department of Psychology, Brooklyn College and the Graduate Center of the City University of New York, New York, USA
E-mail: AREBER@brooklyn.cuny.edu

Martin Redington, Department of Psychology, University College London, 26 Bedford Way, London WC1E 6BT, UK
E-mail: m.redington@ucl.ac.uk

David Shanks, Department of Psychology, University College London, 26 Bedford Way, London WC1E 6BT, UK
E-mail: d.shanks@ucl.ac.uk

Martial Van der Linden, Neuropsychology Unit, University of Liège, 4000 Liège, Belgium
E-mail: mvanderlinden@ulg.ac.be

Annie Vinter, Universite de Bourgogne, LEAD/CNRS, 6 Boulevard Gabriel, 21000 Dijon, France
E-mail: annie.vinter@u-bourgogne.fr

List of figures and tables

Foreword

I am delighted to be able to write the foreword for this collection of sterling papers on what has become one of cognitive psychology's most vigorously researched and vociferously debated topics. I feel a special kind of bond with the issues that have been raised by the contributors and, I hope, I will be excused a burst of nostalgia. Back in 1965, I turned in to the faculty at Brown University a Master's thesis with the title "Implicit learning of artificial grammars". It was not well received. The faculty at Brown were not alone in their misgivings. A long editorial battle ensued before the work was published (Reber, 1967) and, when it did arrive in print, it stirred few passions.

So, it is with considerable interest that I look back on my long involvement with the issue of implicit learning and muse over how much has changed. The fundamental question remains pretty much the same: How is knowledge of complex stimulus displays acquired, encoded, and utilised largely independent of conscious awareness of both the process and the products of acquisition? But the range of issues that has emerged surrounding this seemingly simple question seems to have no bounds and the debates that have been stimulated reach into areas far remote from anything envisioned three decades ago.

As forewords are largely unedited, I am going to take advantage of this opportunity and go on a bit of an intellectual wander. I think I understand why some of the issues that have emerged as points of dispute have stoked controversy and I hope I can provide an overview of why this particular volume is of such importance—and where we need to go from here. There seem to me to be several easily identifiable issues.

(1)   Does implicit learning exist as a non-trivial process? Let's assume that this one gets a thumbs-up from the psychological community. If it didn't, it would be hard to understand what all the fuss has been about. Better to have left that original paper buried in the dark recesses of the library, its pages yellowed and crumbling.

(2)   If we buy the argument that implicit learning *is* a non-trivial process, what exactly do we mean by this? Let's face it, no one doubts that our livers are doing their thing quite nicely without any top–down modulating efforts of consciousness. Surely stuff goes on that is outside of awareness. Now, where folks start getting a little testy is when it is suggested that these implicit processes might yield abstract representations with symbolic content. As John Kihlstrom has oft noted, there is something about the possibility of a smart unconscious that makes people uneasy.

One of my long-standing interests is the history of psychology. My rambles around this literature have convinced me that our discipline is nothing more (or less) than the bastard offspring of the union of philosophy and physiology. The physiological contribution made our science experimental and laboratory based. There is little controversy here and we are, for the most part, grateful for the emphasis.

The difficulties came from the other parent. The philosophical foundation that fostered us had two branches, a continental arm that traces itself back to Descartes and Leibniz and an off-shore line with roots in British empiricism, whose champions include, among others, Locke, Hume, and Berkeley. These two traditions didn't agree on much, that's for certain. One was dualistic, one monistic; one embraced volition and free will, the other determinism; one was romantic, the other naturalistic; one tilted toward nativism, the other environmentalism; one retarded the emergence of psychology as a distinct discipline, the other nurtured and stimulated it.

But there was one common theme: in both, consciousness and cognition were seen as coterminous. If some mental act were to be seen as cognitive, if some process or mechanism or the products of that process or mechanism could be viewed as part of the "higher mental processes", then you could be certain that it was available to consciousness and to introspection. The abstract and the symbolic were confined to the privileged realm of consciousness. The unconscious, the implicit, the procedural elements of human conduct were primitive, unthinking, elemental, and reflexive. The indubitable, in Descartes' famous stab at scepticism, was the conscious mind. And, as Daniel Dennett (1987) put it, to a Lockean the notion of unconscious thought was "incoherent, self-contradictory nonsense". From this point of view the notion that any interesting mental event could be opaque to consciousness was near heresy.

In a similar vein, it is my read on history that the criticism and abuse that was heaped upon Sigmund Freud's early work was not because of his infusing of sex and sexuality into every psychic corner, but was caused by his truly astonishing argument that the mind was not rational, that we were driven by base motives over which we had little control and which functioned very much outside the reach of normal consciousness. We have our history and it follows us.

(3)   Of course, in the end, the question of just how smart the implicit system is is, as we like to say, an empirical question. As our various authors suggest, we're still nowhere near a definitive answer. Otherwise there wouldn't be a need for this volume. So, while awaiting a final decision, I'd like to pose some questions.

How do children acquire language? What mechanisms guide the processes by which we become socialised? How do we learn to adapt to novel cultures and subcultures? How do we come to know and feel comfortable with highly complex stimulus domains such as those expressed in art, music, and literature? Through what system(s) does our sense of aesthetics develop? How do we formulate our hypotheses when we do science? How do we come to play complex games with high levels of skill?

It seems clear that implicit acquisitional mechanisms play a role in these varied domains. Whether it is a major role or a minor role is not always clear and, no doubt, the various forums will display distinct patterns. Natural language learning in children, particularly the syntactic components, is probably driven largely by implicit processes, as is early socialisation. The top–down, conscious modulating mechanisms just aren't in place yet. At the other end of this spectrum, becoming a successful scientist surely requires the development of sophisticated, consciously held knowledge bases—although the tacit dimension almost certainly plays a strong role. Interestingly, in both cases the representational products are abstract and symbolic.

(4)   What is the link between implicit learning and implicit memory? In more than a few places people treat them as equivalent, or nearly so. While it is certainly true that implicit learning typically yields implicit memories, it is not clear that the representations that are the focus of study in the typical implicit memory experiment are the same kind of mental critter that falls under the empirical microscope in the inquiries into implicit learning.

For the most part, the literature on implicit memory points to the conclusion that representations are fairly concrete in nature, leashed to the physical form of the input stimulus. As many have reported, if, in the prototypical implicit memory experiment, you degrade or modify superficial features of probe stimuli, performance is diminished. This result can be quite striking. The effect of implicitly held knowledge of a list of words drops off significantly with such trivial changes as changing the typeface in which they are presented during subsequent testing. Findings such as these have led to the conclusion that implicit memorial representations are relatively inflexible. And, as the hallmark of the abstract and the symbolic is that it is flexible, implicit memories must be non-abstract and non-symbolic.

If you feel the logic of this syllogism slipping, you're right. But it isn't just logic, there is a bigger problem, a methodological one. In the typical implicit memory experiment there is no "real" learning. Rather, episodic tags are put upon previously encoded knowledge. If you are presented with the word "alligator" in a list, your learning is restricted to the fact that "oh, okay, I'm supposed to remember that *alligator*, that greenish collection of teeth with legs and a bad attitude, is on the list this character wants me to memorise". And as virtually every subject will engage in some kind of mnemonicising (if you will allow this neologism), stored representations will tend to have an inflexible character and any change in format will, of necessity, reduce the later impact of the stored episode.

On the other hand, in the typical implicit learning setting, new knowledge *is* acquired. Arbitrary sequences are scanned and upcoming events anticipated, artificial grammars that display structural characteristics are learned and their representations used for decision making, melodic patterns are encoded and preference judgements are based upon them, phonetic sequences are captured and violations of underlying patterns are noticed. Infants, adults, the aged, the psychiatrically compromised, and the neurologically impaired all show these effects.

How the representations from these acquisitional experiences are formed is a complex issue but there are hints. A couple of years back, Lou Manza and I (Manza & Reber, 1997) showed that we could encourage abstract representations in an artificial grammar learning study simply by presenting the learning stimuli in two different instantiations. If you see strings like XXRTRXV and QQWMWQP—where individual letters have shared privileges of occurrence—it encourages representations that are not tied to the physical form of the inputs.

Assuming that the evidence for instantiated implicit representations from the implicit memory literature implies that all implicit representations are non-abstract and non-symbolic might not be the best way to approach this issue.

(5) We, like it or not, are the products of a dizzyingly complex evolutionary history. One pretty good heuristic that we need to keep in mind is that our theories of cognitive function need to make biological sense. Models of memory that assume unitary structures are problematical. It is virtually certain that the sophisticated consciousness that so fascinated

Descartes and Locke, and around which so much of our recent efforts turn, is an evolutionary Johnny-come-lately, having showed up about ten geological minutes ago. If it turns out that all the phylogenetically antecedent representational systems are inflexible and intimately tied to the physical form of the inputs, I'll be more than just surprised. Even *Aplysia californica* shows stimulus generalisation and my bet is that a frog's phenomenal visual experience is pretty much like that of a blindsight patient.

The patterns of covariation among the elements of the environments that we live in are under constant flux. Any representational system, even the most basic and cognitively unadorned, must be sensitive to these variations. And as implicit learning is essentially the detection of patterns of covariation among elements in stimulus displays (the one point that most of us do agree on), to be viable, the representational mechanism must be able to capture random adjustments in form and structure.

(6)   Finally, I wonder just exactly what do we mean when we maintain that a representation is abstract and/or symbolic? The term "abstract" comes from the Latin for "drawn away" and usage turns on the notion that for qualities of objects, events, or phenomena to be abstract is to regard them as separate from the specific objects, events, or phenomena themselves. "Symbolic" has a more checkered etymology but the essential notion is captured by a similar idea. An action, an idea, an utterance, a mental state can be regarded as symbolic if it signifies actions, ideas, utterances, or mental states beyond or distinct from those so denoted (Reber & Reber, 2001).

But neither of these notions has firm definitional boundaries. Being abstract is not like being pregnant. There's a lot of nuance here. In many experiments in implicit learning, representations are formed that have a measure of abstractness or symbolic content. We see this when we observe transfer of structural knowledge across stimulus domains, or when subjects mistakenly recognise unviewed prototypes as familiar, or when so many instances of a category pile up mentally that we lose track of specifics.

We don't want to be seduced by one of psychology's worst conceptual errors, the "polarity fallacy", where we go after our prey believing it be either one thing or another without appreciating that it is, in all likelihood, a bit of each. The abstract and the symbolic are dimensions along which representations can fall. Bruce Whittlesea has been counselling us for some time now to pay more attention to the demand characteristics of our experimental settings. I think he is right, and the arguments both for and against the formation of abstract representations are often unhelpful because of a misplaced search for "either/or" rather than "how much".

There are other points that still nag but I suspect I am beginning to wear out my welcome. Let me end by thanking both the editors of this superb collection for allowing me the privilege of writing this foreword, and the various authors for their often elegant and challenging arguments. It's been a really interesting couple of decades with, hopefully, more to come.

Arthur S. Reber
Brooklyn College and the Graduate
Center of the City University of New York

REFERENCES

Dennett, D.C. (1987). Consciousness. In G.L. Gregory (Ed.). *The Oxford companion to the mind* (pp. 161–164). New York: Oxford University Press.

Manza, L. & Reber, A.S. (1997). Representing artificial grammars: Transfer across stimulus forms and modalities. In D.C. Berry (Ed.) *How implicit is implicit learning?*. London: Oxford University Press.

Reber, A.S. (1967). Implicit learning of artificial grammars. *Journal of Verbal Learning and Verbal Behavior*, 6, 855–863.

Reber, A.S. & Reber, E.S. (1999). *Dictionary of psychology*, 3rd Edition. London: Penguin Books.

Introduction

Robert M. French
Department of Psychology, University of Liège, Belgium

Axel Cleeremans
Cognitive Science Research Unit, Université Libre de Bruxelles, Belgium

The study of consciousness spans a host of disciplines ranging from philosophy to neuroscience, from psychology to computer modelling. Arguments about consciousness run the gamut from tenuous, even ridiculous, thought experiments to the most rigorous neuroscientific experiments. This book offers a novel perspective on many fundamental issues about consciousness based on empirical, computational, and philosophical research on implicit learning—learning without conscious awareness of having learned.

There are many profound and interesting issues involving consciousness that fall within the purview of serious science. Indeed, the "search for the neural correlates of consciousness" has now become a major endeavour in the cognitive neurosciences, as evidenced by countless articles, major books, and scientific meetings. This spectacular renewed interest in the biological bases of consciousness can no doubt be attributed to the increasingly widespread availability of sophisticated brain imaging techniques, which, for the first time, make it possible to conduct detailed explorations of the correspondences between subjective (i.e. mental) and objective (i.e. neural) states. This empirical programme, however, cannot in and of itself answer all the questions one might have about consciousness. Consciousness, indeed, is a complex phenomenon that poses unique conceptual and methodological challenges. A first challenge is conceptual: How do we best characterise the various dimensions of consciousness? Consciousness is not a single thing but includes different dimensions, such as subjective experience, intentional control and attention, and self-consciousness. Whether these different dimensions of consciousness are dissociable, and whether or not they involve the same neural mechanisms, are questions that continue to elicit lively debate among philosophers, cognitive psychologists, and neuroscientists alike. A second challenge is methodological: How do we best differentiate between conscious and unconscious cognition? What operational criteria should we use to decide whether a subject is conscious of some aspect of a particular situation? To what extent is unconscious cognition possible?

As it turns out, implicit learning is one of the paradigms (along with subliminal perception) in which such issues have been explored most thoroughly. Because the field as a whole has been particularly concerned with the delicate methodological issues involved in attempting to establish relationships between subjective and objective measures of performance, it is also one of the most interesting paradigms through which to start exploring consciousness itself. This book is an attempt to come to grips with some of the most significant issues surrounding implicit learning and its relationship to conscious awareness. By bringing together a number of the most important figures in implicit learning research, we have attempted to present the major trends in the field and to show how these trends might gradually be converging towards a consensus. The methods involved in these explorations range from the philosophical to the clinical and from the experimental to the computational. As editors, we have resisted any attempt to select our authors based on any particular conceptual framework or point of view. Rather, we felt that it was important to present a broad spectrum of approaches to this fascinating area, with a specific focus on integrating contributions that address the three central issues raised by the large body of research on implicit learning, namely: (1) to what extent can learning be unconscious? (2) what is the nature of the knowledge acquired in implicit learning situations? and (3) to what extent should implicit and explicit learning be characterised as involving separable, independent processing systems?

The field of implicit learning can reasonably be said to begin with the publication of Arthur Reber's 1967 paper entitled "Implicit learning of artificial grammars". Reber himself begins our book with a series of reflections that not only cover the 35 years since his seminal paper appeared, but also identify what he considers to be the central issues that will set the agenda for future research in the field.

Axel Cleeremans and Luis Jiménez then attempt to develop an overall framework for implicit learning. Their central thesis is that mechanisms underlying both conscious and unconscious (i.e. explicit and implicit) learning are really the same and that it really is only a difference of degree that gives rise to one type of learning or the other. They regard the central function of conscious awareness to be an evolutionary adaptive means of providing us with flexible control of our behaviour. Given the importance of consciousness to their account of implicit/explicit learning, the authors spend a considerable amount of time discussing questions related to consciousness, in general, and computational accounts of consciousness, in particular. One of their central claims is that consciousness is not an all-or-nothing process, but is rather a multi-faceted, graded phenomenon. This contrasts rather sharply with one major perspective, represented in these pages, that denies the existence of unconscious mental representations. For Cleeremans and Jiménez there is an ongoing and interactive relationship between consciousness and learning. While they take a dynamic approach to learning, they are not hardcore advocates of a "dynamical systems" approach to cognition. Rather, they believe in the existence of graded, internal representations of an external reality, very much in keeping with the philosophy of the distributed neural network models that have been on the scene for the past two decades.

Cleeremans and Jiménez spell out the interaction between learning and consciousness and claim, significantly, that the extent to which a particular representation is available to consciousness depends on its quality (defined in terms of activation level, stability in time, and contextual distinctiveness), that learning gradually produces better adapted representations, and that the function of consciousness is to control those representations that are able to influence behaviour. They appeal to a "representation-quality" model of conscious awareness to make their case for implicit learning, to wit: If the quality of a learned representation is good enough, it is perceived consciously; if not, it will remain unconscious (and thus learning, in this case, will have been implicit). They describe an elegant experiment in which a technique called the Process Dissociation Procedure is used to show that learning remains largely implicit as long as the cognitive system is not given enough time to develop high quality representations. In summary, this chapter brings a large body of theoretical as well as empirical evidence to bear on their central claim that conscious and unconscious awareness—and the associated types of learning—merely represent different points on the same continuum of underlying neural mechanisms.

The pendulum swings back from Cleeremans and Jiménez's graded, dynamic stance to Pierre Perruchet and Annie Vinter's denial of unconscious mental representations. Their view is unambiguous in the extreme: "Processes and mechanisms responsible for the elaboration of knowledge are intrinsically unconscious, and the resulting mental representations and knowledge are intrinsically conscious. No other components are needed". In other words, at the heart of their position is the explicit refutation of the notion of unconscious representations. Perruchet and Vinter point to an overwhelming body of evidence that shows that attention to the initial sensory data is necessary for improved performance on implicit learning tests. But this would seem to lead to what appears to be a major paradox: Why should the initial coding of the sensory data require conscious attention whereas all the subsequent operations performed on those data require none?

They provide a two-fold answer to this question via the notion of self-organisation of perceptual experience and the results of a computational model, PARSER. They begin by showing how chunking and segmentation in an undifferentiated stream of utterances gradually emerges both in humans and in their model. One of their key claims is that the discovery of words results from the fact that "the probability of repeatedly selecting the same group of syllables by chance is higher if these syllables form intra-word rather than between-word components". They extend this principle of word segmentation to world segmentation and arrive, perhaps unwittingly, at a restatement of the underlying theoretical principle for the emergence of Roschian basic level categories—namely, that a basic level category is a category grouping where the ratio of inter-category variance to intra-category variance is maximised. Perruchet and Vinter suggest that this unconscious process of self-organisation of perceptual experience gives rise to conscious representations of sensory input. In short, implicit learning is better conceived of as a transformation of conscious experience through the action of elementary associative learning and memory processes acting on components of these experiences. In this respect at least, there is significant agreement between this framework and that of Cleeremans and Jiménez: Both proposals indeed assume that implicit learning shapes conscious experience.

The next chapter, authored by Zoltán Dienes and Josef Perner, returns the discussion to a more foundational level. Dienes and Perner are essentially concerned with developing a carefully crafted definitional framework for explicit and implicit learning, providing a detailed exploration of the relationships between representation, consciousness, metacognition and, of course, implicit/explicit learning. On the matter of representation, they adopt a functionalist stance: representations represent something because of the functional role they play in the cognitive economy. In this they follow Fred Dretske and claim that "A represents B just in case A has the function of indicating B". Dienes and Perner maintain that this definition of representation is broad enough to encompass what cognitive scientists generally mean by representation. (Later in their chapter they tackle the harder question of what makes certain representations conscious and others not.) Based on this definition, they delineate explicit from implicit representations as follows: "Any environmental feature or state of affairs that is not explicitly represented but forms part of the representational content is represented implicitly". The idea here is that when learning a piece of knowledge, K, any information that is a necessary supporting fact of K, but is not present explicitly in K, is implicit knowledge. Thus, implicit in the fact that "Bill is a bachelor", is the necessary supporting fact that Bill is male, even though this is not explicitly represented in the original statement.

The authors then go on to clarify the notion of explicit representation and suggest three levels of explicitness, tying them to consciousness by means of second-order knowing, i.e. knowing that we know. For them, a second-order thought is always necessary for conscious awareness of an event and fully explicit knowledge is necessary for any knowledge to be conscious knowledge. They show how the distinction between declarative knowledge and procedural knowledge fits into this framework. Next, two types of voluntary control are introduced and related to metacognition, the essence of which, they believe, consists of monitoring and control. This then gives them a yardstick by which to judge implicitness: implicit processes essentially lack various degrees of metacognition, while explicit processes centrally involve metacognition. Finally, the authors define implicit learning within the framework they have built up: Implicit learning is a type of learning that results in knowledge "which is not labelled as knowledge by the act of learning itself", whereas explicit learning results in knowledge that is so labelled. In short, explicit learning produces conscious, fully explicit knowledge; implicit learning produces knowledge of which we are unaware. Importantly, Dienes and Perner bring a wealth of experimental data to buttress their claims and distinctions. Unlike Perruchet and Vinter, they firmly believe that implicit representations, even though they do not constitute conscious knowledge, can control action.

In the next chapter David Shanks, Theresa Johnstone, and Annette Kinder introduce an "episodic-processing account" of implicit learning. This chapter amounts to a frontal assault on dual-system accounts of learning that assume the existence of separate learning systems for implicit (general, abstract, procedural) knowledge and explicit (episodic, specific, declarative) knowledge. They begin by laying out four major claims of proponents of dual-system theories. Their episodic-processing account is then compared to rule-abstraction accounts of learning, and areas in which these accounts disagree are pinpointed. Specifically, these differences involve whether we process episodes or use rules, as well as the degree to which the test instructions elicit an implicit or explicit expression of the knowledge.

They consider possible forms of knowledge that could be used in classification and recognition tasks, starting with abstract-rule knowledge and evidence for it from cross-modality transfer results. The authors reject these results, claiming that ultimately there is little, if any, evidence for cross-modality transfer. They move on to strict exemplar-based accounts of knowledge in which classification of new items is achieved based on their similarity in memory to specific stored training examples. Next, they examine the notion that participants learn about the frequency of occurrence of fragments (two- and three-letter strings) in the training strings and classify new strings based on these fragments. Finally, evidence that classification is done by a combination of rules and fragments of knowledge is briefly reviewed.

The introduction of Shanks and colleagues' episodic-processing framework follows. This account suggests: (1) that processing knowledge is acquired in addition to structural knowledge of the training stimuli; (2) that training instructions significantly influence how the training items are encoded; and (3) that the same knowledge can be used either implicitly or explicitly depending how this knowledge was acquired. In particular, on this account, participants learn the particular aspects of the stimuli that are relevant to the task they are engaged in, which provides affordances for subsequent, related tasks.

Finally, the authors consider the case for the existence of two distinct learning systems, based on a particular dissociation in amnesics—namely, that it has been shown repeatedly that, while amnesics' declarative memory may be poor, their non-declarative memory frequently remains largely intact. The authors point out a number of problems with Knowlton and Squire's well-known 1993 study of amnesics that led them to argue for a dual-memory system. Shanks and his colleagues then point to two single-system models capable of reproducing the dissociations that Knowlton and Squire observed. The first single-system model they discuss is Nosofsky's Generalized Context Model, followed by their own model, an Elman network, that also shows this dissociation. Their model shows excellent fit to data and they conclude, reasonably, that a dual-memory system is not necessary to account for the amnesic dissociation data.

Martin Redington and Nick Chater consider the notion of knowledge representation and transfer in their chapter. They begin by reviewing what is normally meant by "transfer" in the artificial grammar learning (hereafter, AGL) paradigm. They continue by suggesting that transfer effects, which they acknowledge exist, are construed by most of the AGL community to demonstrate that the knowledge learned is represented in terms of rules encoded in a "surface-independent" format (i.e. not in its original form, but rather in an abstract form). The authors take issue with this claim, and argue instead that surface-independence and rule-based knowledge are orthogonal concepts. They go on to identify three distinct kinds of representation in the AGL literature—namely, knowledge of whole exemplars, knowledge of fragments of the training items, and rule-based knowledge. Their claim is that all three kinds of knowledge can, in principle, be tied either to a particular kind of surface encoding or, alternatively, can be encoded in a surface-independent manner. In other words, the manner of encoding is independent of type of knowledge encoded.

Transfer and surface-independent encoding is then discussed at length, accompanied by various accounts of transfer, for each of which Redington and Chater show that the knowledge acquired is bound to the original surface form of the training items. They tie this to the broader issue of knowledge representation in AGL and reiterate their claim that the mere existence of transfer does not necessarily imply that the knowledge learned is encoded in a surface-independent manner. They point to both empirical as well as computational studies that emphasise the importance, possibly the necessity, of surface-based knowledge encoding. The authors then discuss in detail an early experiment by Arthur Reber that purported to show strong evidence for surface-independent knowledge. However, the authors were unable to replicate Reber's results in two separate experiments and they conclude, modestly, that their results leave Reber's findings "open to question". In summary, their results show that "once the surface form of the materials is changed, any memorisation advantage for previous expo- sure to the grammar disappears", which argues strongly against surface- independent encoding of knowledge under normal implicit learning conditions.

Redington and Chater then review the question of surface-independent knowledge acquisition being dependent on the context of learning and the age of acquisition of the knowledge. They accept that, under certain specific conditions, surface-independent knowledge acquisition might be possible. They conclude with a discussion of "lazy" and "eager" learning in which the learner stores information, in the former case, largely in unprocessed form and, in the latter, actively attempts to extract regularities from new items. According to the authors, it is likely that we use some mixture of these two learning processes when acquiring new information from our environment. They argue that if these processes are active for learning, in general, they are probably active for implicit learning in particular. They conclude this chapter with the suggestion that, possibly, the ability to find abstract regularities (i.e. surface-independent encoding) could obtain in adults using more natural, speech-like materials.

Finally, the book concludes with an empirically oriented, clinical chapter by Thierry Meulemans and Martial Van der Linden. The main purpose of their chapter is to present data obtained from amnesic patients that bear on the debate about the implicit versus explicit nature of knowledge acquired in implicit learning tasks. Specifically, these patients are dramatically impaired for explicit (episodic) memory tasks, while their performance on implicit memory tasks, such as AGL and serial reaction time tasks, is largely preserved. In addition to their review of the literature on implicit learning in amnesia, the authors also present a study in which they explore the implicit learning abilities of amnesic patients by using an AGL task in which the test strings were constructed in such a way that grammaticality judgements could not be based on superficial features of the learning strings. They also investigate the validity of an explicit sequence generation task in order to assess the explicit knowledge acquired in an artificial grammar learning task. Using the AGL paradigm, the authors show that amnesic patients and controls performed at the same level during the classification task, whereas amnesic patients performed worse than controls on the generation task. Their results also showed that performance in the generation task is directly related to information learned during the study phase, and not to information presented during the classification phase. Moreover, there was no correlation between the implicit and explicit measures. These results are compatible with the hypothesis of the existence of two different kinds of representation in artificial grammar learning: the first based on processes involving fragment-specific knowledge (the chunks, which can be accessed explicitly), the second based on the learning of simple associations and more complex conditional relations between elements. Patients' performance on the classification task depends primarily on this latter mechanism, which seems to be preserved in amnesia and which can therefore be considered as being implicit.

In conclusion, we hope to have convinced our readers of the importance of a broad, multidisciplinary approach to the study of implicit learning and consciousness. We believe that new tools, in particular neural imaging and sophisticated neural network models implemented on ever more powerful computers, will bring us closer to a consensus on precisely what is meant by implicit learning, on how to best measure it, and on its relation to consciousness. This book represents a small step in that direction.

ACKNOWLEDGEMENTS

The editors would especially like to thank Tim Valentine and Vivien Ward for their contribution to the negotiations that made this book possible in the first place. Thanks to Rachel Brazil for actually getting the book into production. We would also like to acknowledge the support of the University of Liège, the Belgian Fund for Scientific Research (FNRS), and a grant from the Belgian government, IAUP 4-19, that made possible the 1998 Implicit Memory and Learning Workshop at the University of Liège, where the idea to bring out this book originated. Finally, we would like to acknowledge the generous support of the European Commission through grant HPRN-CT-2000-00065 to Robert French. Axel Cleeremans is a Research Associate of the National Fund for Scientific Research (Belgium).

Robert M. French
Axel Cleeremans
Liège, Brussels, May 2001

CHAPTER ONE

Implicit learning and consciousness: A graded, dynamic perspective

Axel Cleeremans
Cognitive Science Research Unit, Université Libre de Bruxelles, Belgium

Luis Jiménez
Facultad de Psicologia, Universidad de Santiago, Spain

INTRODUCTION

Although the study of implicit learning is nothing new, the field as a whole has come to embody—over the last decade or so—ongoing questioning about three of the most fundamental debates in the cognitive sciences: (1) the nature of consciousness; (2) the nature of mental representation (in particular the difficult issue of abstraction); and (3) the role of experience in shaping the cognitive system. Our main goal in this chapter is to offer a framework that attempts to integrate current thinking about these three issues in a way that specifically links consciousness with adaptation and learning. Our assumptions about this relationship are rooted in further assumptions about the nature of processing and of representation in cognitive systems. When considered together, we believe that these assumptions offer a new perspective on the relationships between conscious and unconscious processing and on the function of consciousness in cognitive systems.

To begin in a way that reflects the goals of this volume, we can ask the question: "What is implicit learning for?" In asking this question, one presupposes that implicit learning is a special process that can be distinguished from, say, explicit learning or, even more pointedly, from learning *tout court*. The most salient feature attributed to implicit learning is, of course, that it is implicit, by which most researchers in the area actually mean unconscious. Hence the question "What is implicit learning for?" is in

1

fact a way of asking about the function of consciousness in learning that specifically assumes that conscious and unconscious learning have different functions. The central idea that we will develop in this chapter is that conscious and unconscious learning are actually two different expressions of a single set of constantly operating graded, dynamic processes of adaptation. Although this position emphasises that conscious and unconscious processing differ only in degree rather than in kind, it is nevertheless not incompatible with the notion that consciousness has specific functions in the cognitive economy.

Indeed, our main conclusion will be that the function of consciousness is to offer flexible adaptive control over behaviour. By adaptive, here, we do not mean simply the possibility for an agent to select one course of action among several possibilities. This, as dozens of computer programs routinely demonstrate, can be achieved without consciousness. Instead, we assume that genuine flexibility necessarily involves phenomenal consciousness (subjective experience), to the extent that successful adaptation in cognitive systems seems to make it mandatory that behavioural changes be based on the rewarding or punishing qualia they are associated with. There would be no point, for instance, in avoiding dangerous behaviour were it not associated with feelings of danger. Learning is thus necessarily rooted, we believe, in the existence of at least some primitive ability for cognitive agents to experience the consequences of their behaviour and to recreate these experiences independently of action. These primitive experiences can then, through more elaborate learning and developmental processes, become integrated into increasingly complex structures that include representations of the self, that is, into a set of representations and processes that enable an agent to entertain a third-person perspective on itself, or, in other words, to look upon itself as though it were another agent. We surmise that any information-processing system that is sufficiently complex to make such processes possible should be characterised as conscious—albeit we might never find out unless this system exhibits the only sort of consciousness that we know of first-hand, that is, human consciousness. We will not discuss this important epistemic debate any further short of noting: (1) that it actually is what the Turing Test is about (see French, 2000, for further discussion of the Turing Test); and (2) that it is perfectly possible to develop simulations of some behaviour that successfully mimics adaptation without requiring qualia, but then, presumably, only at a level of description that would fail to pass more elaborate testing.

Our primary goal in this chapter will thus be to outline a novel framework with which to think about the relationships between learning and consciousness. In the next section, "Adaptation, adaptive changes, and learning", we propose to define learning as "a set of philogenetically advanced adaptation processes that critically depend on an evolved sensitivity to subjective experience so as to enable agents to afford flexible control over their actions in complex, unpredictable environments". We continue by discussing the implications of such a definition of learning on current debates about: (1) the nature of phenomenal experience (in the third section, "Consciousness"); and (2) the functions of consciousness in cognitive systems (in the fourth section, "The function of consciousness"). In the next section, "The framework", we turn to an overview of our own proposal. We continue by briefly illustrating how our framework can be used to understand diverse phenomena in domains such as priming, implicit learning, automaticity and skill acquisition, or development ("Implications"). We conclude the chapter, in which we consider issues that the framework does not address. We should add that this chapter is by no means intended to offer a complete overview of all relevant phenomena and theories, but rather to convey the flavour of what we believe to be an alternative framework in which to consider some of the central issues in the domain of implicit learning.

ADAPTATION, ADAPTIVE CHANGES, AND LEARNING

Mounting evidence suggests not only that the brain is far more plastic than previously thought, but also that the effects of learning can be tracked all the way down to the organisation of local connectivity. To wit: Expert string players exhibit larger-than-normal areas of the somatosensory cortex dedicated to representing input from the fingering digits (Elbert, Pantey, Wienbruch, Rockstroh, & Taub, 1995). Likewise, not only is posterior hippocampus—a region of the brain involved in episodic and spatial memory—enlarged in experienced taxi drivers compared to subjects who do not have extensive experience in memorising complex maps, but the observed size differences further depend on the amount of driving experience (Maguire et al., 2000). There is also considerable evidence that the brain can recover in various flexible ways after trauma, and even suggestions that the very organisation of the somatosensory cortex (the famous Penfied homunculus) depends on prenatal sensory experience (Farah, 1998). More recently, suggestive evidence for neurogenesis was also found in humans (Eriksson et al., 1998), a finding that overturned decades of unquestioned—but, as it turns out, erroneous—assumptions about the lack of regenerative cellular processes in the adult brain. These often spectacular findings all reassert that adaptation plays a fundamental role in cognition, and that its effects can be traced all the way down to the manner in which specific neural circuits are organised.

Given this plethora of new findings hinting that the brain adapts constantly to the environment that it is immersed in, what can we say about the relationships between learning and consciousness? Should we consider processes of adaptation in general to be distinct from processes of learning? Is it the case, as some authors contend (see Chapter 2 and also Shanks & St John, 1994) that learning is always accompanied by conscious awareness? One can ask the question in another way: Why *should* behaviour always be available to conscious control? It might seem particularly adaptive for complex organisms to be capable of behaviour that does not require conscious control, for instance because behaviour that does not require monitoring of any kind can be executed faster or more efficiently than behaviour that does require such control. Reflexes such as withdrawing one's hand from a fire are good instances of behaviours that have presumably evolved to the point that they have been incorporated in the functional architecture of an organism's central nervous system and cannot be controlled any longer (or perhaps, only with extensive training on self-control techniques).

The relative accessibility of different actions to conscious awareness suggests that an important distinction between adaptation in general and learning is, precisely, the extent to which consciousness accompanies each. Learning, according to many standard definitions (e.g. Anderson, 1995; Klein, 1991; Tarpy, 1997), constitutes a subset of philogenetically advanced adaptation processes that are characteristic of so-called "cognitive systems", and through which relatively permanent and generally adaptive changes in the behaviour or dispositions of the organism arise as the result of their previous "experiences" with the environment in which they are immersed. From such a definition, it follows that the distinction between learning phenomena and the superordinate class of adaptation phenomena to which they belong depends on the "cognitive" status of the systems in which such learning occurs, and on the ability of these systems to enjoy a particular kind of sensitivity—"experience". Thus, however many reasons there might be to consider adaptation and learning as fundamentally rooted in the same mechanisms, we do not think that learning can simply be equated with adaptation. Adaptation, indeed, is a very broad concept. When taken to its limit, it might be used to refer to any dynamic relationship between an object and its environment through which: (1) the object changes its states and dispositions; (2) the object does this as a result of its prior sensitivity to the environment; and (3) the object does it in a way that continuously modifies this sensitivity. It should be clear that, by this definition, even inanimate objects such as rocks, thermostats, or computer programs all exhibit patterns of adaptation. Indeed, erosion in rocks, the switch of a relay in a thermostat, or the occurrence of specific digital states in computers, can all be characterised as adaptive "responses" to changing environmental conditions, to the extent that they modify the systems' future sensitivity to the re-occurrence of the same environmental conditions. In living systems, these processes of adaptation are further subject to continuous evolution on a species basis through the laws of natural selection.

Is it reasonable to consider such processes as processes of learning? Consider again standard definitions of learning. What, exactly, in these definitions, does "experience" refer to? Should our "experiences" as human beings be considered as similar to those of stones and amoebas? Certainly not. However, the literature about learning is in general conspicuously prone to conflate the term "experience" with any other kind of phenomenally neutral sensitivity that produces relatively permanent and adaptive changes in the responses of a system. For instance, even though neither machines nor neurovegetative systems are generally considered to be endowed with subjective experience, there is at least one journal that is entirely devoted to "Machine Learning". It is also relatively easy to find articles in psychological journals in which the changes produced in our neurovegetative systems in response to their environment are analysed as examples of learning (Ader & Cohen, 1985).

While this conflation between "experience" and "mere sensitivity" has had the merit of emphasising that there is a continuity between the processes of change that occur in different natural or artificial systems, it also blurs the distinction between learning and adaptation phenomena in general. In so doing, it has also further contributed to doing away with the distinction between cognitive and non-cognitive systems. Dennett (1996), in particular, has made this conflation completely explicit by assuming that the differences between cognitive and non-cognitive systems (e.g. between most animals and plants) might be only in the eye of the beholder. Indeed, according to Dennett, the main difference between animals and plants is that we tend to adopt an intentional stance when analysing animals' behaviour but do not do so when it comes to understand the dynamics of plant adaptation. As he boldly puts it, there is no reason to dispute the claims that plants should be considered as extremely slow animals whose "experiences" are overlooked because of our "temporal scale" chauvinism (Dennett, 1996) and that libraries should be viewed as cognitive systems that use researchers as tools to reproduce themselves (Dennett, 1991).

While this conclusion strikes many of us as bluntly absurd, perhaps its absurdity should be taken as an indication that we need to revisit the notion of "experience" and, in so doing, attempt to carefully delineate what it entails. Indeed, if learning is a fundamental element of what it takes for a system to be "cognitive" (Dretske, 1988), it might also be the case that the nature of the phenomenal states upon which learning operates is essential to distinguish it from other processes of adaptation. This analysis thus forces us to look into the nature of phenomenal experience in some detail. That is what we attempt to do in the next section.

CONSCIOUSNESS

What is consciousness? While it would be foolish even to attempt to answer this question in this chapter, it might nevertheless be useful to offer guidelines about the sorts of explanations we are looking for, and about which of these are relevant to the study of implicit learning. In the following, we briefly discuss three aspects of consciousness that often tend to be overlooked in discussions of implicit learning: (1) the fact that consciousness is not a unitary phenomenon; (2) the fact that consciousness is graded; and (3) the fact that consciousness is dynamic.

Consciousness is not a unitary phenomenon

Consciousness is not a unitary concept but instead includes different dimensions. Block (1995), for instance, distinguishes between access consciousness, phenomenal consciousness, monitoring consciousness, and self consciousness. Everybody agrees that the most problematic aspect of consciousness is phenomenal consciousness, or subjective experience, that is, the fact that information processing is accompanied by qualia—elements of conscious imagery, feelings, or thoughts that together appear in our mind to form a coherent impression of the current state of affairs.

   In the specific context of research about implicit learning, the central question is thus: Can changes in behaviour occur without correlated changes in subjective experience, and are these changes best characterised as mere adaptation or as learning? This, at it turns out, is also one of the central questions in the ongoing "search for the neural correlates of consciousness" (Crick & Koch, 1990) that has been the focus of so much recent empirical research about consciousness in the cognitive neurosciences. In an excellent overview, Frith, Perry, and Lumer (1999) have suggested organising paradigms through which to study the "neural correlates of consciousness" in nine groups resulting from crossing two dimensions: (1) three classes of psychological process involving, respectively, knowledge of the past, present, and future—memory, perception, and action; and (2) three types of cases where subjective experience is incongruent with the objective situation—cases where subjective experience fails to reflect changes in either (i) the stimulation or (ii) the behaviour, and (iii) cases where subjective experience changes whereas stimulation and behaviour remain constant.

   The paradigmatic example of the third situation is binocular rivalry, in which an unchanging compound stimulus consisting of two elements, each presented separately and simultaneously to each eye, produces spontaneously alternating complete perceptions of each element. By asking participants to indicate which stimulus they perceive at any moment, one can then hope to establish which regions of the brain exhibit activity that correlates with subjective experience and which do not, in a situation where the actual stimulus remains unchanged. Frith et al. go on by delineating many other relevant empirical paradigms involving both normal subjects and patients suffering from a variety of neuropsychological syndromes. While reviewing these different paradigms in detail goes far beyond the scope of this chapter, it is interesting to note that implicit learning, in their analysis, constitutes one example of cases where subjective experience remains constant while behaviour changes. The study of implicit learning is thus highly relevant to the study of consciousness in general.

In addition to the well-known difficult challenges involved in designing empirical paradigms suitable for the exploration of differences between conscious and unconscious processing (see Cleeremans, 1997, for an overview of these issues), the study of consciousness also notoriously involves a great deal of conceptual issues. In this respect, it is worth pointing out that current theories of consciousness make sometimes very contrasted assumptions about its underlying mechanisms. For instance, Farah (1994) proposed to distinguish between three types of neuroscientific accounts of consciousness: "Privileged Role" accounts, "Integration" accounts, and "Quality of Representation" accounts. "Privileged Role" accounts take their roots in Descartes' thinking and assume that consciousness depends on the activity of specific brain systems whose function it is to produce subjective experience. "Integration" accounts, in contrast, assume that consciousness depends only on processes of integration, through which the activity of different brain regions can be synchronised or made coherent so as to form the contents of subjective experience. Finally, "Quality of Representation" accounts assume that consciousness depends on particular properties of neural representations, such as their strength or stability in time.

In a recent overview article (Atkinson, Thomas, & Cleeremans, 2000; see also O'Brien & Opie, 1999), we proposed to organise computational theories of consciousness along two dimensions: (1) a *process* versus *representation* dimension, which opposes models that characterise consciousness in terms of specific processes operating over mental representations to models that characterise consciousness in terms of intrinsic properties of mental representations; and (2) a *specialised* versus *nonspecialised* dimension, which contrasts models that posit information-processing systems dedicated to consciousness with models for which consciousness can be associated with any information-processing system, as long as this system has the relevant properties. Farah's three categories can be subsumed in this analysis in the following manner: "Privileged Role" models, which assume that some brain systems play a specific role in subtending consciousness, are specialised models that can be instantiated either through vehicle or through process principles; "Quality of Representation" models, on the other hand, are typical vehicle theories in that they emphasise that what makes some representations available to conscious experience are properties of those representations rather than their functional role; finally, "Integration" models are examples of non-specialised theories, which can again be either instantiated in terms of the properties of the representations involved or in terms of the processes that engage these representations.

Atkinson et al.'s (2000) analysis thus offers four broad categories of computational accounts of consciousness:

(1) *Specialised vehicle theories*: assume that consciousness depends on the properties of representations that are located within a specialised system in the brain. An example of such accounts is Atkinson and Shiffrin's (1971) model of short-term memory, which specifically assumes that representations contained in the short-term memory store (a specialised system) become conscious only if they are sufficiently strong (a property of representations).

(2) *Specialised process theories*: assume that consciousness arises from specific computations that occur in a dedicated mechanism, as in Schacter's (1989) Conscious Awareness System (CAS) model. Shacter's model indeed assumes that the CAS's main function is to integrate inputs from various domain-specific modules and to make this information available to executive systems. It is therefore a specialised model in that it assumes that there exist specific regions of the brain whose function it is to make their contents available to conscious awareness. It is a process model to the extent that any representation that enters the CAS will become available to conscious awareness in virtue of the processes that manipulate these representations, and not in virtue of properties of those representations themselves.

(3) *Non-specialised vehicle theories*: include any model that posits that availability to consciousness depends only on properties of representations, regardless of where in the brain these representations exist. O'Brien and Opie's (1999) "connectionist theory of phenomenal experience" is the prototypical example of this category, to the extent that it specifically assumes that any stable neural representation will both be causally efficacious and form part of the contents of phenomenal experience.

(4) *Non-specialised process theories*: assume that representations become conscious whenever they are engaged by certain specific processes, regardless of where these representations exist in the brain. Most recent proposals fall into this category. Examples include Tononi and Edelman's (1998) "dynamic core" model; Crick and Koch's (1995) idea that synchronous firing constitutes the primary mechanisms through which disparate representations become integrated as part of a unified conscious experience; and Grossberg's (1999) characterisation of

consciousness as involving processes of "resonance" through which representations that simultaneously receive bottom–up and top–down activation become conscious because of their stability and strength.

While most recent neurocomputational models of consciousness fall into the last category, several proposals also tend to be somewhat more hybrid, instantiating features and ideas from several of the categories described by Atkinson et al. (2000). Baars' influential "Global Workspace" model (Baars, 1988), for instance, incorporates features from specialised process models as well as from non-specialised vehicle theories, to the extent that the model assumes that consciousness involves a specialised system (the global workspace), but also characterises conscious states in terms of the properties associated with their representations (i.e. global influence and widespread availability) rather than in terms of the processes that operate on these representations. Likewise, Dehaene and Naccache's recent "neural work-space" framework (Dehaene & Naccache, 2001) assumes that consciousness depends: (1) on the existence of a distributed system of long-range connectivity that links many different specialised processing modules in the brain; and (2) on the simultaneous bottom–up and top–down activation of the representations contained in the linked modules. Thus, this model acknowledges both the existence of specific, dedicated mechanisms to support consciousness and the specific properties of representations (e.g. their strength or stability) brought about by specific processes (e.g. resonance).

These various tentative accounts of the neural or computational mechanisms of consciousness are highly relevant to the study of implicit learning because any theory of the mechanisms through which implicit learning occurs necessarily also has to make corresponding assumptions about the mechanisms of consciousness. As we shall see later (pp. 12–14), however, most existing theories of implicit learning tend to be rather mute about their implications with respect to the study of consciousness. Indeed, most of the debate in the psychological literature about the relationships between conscious and unconscious processing has been dedicated to addressing methodological rather than conceptual issues. While these methodological debates are of central importance, we also believe that addressing the conceptual issues is essential.

Consciousness is graded

A second central aspect of conscious experience—and one that is also particularly relevant for behavioural studies of implicit cognition—is that consciousness is not an all-or-none process or property but that it affords many degrees and components. Conscious experience, however unified it appears to us, is not a single thing. Any theory of consciousness therefore has to answer questions about how the various elements of conscious experience are integrated with each other so as to form a unified whole, and about how to best think about the relative complexity of different sorts of conscious experiences. In other words: How does one go from the simple experiences that a snail might enjoy of its surroundings to the considerably more complex experience produced by your reading these words? How does one account for the differences between the sort of consciousness that infants undoubtedly possess to the sort of verbally rich consciousness that adults enjoy? Process and vehicle theories of consciousness make very different assumptions about these questions. For O'Brien and Opie (1999), for instance, the graded character of conscious experience is readily accommodated by vehicle theories, to the extent that properties of representations such as strength or stability in time can easily be mapped onto corresponding degrees or components of conscious awareness. This mapping is somewhat more delicate for what we have called process theories, even though at first sight these appear to offer an appealing set of conceptual principles with which to understand how conscious experience can increase in complexity through development or learning.

Dienes and Perner (1999) have recently pursued this goal in their theory of explicit and implicit knowledge, and "higher-order thought" (HOT) theories of consciousness in general can be described as relying on this principle (e.g. Rosenthal, 1986, 1997). However, what is harder to accept from such accounts of subjective experience is that its phenomenal character could be brought about in the first place from a series of computational processes performed on otherwise non-phenomenal representations. Indeed, and however much one might disagree with the specific way in which this thought experiment was framed, Searle's Chinese Room argument showed us more than 20 years ago that the phenomenal properties of experience seem not to be the sort of stuff that one might expect to obtain by mere shuffling of formal representations or symbols, no matter how convoluted, recurrent, or complex the relation among these symbols may turn out to be (Searle, 1980, 1992, 1999). Neither semantics nor phenomenal experience can emerge out of syntax. Symbols need to be grounded. Hence, if this intuition is right, a pure process theory could never tell us the last word in accounting for the first principles of consciousness.

Vehicle theories, it therefore appears, seem to be the best candidates to account for the emergence of the first elements of subjective experience which, through processes of learning, development, and socialisation, subsequently provide the appropriate foundations for the emergence of more elaborated forms of consciousness. It must be made clear at this point that by "vehicle theories" we refer to any theory that assumes that experience is not merely a relational or syntactic property that could be realised through any representational vehicle, but that claims instead that experience arises in a specific medium (e.g. neural) and as a result of processes that are proper to this medium.[1]

Consciousness is dynamic

For the sake of discussion, let us simply accept that phenomenal experience arises as the result of some neural processes. What, then, might be the functions fulfilled by phenomenal experience? What is it about experience that makes it play a special role in distinguishing between learning and mere adaptation? These questions are in fact questions about a third aspect of consciousness, that is, its dynamical character. Most discussions of consciousness tend to analyse it as a static property of some processes or representational states. However, it is obvious that consciousness is a phenomenon that is highly dynamical: What I am aware of now I might be unaware of at the next moment. Likewise, what I am aware of at some point in time when learning a new skill is not identical with what I will be aware of after I have mastered the skill. Thus, we believe that processes of change are central to our understanding of consciousness, and that an analysis of its possible functions should therefore be rooted in an analysis of the role that learning and adaptation play in shaping action.

THE FUNCTION OF CONSCIOUSNESS: COMMANDER DATA MEETS THE ZOMBIES

The findings briefly overviewed on page 3 raise the question of what the role of consciousness might be in adaptation and learning. We concluded that a significant difference between adaptation and learning is whether or not consciousness is involved. In this section, we attempt to reflect upon the function that consciousness might have in information processing. In so doing, we suggest that most existing theories of the relationships between conscious and unconscious processing have simply failed to give consciousness a clear functional role.

In a recent overview article, Dehaene and Naccache (2001, p. 31) conclude that "The present view associates consciousness with a unified neural workspace through which many processes can communicate. The evolutionary advantages that this system confers to the organism may be related to the increased independence that it affords". Dehaene and Naccache thus suggest that consciousness allows organisms to free themselves from acting out their intentions in the real world, relying instead on less hazardous

---

[1] This does not necessarily imply that artificial consciousness is not possible, but simply that the relevant processes cannot consist simply of symbol manipulation.

simulation made possible by the neural workspace. While we certainly agree with this conclusion, it begs the question of how consciousness came to play these functions in the first place. Are there any adaptive or evolutionary causes that would favour the emergence of unifying control systems characterised by conscious states, and that could go beyond what local adaptive processes can do by forcing large parts of the nervous system to work together in a coherent direction for some fractions of seconds? How can these coherent, resonant, synchronous, reverberant, or otherwise conscious states of the system come to reflect the most adaptive representation of the current situation, given that "what is most adaptive" continuously changes?

As discussed by Perruchet and Vinter (Chapter 2), the answers to these questions are intimately related to the dynamics between learning and consciousness: On the one hand, phenomenal consciousness provides the cognitive system with an adapted, global representation of the current situation so that learning mechanisms operate on the best possible representations. On the other hand, learning changes these representations in increasingly adaptive ways. From this perspective, then, the central function of consciousness is to offer flexible, adaptive control over behaviour.

This complex, dynamical relationship between consciousness and learning has, however, often tended to be overlooked in classical models of cognition. As argued in Cleeremans (1997) and also in Jiménez and Cleeremans (1999), this is most likely due to the fact that classical models of cognition (the "Computational Theory of Mind", see Fodor, 1975) take it as a starting point that cognition is symbol manipulation. As we will try to highlight in the next few paragraphs, we surmise that if one takes cognition to be exclusively and exhaustively about symbol manipulation, then there are but a few conceptual possibilities with which to think about differences between conscious and unconscious states.

Cognitive scientists concerned with the relation between consciousness and cognition generally tend to oscillate between two extreme (and admittedly caricatural) positions, which we have dubbed "Commander Data" and "Zombie" theories of cognition. Star Trek's character Data is an android whose bodily and cognitive innards are fully transparent to himself. Except in rare circumstances (which systematically tend to be described as the result of some sort of dysfunction), Data is thus capable of describing in uncanny detail each and every aspect of his internal states: How much force he is applying when attempting to pry open a steel door, how many circuits are currently active in his positronic brain, or the number of times over the last 10 years he smelled a particular scent, and in which circumstances he did so. Commander Data theorists likewise assume that cognition is fully transparent, that is: (1) that whatever knowledge is expressed through behaviour is also transparently available to introspection; and (2) that consciousness reigns supreme and allows access, with sufficient effort or attention, to all aspects of our inner lives. This perspective is what Broadbent described as the "common sense" view of cognition, according to which "people act by consulting an internal model of the world, a database of knowledge common to all output processes, and manipulating it to decide on the best action" (Broadbent, Fitzgerald, & Broadbent, 1986, p. 77).

In contrast, the famed philosophical zombies (Chalmers, 1996) are perfectly opaque, and in this sense instantiate absolutely implicit beings: Whatever internal knowledge currently influences their behaviour can neither be explicit nor conscious because, by definition, they lack conscious experience. Zombie theorists thus take it as a starting point that consciousness has an epiphenomenal character: There is a zombie within you and, although you might not be aware of its existence, it could in fact be responsible for most of your actions. It is capable of processing all the information you can process in the same way that you do, with one crucial difference: "All is dark inside" (Chalmers, 1996, p. 96); your zombie is unconscious. From this perspective then, cognition is inherently opaque, and consciousness, when present, offers but a very incomplete and imperfect perspective on internal states of affairs.

Needless to say, both of these perspectives are profoundly unsatisfactory. On the one hand, Zombie perspectives (ZP) ascribe no role whatsoever to consciousness in information processing, threaten to rob us of free will, and—because it is absurd to deny consciousness altogether—are ultimately forced to assume the existence of equally powerful conscious and unconscious systems. On the other hand, Commander Data perspectives (CDP), by assuming that all of cognition is conscious, paradoxically likewise depict consciousness as epiphenomenal. Crucially, both perspectives assume that consciousness does not change cognition in any principled way, and hence that *consciousness plays no functional role* beyond that of a epiphenomenon that accompanies either a functionally redundant subset of ZP or all CDP cognitive events.

On the face of the deeply counterintuitive flavour of both perspectives, it seems surprising to see that the past few years have witnessed the appearance of several broad theoretical proposals that intentionally or inadvertently endorse either of these perspectives. Some of these proposals are based on empirical evidence, and argue that there is in fact no evidence for unconscious influences in cognition. Thus for instance, Holender (1986), based on an extensive review of the subliminal perception literature, found no evidence for the existence of unconscious priming. Holender (1992) further proposed that many congruency effects observed in priming experiments can be accounted for by conflicts between conscious contents, that is, without appealing to the effects of unconscious influences. Likewise, Shanks and St John (1994), expanding on the perspective offered by Brewer

(1974), concluded their target article dedicated to implicit learning with the statement that "Human learning is almost invariably accompanied by conscious awareness" (p. 394).

Other proposals are more conceptual in nature. For instance, O'Brien and Opie (1999) propose that the contents of phenomenal consciousness include all stable neural states, and that it is only those stable states that are "causally efficacious", that is, susceptible to influence further processing and, ultimately, behaviour. Perruchet and Vinter (1998 and Chapter 2), consider that unconscious influences on behaviour should be ascribed exclusively to non-cognitive, neural processes and state that "Mental life [. . .] is co-extensive with consciousness" (Perruchet, personal communication; see also Dulany, 1997). Finally, Dienes and Perner's (1999) recent "theory of implicit and explicit knowledge", although carefully delineating the various ways in which knowledge can be cast as implicit or explicit, also seems to take it as a starting point that causally efficacious knowledge is always explicit in some sense, that is, at least at the specific level that is needed to account for the observed behavioural effects, and hence ends up, we believe, inadvertently painting a picture of cognition in which the implicit again plays no functional role in cognition.

It should be pointed out that if the emphasis of these theories on the "transparent" character of cognition can be seen as a normal swing of the conceptual pendulum, there is nevertheless something paradoxical about the emergence of such proposals at a time when the importance of unconscious processing in cognition finally appears to have gained some form of recognition in dozens of articles, books, and conferences.

The debate, we believe, is not so much rooted in equivocal empirical findings but rather in the deep conceptual problems associated with the notion of unconscious representation. Hence, defenders of the claim that cognition can be unconscious often succumb to some version of the ZP, while defenders of the opposite view can often be taken to endorse some variant of the CDP. Crucially, we believe that both these general frameworks are, in fact, based on the classical assumption that *cognition involves symbol manipulation*, and hence that their only way to separate conscious from unconscious cognition is to assume that unconscious cognition is just like conscious cognition, but only minus consciousness (Searle, 1992).

THE FRAMEWORK

We would now like to sketch out an alternative, subsymbolic, framework through which to think about the relationship between learning and consciousness—one that we believe offers a clear function to consciousness by linking it with adaptability in cognitive systems, while at the same time leaving open the possibility for adaptive changes to occur without consciousness.

If our central assumption that the function of consciousness is to offer adaptive control over behaviour is correct, then consciousness is necessarily closely related to processes of learning, because one of the central consequences of successful adaptation is that conscious control is no longer required over the corresponding behaviour. We therefore believe that it makes sense to root accounts of consciousness in accounts of how change occurs in cognitive systems.

Like Perruchet and Vinter (Chapter 2), we assume that there is a dynamic relationship between consciousness and learning such that: (1) awareness of a particular state of affairs triggers learning; and (2) that this learning in turn changes the contents of subjective experience so as to make these contents more adapted. However, and this is an important departure from Perruchet and Vinter's framework, we also assume that learning has additional obligatory indirect effects that can fail to enter awareness. In other words, learning is not *just* about modifying conscious experience, as Perruchet and Vinter seem to assume. Thus, when I learn about cats, I also learn indirectly about dogs and other animals, because the corresponding representations are all linked together by virtue of being embedded in distributed representational systems. These indirect effects of conscious learning need not themselves be conscious, particularly if they are weak.

We will return to these issues in the general discussion. At this point, we would like to introduce the set of assumptions that together form our framework. In the following, we present these assumptions in four groups: Assumptions about information processing (P1–4), about representation (R1–3), about learning (L1–3), and, finally, about consciousness (C1–5).

Assumptions about information processing

Consistent with well-known ideas in the connectionist literature (e.g. Rumelhart & McClelland, 1986), we will assume the following without further discussion:

P1. *The cognitive system is best viewed as involving a large set of interconnected processing modules organised in a loose hierarchy. Each module in turn consists of a large number of simple processing units connected together.*

P2. *Long-term knowledge in such systems is embodied in the pattern of connectivity between the processing units of each module and between the modules themselves.*

P3. *Dynamic, transient patterns of activation over the units of each module capture the results of information processing conducted so far.*

P4.   *Processing is graded and continuous: Connected modules continuously influence each other's processing in a graded manner that depends on the strength of the connection between them and on the strength of the activation patterns that they contain.*

Assumptions about representation

Representation is one of the most difficult issues to think about in the cognitive sciences because it is often hard to delineate exactly which states should be properly taken to be representational (see Dienes & Perner, Chapter 3, for a detailed discussion of representation). In the following, and in contrast to purely dynamical approaches, we take the perspective that representations are necessary as mediating states through which the intermediate results of processing can be captured, thereby making it possible for complex tasks to be decomposed into modular components.

R1.   *Representations consist exclusively of the transient patterns of activation that occur in distributed memory systems.*

This assumption is a central one in our framework because it contrasts with other recent proposals (e.g. Dienes & Perner, Chapter 3). In particular, we do not think that the knowledge that is embedded in the pattern of connectivity between units of a module, or between modules themselves, is representational in the same manner that patterns of activation are. Indeed, while such knowledge can be analysed as representational from a third-person perspective (because the connection between two units, for instance, can be described as representing the fact that the units' activities are correlated), it is never directly available to the system itself. In other words, such knowledge is knowledge "in the system" rather "for the system" (see Clark & Karmiloff-Smith, 1993). Knowledge embedded in connections weights can thus only be expressed dynamically, over the course of some processing, when the corresponding representations form over a given set of processing units. These representations can then in turn influence further processing in other modules. Importantly, and in contrast to thoroughly classical approaches in cognitive science, the extent to which representations can influence processing in such systems never depends on representations being interpreted by a "processor".

R2.   *Representations are graded: They vary on several dimensions that include strength, stability in time, and distinctiveness.*

Patterns of activation in neural networks and in the brain are typically distributed and can therefore vary on a number of dimensions, such as their stability in time, their strength, or their distinctiveness. Stability in time refers to how long a representation can be maintained active during processing. There are many indications that different neural systems involve representations that differ along this dimension. For instance, the prefrontal cortex, which plays a central role in working memory, is widely assumed to involve circuits specialised in the formation of the enduring representations needed for the active maintenance of task-relevant information.

Strength of representation simply refers to how many processing units are involved in the representation, and to how strongly activated these units are. As a rule, strong activation patterns will exert more influence on ongoing processing than weak patterns.

Finally, *distinctiveness* of representation refers to the extent of overlap that exists between representations of similar instances. Distinctiveness has been hypothesised as the main dimension through which cortical and hippocampal representations differ (McClelland, McNaughton, & O'Reilly, 1995; O'Reilly & Munakata, 2000), with the latter becoming active only when the specific conjunctions of features that they code for are active themselves.

In the following, we will collectively refer to these different dimensions as "quality of representation" (see also Farah, 1994) For our purposes, the most important notion that underpins these different dimensions is that representations, in contrast to the all-or-none propositional representations typically used in classical theories, instead have a *graded* character, which enables any particular representation to convey in a natural manner the extent to which what it refers to is indeed present. A second important aspect of this characterisation of representational systems in the brain is that representations are *complex, distributed objects* that systematically tend to involve many processing units.

R3.   *Representations are dynamic, active, and constantly causally efficacious.*

This assumption simply states that memory traces, far from being static propositions waiting to be accessed by some process, instead continuously influence processing regardless of their strength, stability, or distinctiveness. This assumption is again central in any connectionist account of cognition. Indeed, it takes its roots in McClelland's analysis of cascaded processing (McClelland, 1979), which, by showing how modules interacting with each other need not "wait" for other modules to have completed their processing before starting their own, demonstrated how stage-like performance could emerge out of such continuous, non-linear systems. Thus, in our framework, even weak, poor-quality traces are capable of influencing processing, for instance through associative priming mechanisms, that is, in conjunction with other sources of stimulation. Strong, high-quality traces, in contrast have generative capacity, in the sense that they can influence performance (i.e. determine responses) independently of the influence of other constraints, that is, whenever their preferred stimulus is present.

Assumptions about learning

Having put in place our assumptions about processing and representation, we now focus on learning mechanisms. We assume the following:

L1.   *Adaptation is a mandatory consequence of information processing.*

Every form of neural information processing produces adaptive changes in the connectivity of the system, through mechanisms such as long-term potentiation (LTP) or long-term depression (LTD) in neural systems, or hebbian learning in connectionist systems. An important aspect of these mechanisms is that they are mandatory in the sense that they take place whenever the sending and receiving units or processing modules are co-active. O'Reilly and Munakata (2000) have described hebbian learning as instantiating what they call model learning. The fundamental computational objective of such unsupervised learning mechanisms is to enable the cognitive system to develop useful, informative models of the world by capturing its correlational structure. As such, they stand in contrast with task learning mechanisms, which instantiate the different computational objective of mastering specific input–output mappings (i.e. achieving specific goals) in the context of specific tasks through error-correcting learning procedures. Regardless of how these two classes of learning mechanisms can be combined, the important point to remember in the context of this framework is that model learning operates whenever information processing takes place, whereas task learning operates only in specific contexts defined by particular goals.

L2.   *Learning is adaptation that specifically involves high-quality representations.*

We assume that learning consists specifically of those adaptation processes that involve high-quality, strong, stable representations. One way to characterise this notion is to appeal to another distinction offered by O'Reilly and Munakata (2000)—that between weight-based and activation-based processing. According to O'Reilly and Munakata (2000, p. 380), "Activation-based processing is based on the activation, maintenance, and updating of active representations to influence processing, whereas weight-based processing is based on the adaptation of weight values to alter input/output mappings". The main advantage of activation-based processing is that it is faster and more flexible than weight-based processing. Speed and flexibility are both salient characteristics of high-level cognition. O'Reilly and Munakata further speculate that activation-based processing is one of the central characteristics of the frontal cortex, and suggest that this region of the brain has evolved specifically to serve a number of important functions related to controlled processing, such as working memory, inhibition, executive control, and monitoring or evaluation of ongoing behaviour. To serve these functions, processing in the frontal cortex is characterised by mechanisms of active maintenance through which representations can remain strongly activated for long periods of time so as it make it possible for these representations to bias processing elsewhere in the brain.

O'Reilly and Munakata point out that a major puzzle is to understand how the frontal cortex comes to develop what they call a "rich vocabulary of frontal activation-based processing representations with appropriate associations to corresponding posterior-cortical representations" (p. 382). Our framework does not solve this difficult chicken-and-egg problem, but simply suggests that early learning or development, which involves mostly weight-based processing, progressively results in the emergence of the strong, high-quality representations that allow activation-based processing and the ensuing flexibility to take place. Language and linguistic representations in general undoubtedly play a major role in making activation-based processing possible.

L3. *Learning has both direct and indirect effects.*

Learning not only has direct effects (i.e. changing the subjective experience that corresponds to the processing of a particular event and modifying the system's response to that event), but it also has indirect effects on how (functionally or physically) similar events are processed. This is again a natural consequence of the assumption that memory systems in general involve distributed, superpositional representations, such that all representations share many processing units, and such that all processing units are involved in many representations. In such representational systems, changes to any particular representation that might arise from learning will necessarily have indirect effects on related representations. Importantly, these indirect effects are mediated by changes in the connection weights shared by the different representations in a given module; in other words, they do not involve direct, simultaneous modification of the corresponding representations. These indirect effects are thus, in our framework, not necessarily accompanied by awareness, because to be accompanied by awareness, their origin and magnitude would have to be identifiable by the agent.

Assumptions about consciousness

So far, we have spelled out a number of assumptions about information processing, representation, and learning. We are now ready to introduce

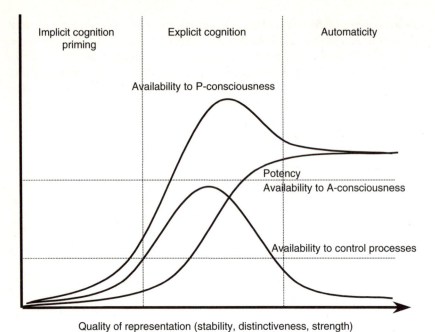

Figure 1.1. Graphical representation of the relationships between quality of representation (the *x*-axis) and their potency, their availability to control, and their availability to subjective experience.

our assumptions about consciousness and its relationship to adaptation and learning processes. The central ideas that we would like to explore are: (1) that the extent to which a particular representation is available to consciousness depends on its quality; (2) that learning produces, over time, higher-quality, adapted representations; and (3) that the function of consciousness is to offer necessary control over those representations that are strong enough to influence behaviour, yet not sufficiently adapted that their influence does not require control anymore.

Figure 1.1 aims to capture these ideas by representing the relationships between quality of representation (*x*-axis) on the one hand and: (1) potency; (2) availability to control; and (3) availability to subjective experience. We discuss the figure at length in the following section. Let us simply note here that the *x*-axis represents a continuum between weak, poor-quality representations on the left and very strong, high-quality representations on the right, and that principle R3 ("Representations are constantly causally efficacious") is captured by the curve labelled "Potency", which assumes that all representations, even weak ones, can influence behaviour to some extent. The general form of the relationship between quality of representation and potency is assumed to be non-linear.

Two further points are important to keep in mind with respect to Figure 1.1. Firstly, the relationships depicted in the figure are intended to represent availability to some dimension of behaviour or consciousness independent of other considerations. Many potentially important modulatory influences on the state of any particular module are thus simply not meant to be captured, neither by Figure 1.1, nor by our framework as we present it here. Secondly, the figure is intended to represent what happens in each of many processing modules involved in any particular cognitive task. Thus, as hinted by assumptions P1–P4, at any point in time there will be many such modules active, each contributing to some extent to behaviour and to conscious experience; each modulating the activity of other modules. With these caveats in mind, let us now turn to our five assumptions about consciousness and its relationship with learning:

C1.   *Consciousness involves two dimensions: Subjective experience and control.*

As argued by many, and most cogently by Block (1995), consciousness involves at least two separable aspects, namely access consciousness (A-consciousness) and phenomenal consciousness (P-consciousness). For Posner and Rothbart (1998), awareness of the sensory world and voluntary control are the two most important aspects of consciousness. According to Block (1995, p. 234), "A perceptual state is access-conscious roughly speaking if its content—what is represented by the perceptual state—is processed via that information processing function, that is, if its content gets to the Executive system, whereby it can be used to control reasoning and behavior". In other words, whether a state is A-conscious is defined essentially by the causal efficacy of that state—the extent to which it is available for global control of action. Control refers to the ability of an agent to control, to modulate, and to inhibit the influence of particular representations on processing. In our framework, control is simply a function of potency, as described in assumption C3. In contrast, P-consciousness refers to the phenomenal aspects of subjective experience: A state is P-conscious to the extent that there is something it is like to be in that state. Although the extent to which potency (i.e. availability to access consciousness), control, and subjective experience (i.e. availability to phenomenal consciousness) are dissociable is debatable, our framework suggests that these three aspects of consciousness are closely related to each other.

C2.   *Availability to consciousness correlates with quality of representation.*

This assumption is also a central one in our framework. It states that explicit, conscious knowledge involves higher quality memory traces than implicit knowledge. "Quality of representation", as discussed in assumption

R3, designates several properties of memory traces, such as their relative strength in the relevant information-processing pathways, their distinctiveness, or their stability in time. Our assumption is consistent with the theoretical positions expressed by several different authors over the last few years. O'Brien and Opie (1999) have perhaps been the most direct in endorsing a characterisation of phenomenal consciousness in terms of the properties of mental representations in defending the idea that "consciousness equals stability of representation", that is, that the particular mental contents that one is aware of at some point in time correspond to those representations that are sufficiently stable in time. Mathis and Mozer (1996) have also suggested that consciousness involves stable representations, but have defined stability more technically than O'Brien and Opie, specifically by offering a computational model of priming phenomena in which stability literally corresponds to the state that a so-called dynamic "attractor" network reaches when the activations of a subset of its units stops changing and settle into a stable, unchanging state.

A slightly different perspective on the notion of "quality of representation" is offered by authors who emphasise not stability but strength of representation as the important feature through which to characterise availability to consciousness. One finds echoes of this position in the writings of Kinsbourne (1997), for whom availability to consciousness depends on properties of representations such as duration, activation, or congruence. Importantly, for both O'Brien and Opie and for Kinsbourne, the contents of subjective experience never depend on representations entering a particular system in the brain—that is, consciousness is conceived as essentially decentralised: Any region of the brain can contribute to the contents of subjective experience so long as its representational vehicles have the appropriate properties.

In Figure 1.1, we have represented the extent to which a given representation is available to the different components of consciousness (phenomenal consciousness, access-consciousness/potency, and control) as functions of a single underlying dimension expressed in terms of the quality of this representation. Availability to access-consciousness is represented by the curve labelled "Potency", which expresses the extent to which representations can influence behaviour as a function of their quality. We simply assume that high-quality, strong, distinctive representations are more potent than weaker representations. "Availability to control processes" is represented by a second curve, so labelled. We simply assume that both weak and very strong representations are difficult to control, and that maximal control can be achieved on representations that are strong enough that they can begin to influence behaviour in significant ways, yet not so strong that they have become utterly dominant in processing. Finally, availability to phenomenal experience is represented by the third curve, obtained by convolving the other two. The underlying intuition, discussed in the context of assumption C4, is that which contents enter subjective experience is a function of both availability to control and of potency.

C3.   *Developing high-quality representations takes time.*

This assumption states that the emergence of high-quality representations (see assumption C2) in a given processing module takes time, both over training or development, as well as during processing of a single event. Figure 1.1 can thus be viewed as representing not only the relationships between quality of representation and their availability to the different components of consciousness, but also as a depiction of the dynamics of how a particular representation will change over the different time scales corresponding to development, learning, or within-trial processing.

Both skill acquisition and development, for instance, involve the long-term progressive emergence of high-quality, strong memory traces based on early availability of weaker traces. Likewise, the extent to which memory traces can influence performance at any moment (e.g. during a single trial) depends both on available processing time and on overall trace strength. We envision these processes of change as operating on the connection weights between units in a connectionist network. They can involve either task-dependent, error-correcting procedures, or unsupervised procedures such as hebbian learning. In either case, continued exposure to exemplars of the domain will result in the development of increasingly congruent and strong internal representations that capture more and more of the relevant variance. Although we think of this process as essentially continuous, we distinguish three stages in the formation of such internal representations (each depicted as separate regions in Figure 1.1): Implicit representations, explicit representations, and automatic representations.

The first region, labelled "Implicit cognition" in Figure 1.1, is meant to correspond to the point at which processing starts in the context of a single trial, or to some early stage of development or skill acquisition. In either case, this stage is characterised by weak, poor-quality representations. A first important point, embodied in assumption R3, is that representations at this stage are already capable of influencing performance, as long as they can be brought to bear on processing together with other sources of constraints, that is, essentially through mechanisms of associative priming and constraint satisfaction. A second important point is that this influence is best described as "implicit", because the relevant representations are too weak (i.e. not distinctive enough) for the system as a whole to be capable of exerting control over them: You cannot control what you cannot identify as distinct from something else. One might even speculate that what enables you to take control of an internal state is precisely the fact that it is capable of triggering responses in and of itself—a speculation that links control with action in a very direct way.

The second region of Figure 1.1 corresponds to the emergence of explicit representations, defined as representations over which one can exert control. In the terminology of attractor networks, this would correspond to a stage during learning at which attractors become better defined—deeper, wider, and more distinctive. It is also at this point that the relevant representations acquire generative capacity, in the sense that they have now accrued sufficient strength to have the potential to determine appropriate responses when their preferred stimulus is presented to the system alone. Because awareness is partially tied to control in our framework, one would thus also be aware both of these internal representations and of their influence on our behaviour. Because one is aware of these representations, one can then also possess meta-knowledge about them, and recode them in various different ways, for instance, as linguistic propositions.

The third region involves what we call automatic representations, that is, representations that have become so strong that their influence on behaviour can no longer be controlled (i.e. inhibited). Such representations exert a mandatory influence on processing. Importantly, however, one is aware both of possessing them (that is, one has relevant meta-knowledge) and of their influence on processing (see also Tzelgov, 1997), because availability to conscious awareness depends on the quality of internal representations, and strong representations are of high quality. In this perspective then, one can always be conscious of automatic behaviour, but not necessarily with the possibility of control over these behaviours.

In our framework, skill acquisition, and development therefore involve a continuum at both ends of which control over representations is impossible or difficult, but for very different reasons: Implicit representations influence performance but cannot be controlled because they are not yet sufficiently distinctive and strong for the system to even know it possesses them. This might in turn be related to the fact that, precisely because of their weakness, implicit representations cannot influence behaviour on their own, but only in conjunction with other sources of constraints. Automatic representations, on the other hand, cannot be controlled because they are too strong, but the system is aware both of their presence and of their influence on performance.

C4. *The function of consciousness is to offer flexible, adaptive control over behaviour.*

Our framework gives consciousness a central place in information processing, in the sense that its function is to enable flexible control over behaviour. Crucially, however, consciousness is not necessary for information processing, or for adaptation in general, thus giving a place for implicit learning in cognition. We believe this perspective to be congruent with theories of adaptation and optimality in general.

Indeed, another way to think about the role of learning in consciousness is to ask: "When does one need control over behaviour?". Control is perhaps not necessary for implicit representations, for their influence on behaviour is necessarily weak (by virtue of the fact that, precisely because they are weak, such representations are unlikely to be detrimental to the organism even if they are not particularly well-adapted). Likewise, control is not necessary for automatic representations, because, presumably, those representations that have become automatic after extensive training should be adapted (optimal) as long as the processes of learning that have produced them can themselves be assumed to be adaptive. Automatic behaviour is thus necessarily optimal behaviour, except, precisely, in cases such as addiction or in laboratory situations where the automatic response is manipulated to be non-optimal, such as in the Stroop situation. Referring again to Figure 1.1, this analysis thus suggests that the representations that require control are the explicit representations that correspond to the central region of Figure 1.1: Representations that are strong enough that they have the potential to influence behaviour in and of themselves (and hence that one should really care about, in contrast to implicit representations), but not sufficiently strong that they can be assumed to be already adapted, as is the case for automatic representations. It is for those representations that control is needed, and, for this reason, it is of these representations that one is most aware.

Likewise, this analysis also predicts that the dominant contents of subjective experience at any point in time consist precisely of those representations that are strong enough to influence behaviour yet weak enough still to require control. Figure 1.1 reflects these ideas by suggesting that the contents of phenomenal experience depend both on the potency of currently active representations and on their availability to control. As availability to control is inversely related to potency for representations associated with automatic behaviour, this indeed predicts weaker availability to phenomenal experience of "very strong" representations as compared to "merely strong" representations. Such "automatic representations" therefore form what Mangan (1993) has called the "fringe of consciousness". In other words, such representations can become conscious if appropriate attention is directed towards their contents—as in cases where normally automatic behaviour (such as walking) suddenly becomes conscious because the normal unfolding of the behaviour has been interrupted (e.g. because I've stumbled upon something)—but they are not normally part of the central focus of awareness nor do they require conscious control.

While the dominant contents of subjective experience can thus be viewed as reflecting the activity of the topmost module in the constantly evolving loose hierarchy of processing modules involved in any particular aspect of information processing, it is also important to note that we assume, in contrast to the position expressed by Perruchet and Vinter in Chapter 2, that complex representations depend on the continued activation of their more elementary components. In other words, while learning certainly results in the elaboration of progressively more complex representations, it neither prevents their components from contributing to subjective experience nor does it eliminate their influence on ongoing processing. This therefore opens the door for the continued—but attenuated, indirect—expression of the representations associated with these lower-level modules.

C5. *Learning shapes conscious experience.*

This assumption, which we adapt from Perruchet and Vinter (Chapter 2) is a corollary of assumption C4: If the function of consciousness is to offer flexible, adaptive control over behaviour, then its contents—the way it reflects the world—should necessarily be shaped by learning so that, at any moment, these contents tend to reflect precisely those aspects of the situation that most require control. This assumption allows us to relate two central aspects of consciousness that have often been considered as independent: subjective experience and control of action—or phenomenal versus access consciousness.

Ways for knowledge to be implicit

In our framework, we emphasised quality of representation as a central dimension through which to account for which representations are likely to enter conscious awareness. It should be clear, however, that we take quality of representation as a **necessary**, but not **sufficient**, condition for conscious awareness. In particular, our framework remains mute with respect to the fate of the high-quality, strong representations that characterise explicit, conscious cognition, short of claiming that it is these representations that are most likely to form the contents of subjective experience. Whether these representations actually enter conscious experience is yet another story—one in which processes of attention and processes of integration undoubtedly play a central role. In this respect, our framework is not inconsistent with recent proposals that emphasise the importance of such processes in the formation of subjective experience. One such recent proposal has been put forward by Dehaene and Naccache (2001). These authors, based on Baars' (1998) notion of "global workspace", propose that conscious awareness depends on the extent to which the contents of the many domain-specific unconscious processing modules that make up our brain can be made accessible globally through specific, dedicated, long-distance neural pathways that interconnect the modules and specific regions of the brain (i.e. essentially prefrontal cortex, anterior cingulate, and other regions connected to both). Availability to the global workspace thus depends on both bottom–up (i.e. input strength) and top–down (i.e. attention) factors. When these two conditions exist, the contents of those modules that connect to the neural workspace would then enter in the stable, resonant, or synchronous states that are assumed to correlate with conscious awareness.

Kanwisher (2001) also discusses the conditions under which particular representations will enter conscious awareness and notes that activation strength alone, although perhaps necessary, is certainly not sufficient. Like Dehaene and Naccache, Kanwisher suggests that awareness also depends on "informational access", that is, on the fact that other parts of the brain/mind have access to the relevant representations. Kanwisher also suggests the accessibility can change over time as a result of practice—a point that we very much agree with—and that an important further factor in determining availability to consciousness is what she calls the "type/token" distinction, that is, the fact that awareness of some perceptual attribute not only requires a strong corresponding representation but also "individuation of that perceptual information as a distinct event" (Kanwisher, 2001, p. 107). In other words, the relevant representation has to be accompanied by relevant meta-knowledge—a point discussed in detail by Dienes and Perner (1999).

Our own framework leaves open four distinct possibilities for knowledge to be implicit:

(1) We assume that the knowledge that is embedded in the connection weights within and between processing modules can never be directly available to conscious awareness and control. This is simply a consequence of the fact that we assume that consciousness necessarily involves representations (patterns of activation over processing units). Because weight-based knowledge is not representational in this specific sense, it follows that it can never contribute directly to the contents of conscious experience. This knowledge will, however, shape the representations that depend on it, and its effects will therefore be detectable—but only indirectly, and only to the extent that these effects are sufficiently marked in the corresponding representations.

(2) We assume that, to enter conscious awareness, a representation needs to be of sufficiently high quality in terms of strength, stability in time, or distinctiveness. Weak representations are therefore poor candidates to enter conscious awareness. This, however, as we repeatedly emphasised, does not necessarily imply that they remain causally inert, for they can influence further processing in other modules, even if only

weakly so. Note that this aspect of our framework differs both from the assumptions put forward by O'Brien and Opie (1999) and from those embodied in Perruchet and collaborators (Perruchet, Vinter, & Gallego, 1997; Perruchet & Vinter, 1998 and Chapter 2).

(3) A representation can be strong enough to enter conscious awareness but fail to be recognised as relevant to the particular situation that is currently unfolding. This case corresponds almost exactly with Kanwisher's "type/token" distinction, and also with aspects of Dienes and Perner's analysis of the differences between implicit and explicit knowledge. Conscious contents, indeed, have to be linked together in a coherent manner before they can be made available globally for conscious report and for the control of action. One should therefore be very careful to distinguish between cases involving awareness of the intention of initiating some behaviour, awareness of the fact that the behaviour is taking place, awareness of the causes of the behaviour, and awareness of the effects of the behaviour. There are thus many opportunities for a particular conscious content to remain, in a way, implicit, not because its representational vehicle does not have the appropriate properties, but because it fails to be integrated with other conscious contents. Dienes and Perner (see Chapter 3) offer an insightful analysis of the different ways in which what we call high-quality representations can remain implicit.

(4) Finally, a representation can be so strong that its influence can no longer be controlled. In these cases, it is debatable whether the knowledge should be taken as genuinely unconscious, because they can certainly become fully conscious as long as appropriate attention is directed to them, but the point is that such very strong representations can trigger and support behaviour without conscious intention and without the need for conscious monitoring of the unfolding behaviour.

Another way to think about these different ways for knowledge to be implicit is to consider the various mechanisms of change suggested by O'Reilly and Munakata (2000). Recall that these authors distinguish between weight-based processing and activation-based processing. Weight-based processing in turn involves model learning (subserved by hebbian-like learning mechanisms) and task learning (subserved by error-correcting learning procedures). From the perspective developed here, activation-based processing and learning will always tend to be associated with awareness—even though it might often be that conscious contents fail to be associated with relevant meta-knowledge and therefore remain implicit. Model learning, in contrast, corresponds to the clearest case of implicit learning, to the extent that it is assumed to be a mandatory consequence of information processing. Such learning, therefore, never depends on the intentions or goals of the agent, and its effects, because they are very gradual, can be expressed in behaviour before they become available to awareness. Task learning, by contrast, is necessarily intentional, and therefore more likely to shape representations in ways that are directly consistent with the current goals of the agent.

IMPLICATIONS

In this section, we offer a necessarily brief and sketchy set of examples where we have found our framework helpful in terms of understanding empirical phenomena such as priming, implicit learning, skill acquisition and automaticity, or development. This short review also gives us the opportunity to link our framework with similar previous accounts of these phenomena and to further contrast our own proposal with other positions.

Priming

In a recent paper, Becker, Moscovitch, Behrmann, and Joordens (1997) describe an attractor, neural-network model of both short- and long-term priming effects that accounts for a large variety of priming phenomena as the result of an automatic process of incremental learning that is based on the same information processing and representational principles that we have just outlined. Becker and colleagues showed that semantic priming can be construed as the automatic deepening of the basin of attraction "of the semantic space for both primes and related targets, and that this effect should primarily manifest itself on semantic-retrieval tasks" (Becker et al., 1997, p. 1062). Their model accurately predicts that performing a semantic task on a target is influenced by having previously performed a similar task on a semantically related prime, even if a number of intervening words are presented between prime and target. Importantly, it also predicts low or null priming effects when long-term semantic effects are tested through a lexical decision task (see also Joordens & Becker, 1997) or when the processing task performed with the primes is not semantic (Friedrich, Henik, & Tzelgov, 1991; Kaye & Brown, 1985; Smith, Theodor, & Franklin, 1983). These results, as well as the successful simulation work, are compatible with our own assumptions in that they suggest: (1) that learning is assumed to be a mandatory consequence of processing; (2) that the effects of learning are particularly focused on those representational features that are relevant to the processing task (and which therefore produce specific experiences); and (3) that these effects are not limited to their most direct consequences—in this case, the episodic recollection that a prime has been presented—but might also produce a host of indirect (priming) effects that are not necessarily mediated by conscious recollection of its cause.

Implicit learning

If priming can be cast as a form of implicit learning, as Becker et al. (1997) suggest, it seems that implicit learning can likewise be depicted as a form of complex relational priming. Indeed, while our framework emphasises that learning results from conscious experience, it also makes it clear that the effects of learning need not be limited to modifying conscious experience. In particular, two important assumptions embodied in our framework are: (1) that adaptation occurs as a mandatory consequence of processing; and (2) that learning has both direct and indirect effects. Three consequences of these assumptions are: (1) that learning can occur without intention to learn; (2) that the changes resulting from learning can remain unconscious at the time of learning; and (3) that such changes can influence subsequent processing even in the absence of awareness that this is so.

Because of the intricate methodological issues involved, it has proved rather difficult to gather supporting evidence for any of these three claims. It is always difficult to assess exactly what participants in an experiment involving learning are actually intending to do. Implicit learning studies have often tried to circumvent this problem by exposing participants to very complex settings in which learning would not be expected to improve through an intentional orientation, but this strategy has not been used often (see Jiménez, Méndez, & Cleeremans, 1996, for one example). However, indirect evidence that people can learn effectively without intending to do so has been obtained through some recent experiments that use dual-cue paradigms, in which the existence of a perfect and explicit predictor of the relevant stimulus dimension can be taken to prevent the deliberate search for more complex contingencies (Cleeremans, 1997; Jiménez & Méndez, 2001). The fact that learning of these complex contingencies can be obtained even under these dual-cue conditions provides us with a clear indication that this learning proceeds regardless of participants' intention to learn. Importantly, however, these results should not be taken as indicating that learning is completely unselective. Indeed, several recent experimental results (Jiménez & Méndez, 1999; 2001; see also Jiang & Chun, in press) indicate convincingly that learning is obtained selectively for those particular features that are relevant to the task(s) at hand and, hence, that learning is deeply modulated by the attentional variables that ultimately determine the learner's experiences.

As we have stated repeatedly, the fact that learning depends on the conscious experiences of the learner does not necessarily entail that all learning should be conscious at the moment of learning, or that they should be conscious to produce any effect on performance. The unconscious nature of the knowledge acquired during training on a sequence learning task has been examined by us in previous studies (e.g. Jiménez et al., 1996) and it has been recently investigated by Destrebecqz and Cleeremans (2001) by adapting Jacoby's process dissociation procedure (PDP).

In a typical sequence learning situation (see Clegg, DiGirolamo, & Keele, 1998), participants are asked to react to each element of a sequentially structured visual sequence of events in the context of a serial reaction time task. On each trial, subjects see a stimulus that appears at one of several locations on a computer screen and are asked to press as fast and as accurately as possible on the key corresponding to its current location. Unknown to them, the sequence of successive locations follows a repeating pattern (Nissen & Bullemer, 1987) and participants learn this pattern, as showed by a progressive decrease in their reaction times, which increase dramatically when the sequential structure of the material is modified (Cohen, Ivry, & Keele, 1990; Curran & Keele, 1993; Reed & Johnson, 1994).

This learning, however, often fails to be expressed through verbal reports (Curran & Keele, 1993; Willingham, Nissen, & Bullemer, 1989)—a dissociation that has led many authors to consider learning in this situation to be implicit. However, many of the relevant studies have been criticised on methodological grounds that would be too long to review in this chapter (but see Cleeremans, Destrebecqz, & Boyer, 1998, for a detailed overview). Suffice it to say that many of the relevant methodological difficulties stem from the fact that most empirical paradigms through which implicit learning has been studied have assumed that one takes specific tasks with either implicit or explicit processing.

To overcome these methodological difficulties, Destrebecqz and Cleeremans (2001) sought to adapt Jacoby's process dissociation procedure (PDP; Jacoby, 1991) to the study of sequence learning. Subjects were first trained, under the incidental learning conditions typical of implicit learning studies, on a second-order conditional sequence. This training occurred under two conditions defined by the length of the response-to-stimulus interval (RSI): One group of participants was trained with a standard RSI of 250 ms, and another was trained with an RSI of 0 ms. For this latter group, the next stimulus therefore appeared on the screen as soon as the previous one had been responded to. Consistent with the ideas embodied in assumption C3 (page 23), we hoped that reducing the time available for processing would selectively impair the development of strong, explicit representations of the links between the temporal context set by previous elements of the sequence and the location of the next stimulus.

To find out about participants' explicit knowledge of the material, Destrebecqz and Cleeremans asked them to perform two generation tasks and a recognition task. The generation task was adapted from Jacoby's PDP, and consisted of both an inclusion task and an exclusion task. In inclusion, participants had to generate a sequence of 96 elements that resembled the training sequence. They were told to base their sequence either on conscious recollection or to guess. Both conscious and unconscious processes can therefore contribute to performance in inclusion. In exclusion, participants were again told to generate a sequence of 96 elements, but this time they were told to produce a sequence that was as different as possible from the training sequence. By assumption, the only way participants can perform this exclusion task successfully is by recollecting the location of the next stimulus and by selecting another location. Failure to exclude can thus be interpreted as reflecting the influence of implicit knowledge. Thus, in this condition, and in contrast to what happens in inclusion, conscious and unconscious components of performance act against each other. Finally, in recognition, participants were presented with 24 sequences of three elements, only 12 of which had actually been part of the training sequence. For each, they had to indicate the extent to which they believed it was part of the training sequence on a 6-point scale.

The results indicated that whereas both groups of participants exhibited some explicit knowledge of the material through the inclusion task, only people trained with an RSI of 250 ms were able to perform successfully in the exclusion task. People trained with an RSI of 0 ms indeed continued to generate material from the training sequence in spite of instructions to the contrary. Further, only participants trained with a 250 ms RSI were able to perform above chance on the final recognition task.

When applied to these data, our framework suggests the following interpretation: People trained with an RSI were given more opportunities to develop and link together high-quality memory traces than people in the no RSI condition. Because awareness depends in part on the quality of stored memory traces, the former will therefore tend to acquire more explicit knowledge than the latter. Importantly, "no RSI" participants do acquire relevant knowledge about the sequence—but in the form of weaker memory traces that are capable of influencing responses only when contextual information is available simultaneously. This knowledge can thus be expressed in the serial reaction time (SRT) task as well as in the generation tasks because, in both cases, responses can be determined based jointly on an external stimulus (self-generated in the case of the generation tasks or produced by the experimental software in the SRT task) and the relevant memory traces. Because these traces are weak, and because controlled processing (and hence awareness) requires high-quality traces to be available, their influence on performance remains undetected and controlled responding is made difficult. The relevant sequential knowledge therefore cannot be inhibited when the generation task is performed under exclusion conditions. Similarly, during recognition, weak memory traces do not allow successful discrimination between old and novel sequences in the absence of perceptual and motor fluency, as was the case in Destrebecqz and Cleeremans's study.

Skill acquisition and automaticity

Skill acquisition refers to extended periods of exposure to a particular domain during which learning occurs. It might involve learning how to use a musical instrument, learning to master a particular athletic skill, or learning natural language. In our framework, skill acquisition thus involves a graded continuum expressed in terms of the relative strength of the underlying representations. This continuum involves weak, implicit representations when learning starts and very strong, high-quality representations when training ends.

Automaticity has often been associated with lack of availability to conscious experience, but some authors (Tzelgov, 1997) have proposed that the defining feature of automatic behaviour should simply be its ballistic properties, that is, the fact that, once initiated, execution of the behaviour can no longer be inhibited until completed. We very much agree with this position. In our framework, the strong representations associated with automatic behaviour are available to subjective experience and form what one could call, along with Mangan (1993), the "fringe" of consciousness. In other words, such representations can become conscious if appropriate attention is directed towards their contents—as in cases where normally automatic behaviour (such as walking) suddenly becomes conscious because the normal unfolding of the behaviour has been interrupted (e.g. because I've stumbled upon something)—but they are not normally part of the central focus of awareness, nor do they require conscious control. This is reflected in our framework by assuming that the contents of phenomenal experience depend both on the potency of currently active representations as well as on their availability to control. As availability to control is inversely related to potency for automatic representations, this indeed predicts weaker availability to phenomenal experience of very strong representations as compared to merely strong representations.

Our framework also predicts that very strong representations are left in place, that is, they become active whenever their preferred stimulus is present. This suggests that what happens over the course of learning a skill is that additional novel ways of inhibiting or otherwise modulating the effects of these very strong representations are found through processes of learning. Consider what happens when you learn to play the piano, for instance. As Karmiloff-Smith (1992) points out, one goes from effortful programming of every movement to a stage where entire sequences of movements can be executed all at once, and then to a later stage where genuine flexibility is achieved. Our suggestion here is that subjective experience at each stage simply reflects the contents of the processing modules that currently contain the most abstract representation of the stimulus. Ability to control the influence of the contents of lower-level modules is thus lost progressively during skill acquisition but, importantly, these contents are still constitutive of subjective experience, if only through their role in supporting higher-level representations.

Development

The notion that development involves continuous changes in the strength or quality of underlying representations is central in many accounts of various relevant phenomena. For instance, McClelland and Jenkins's (1991) connectionist model of developmental changes in the balance beam task is rooted in the idea that experience at solving balance beam problems results in the progressive differential strengthening of the internal representations of the weight and distance information. The relatively systematic sequence of stages observed through development in the emergence of mastery on this task, which exhibits various patterns of ability to solve specific problems, can thus simply be accounted for by competition between the information-processing pathways corresponding to each dimension. In other words, this account of the emergence of skilled behaviour at mastering balance beam tasks is entirely strength-based.

Munakata and collaborators (Munakata, McClelland, Johnson, & Siegler, 1997) have likewise proposed a novel account of the development of object permanence during infancy (see also Mareschal, Plunkett, & Harris, 1999) in which the notion of strength of representation also plays a central role. Classical theories of object permanence assume that at some early point during development, children "acquire the concept" that objects continue to exist when out of view. The crucial point here is that this knowledge is assumed to be of a conceptual nature: Children are taken to be constantly developing explicit theories about their environment, and their theories can be described as consisting of a set of all-or-none beliefs about the way the world works. In stark constrast, Munakata et al. (1997) suggested that the progressive emergence of appropriate anticipatory responses in situations where a moving object temporarily disappears behind a screen can emerge simply out of the operation of prediction-driven mechanisms such as insantiated in the Simple Recurrent Network (Elman, 1990; see also Cleeremans, Servan-Schreiber, & McClelland, 1989). Most importantly, Munakata et al. showed how the model, when trained on such a prediction task, develops progressively stronger, higher-quality representations of the object while it is hidden, and how this progressive strengthening of the model's internal representations can be related to the development of knowledge about object permanence. Another important aspect of this work was the demonstration that the very same principles—strength of internal representation—could account for observed dissociations between different measures (e.g. looking times versus reaching behaviour) of children's ability to exhibit knowledge of object permanence. It is interesting to note that, in many ways, the debates elicited in the developmental literature by the empirical findings related to object permanence mirror those taking place in the field of implicit learning about whether or not subjects are best described as "knowing the rules of the grammar".

A central idea that both of these models illustrate is that continuous changes along one dimension can exert non-linear effects on the overall behaviour of the system when interactions between several dimensions are considered. In other words, all-or-none behaviour can be rooted in continuous, graded changes in some relevant underlying dimension.

Finally, with respect to the development of explicit, conscious representations in cognitive systems, our framework can also be linked in interesting ways with the processes of representational redescription envisioned by Karmiloff-Smith (1992) as the main process of change during development. A crucial claim embodied in the assumptions that underpin the notion of representational redescription is that learning is success-driven, that is, behavioural mastery of a particular skill does not constitute a signal for learning to stop but rather a signal for further learning to occur on the internal representations through which mastery was achieved. Representational description, according to Karmiloff-Smith, is a ". . . process of 'appropriating' stable states to extract the information they contain, which can then be used more flexibly for other purposes" (p. 25). Thus, representations change over development in such a manner that previously implicit dimensions of the problem, which are sufficient to achieve behavioural success, become progressively explicit and hence available for global control of action and for verbal report. Finally, our framework is also congruent with the idea that modules, in general, are a product of learning and development rather than their starting point.

DISCUSSION: WHAT WE LEAVE BEHIND

In this chapter, we have attempted to outline a framework that offers a clear functional role to consciousness by linking conscious awareness with adaptation in general, and with learning in particular. We have argued that if we take consciousness as the only mechanism through which flexible control can be achieved over action, then it follows that learning should be the most important factor that determines the contents of conscious experience. Learning thus shapes consciousness, and consciousness, in turn, reflects the adapted appreciation of the dynamics of the current situation that is necessary to make flexible control over action possible (see also Perruchet and Vinter, Chapter 2). Our framework as it stands, however, does not address *how* the contents of consciousness are shaped by experience; it merely suggests the conditions under which representations are most likely to become part of conscious experience, and, importantly for our purposes, it also roots the emergence of conscious awareness into thoroughly subsymbolic mechanisms.

Further, our framework does not assume that there is a strong distinction between conscious and non-conscious aspects of cognition. Rather, it assumes that conscious and unconscious aspects of cognition are simply that—*aspects* of a single set of underlying neural mechanisms. Again, this position does not deny (far from it) that there are qualitative differences between conscious and unconscious computations, but simply emphasises that such differences are rooted in the non-linear properties of otherwise graded, continuous representation and processing systems. The most important implication of these assumptions in the context of implicit learning research is that our framework leaves open the possibility for change to occur without intention and without concurrent awareness that change is taking place.

"What we leave behind", then, is a large set of unanswered questions about the fate of what we have called "explicit representations"—those representations that we assume constitute the best candidates to form the contents of phenomenal experience. However, we hope to have convinced readers that: (1) understanding conscious (symbolic) cognition necessarily involves rooting this understanding in an analysis of implicit (subsymbolic) cognition; and (2) understanding processes of learning is fundamental for any theory of consciousness. In this respect, the study of implicit learning has a bright future, for it is through the development of sensitive paradigms to explore the differences between conscious and unconscious cognition that one can best contribute to the search for the neural correlates of consciousness.

ACKNOWLEDGEMENTS

Axel Cleeremans is a research associate with the National Fund for Scientific Research (Belgium). This work was supported by a grant from the Université Libre de Bruxelles in support of IUAP program P4/19, by grant HPRN-CT-2000-00065 from the European Commission, and by DGES Grant PB97-0525 from the Ministerio de Educación y Cultura (Spain) to Luis Jiménez.

REFERENCES

Ader, R., & Cohen, N. (1985). CNS–immune system interactions: Conditioning phenomena. *Behavioral and Brain Sciences, 8,* 379–394.

Anderson, J.R. (1995). *Learning and memory*. New York: Wiley.

Atkinson, A., Thomas, M., & Cleeremans, A. (2000). Consciousness: Mapping the theoretical landscape. *Trends in Cognitive Sciences, 4*(10), 372–382.

Atkinson, R.C., & Shiffrin, R.M. (1971). The control of short-term memory. *Scientific American, 224*, 82–90.

Baars, B. (1988). *A cognitive theory of consciousness*. Cambridge: Cambridge University Press.

Becker, S., Moscovitch, M., Behrmann, M., & Joordens, S. (1997). Long-term semantic priming: A computational account and empirical evidence. *Journal of Experimental Psychology: Learning, Memory and Cognition, 23*, 1059–1082.

Block, N. (1995). On a confusion about a function of consciousness. *Behavioral and Brain Sciences, 18*, 227–287.

Brewer, W.F. (1974). There is no convincing evidence for operant or classical conditioning in adult humans. In W.B. Weimer & D.S. Palermo (Eds.), *Cognition and the symbolic processes*. Mahwah, NJ: Lawrence Erlbaum Associates Inc.

Broadbent, D.E., Fitzgerald, P., & Broadbent, M.H.P. (1986). Implicit and explicit knowledge in the control of complex system. *British Journal of Psychology, 77*, 33–50.

Chalmers, D.J. (1996). *The conscious mind: In search of a fundamental theory*. Oxford: Oxford University Press.

Clark, A., & Karmiloff-Smith, A. (1993). The cognizer's innards: A psychological and philosophical perspective on the development of thought. *Mind and Language, 8*, 487–519.

Cleeremans, A. (1997). Principles for implicit learning. In D.C. Berry (Ed.), *How implicit is implicit learning?* (pp. 195–234). Oxford: Oxford University Press.

Cleeremans, A., Destrebecqz, A., & Boyer, M. (1998). Implicit learning: News from the front. *Trends in Cognitive Sciences, 2*, 406–416.

Cleeremans, A., Servan-Schreiber, D., & McClelland, J.L. (1989). Finite state automata and simple recurrent networks. *Neural Computation, 1*, 372–381.

Clegg, B.A., DiGirolamo, G.J., & Keele, S.W. (1998). Sequence learning. *Trends in Cognitive Science, 2*, 275–281.

Cohen, A., Ivry, R.I., & Keele, S.W. (1990). Attention and structure in sequence learning. *Journal of Experimental Psychology: Learning, Memory and Cognition, 16*, 17–30.

Crick, F., & Koch, C. (1990). Towards a neurobiological theory of consciousness. *Seminars in the Neurosciences, 2*, 263–275.

Crick, F., & Koch, C. (1995). Are we aware of neural activity in primary visual cortex? *Nature, 375*, 121–123.

Curran, T., & Keele, S.W. (1993). Attentional and nonattentional forms of sequence learning. *Journal of Experimental Psychology: Learning, Memory and Cognition, 19*, 189–202.

Dehaene, S., & Naccache, L. (2001). Towards a cognitive neuroscience of consciousness: Basic evidence and a workspace framework. *Cognition, 79*, 1–37.

Dennett, D.C. (1991). *Consciousness explained*. Boston, MA: Little, Brown & Co.

Dennett, D.C. (1996). *Kinds of minds: Towards an understanding of consciousness*. New York: Basic Books.

Destrebecqz, A., & Cleeremans, A. (2001). Can sequence learning be implicit? New evidence with the process dissociation procedure. *Psychonomic Bulletin & Review, 8*(2), 343–350.

Dienes, Z., & Perner, J. (1999). A theory of implicit and explicit knowledge. *Behavioral and Brain Sciences, 22*, 735–808.

Dretske, F. (1988). *Explaining behavior*. Cambridge, MA: MIT Press.

Dulany, D.E. (1997). Consciousness in the explicit (deliberative) and implicit (evocative). In J.D. Cohen & J.W. Schooler (Eds.), *Scientific approaches to the study of consciousness* (pp. 179–212). Mahwah, NJ: Lawrence Erlbaum Associates Inc.

Elbert, T., Pantey, C., Wienbruch, C., Rockstroh, B., & Taub, E. (1995). Increased cortical representation of the fingers of the left hand in string players. *Science, 270*, 305–307.

Elman, J.L. (1990). Finding structure in time. *Cognitive Science, 14*, 179–211.

Eriksson, P.S., Perfilieva, E., Björk-Eriksson, T., Alborn, A.-M., Nordborg, C., Peterson, D.A., & Gage, F.H. (1998). Neurogenesis in the adult hippocampus. *Nature Medicine, 4*(11), 1313–1317.

Farah, M.J. (1994). Visual perception and visual awareness after brain damage: A tutorial overview. In C. Umiltà & M. Moscovitch (Eds.), *Attention and Performance XV: Conscious and nonconscious information processing* (pp. 37–76). Cambridge, MA: MIT Press.

Farah, M.J. (1998). Why does the somatosensory homunculus have hands next to face and feet next to genitals: A hypothesis. *Neural Computation, 10*(8), 1983–1985.

Fodor, J. (1975). *The language of thought.* New York: Harper & Row Publishers Inc.

French, R.M. (2000). The Turing test: The first 50 years. *Trends in Cognitive Sciences, 4*(3), 115–122.

Friedrich, F.J., Henik, A., & Tzelgov, J. (1991). Automatic processes in lexical access and spreading activation. *Journal of Experimental Psychology: Human Perception and Performance, 17*, 792–806.

Frith, C., Perry, R., & Lumer, E. (1999). The neural correlates of conscious experience: An experimental framework. *Trends in Cognitive Sciences, 3*, 105–114.

Grossberg, S. (1999). The link between brain learning, attention, and consciousness. *Consciousness and Cognition, 8*, 1–44.

Holender, D. (1986). Semantic activation without conscious activation in dichotic listening, parafoveal vision, and visual masking: A survey and appraisal. *Behavioral and Brain Sciences, 9*, 1–23.

Holender, D. (1992). Expectancy effects, congruity effects, and the interpretation of response latency measurement. In J. Alégria, D. Holender, J.J.D. Morais, & M. Radeau (Eds.), *Analytic approaches to human cognition* (pp. 351–375). Amsterdam: Elsevier.

Jacoby, L.L. (1991). A process dissociation framework: Separating automatic from intentional uses of memory. *Journal of Memory and Language, 30*, 513–541.

Jiang, Y., & Chun, M. (in press). Selective attention modulates implicit learning. *Quarterly Journal of Experimental Psychology.*

Jiménez, L., & Cleeremans, A. (1999). Fishing with the wrong nets: How the implicit slips through the representational theory of mind. *Behavioral and Brain Sciences, 22*, 771.

Jiménez, L., & Méndez, C. (1999). Which attention is needed for implicit sequence learning? *Journal of Experimental Psychology: Learning, Memory, and Cognition, 25*, 236–259.

Jiménez, L. & Méndez, C. (2001). Implicit sequence learning with competing explicit cues. *Quarterly Journal of Experimental Psychology (A), 54*(2), 345–369.

Jiménez, L., Méndez, C., & Cleeremans, A. (1996). Comparing direct and indirect measures of sequence learning. *Journal of Experimental Psychology: Learning, Memory, and Cognition, 22*, 948–969.

Joordens, S., & Becker, S. (1997). The long and short of semantic priming effects in lexical decision. *Journal of Experimental Psychology: Learning, Memory, and Cognition, 23*, 1083–1105.

Kanwisher, N. (2001). Neural events and perceptual awareness. *Cognition, 79*, 89–113.

Karmiloff-Smith, A. (1992). *Beyond modularity: A developmental perspective on cognitive science.* Cambridge, MA: MIT Press.

Kaye, D.B., & Brown, S.W. (1985). Levels and speed of processing effects on word analysis. *Memory and Cognition, 13*, 425–434.

Kinsbourne, M. (1997). What qualifies a representation for a role in consciousness? In J.D. Cohen & J.W. Schooler (Eds.), *Scientific approaches to consciousness* (pp. 335–355). Mahwah, NJ: Lawrence Erlbaum Associates Inc.

Klein, S.B. (1991). *Learning: principles and applications.* New York: McGraw Hill.

Maguire, E.A., Gadian, D.G., Johnsrude, I.S., Good, C.D., Ashburner, J., Frackowiak, R.S.,

& Frith, C.D. (2000). Navigation-related structural change in the hippocampi of taxi drivers. *Proceedings of the National Academy of Sciences of the U.S.A.*, *10*, 1073.

Mangan, B. (1993). Taking phenomenology seriously: The "fringe" and its implication for cognitive research. *Consciousness and Cognition*, *2*, 89–108.

Mareschal, D., Plunkett, K., & Harris, P. (1999). A computational and neuropsychological account of object-directed behaviours in infancy. *Developmental Science*, *2*, 306–317.

Mathis, W.D., & Mozer, M.C. (1996). *Conscious and unconscious perception: A computational theory*. Paper presented at the Proceedings of the Eighteenth Annual Conference of the Cognitive Science Society, Hillsdale, NJ.

McClelland, J.L. (1979). On the time-relations of mental processes: An examination of systems in cascade. *Psychological Review*, *86*, 287–330.

McClelland, J.L., & Jenkins, E. (1991). Nature, nurture, and connectionism: Implications for connectionist models of development. In K.V. Lehn (Ed.), *Architectures for intelligence—the twenty-second (1988) Carnegie Symposium on Cognition*. Hillsdale, NJ: Lawrence Erlbaum Associates Inc.

McClelland, J.L., McNaughton, B.L., & O'Reilly, R.C. (1995). Why there are complementary learning systems in the hippocampus and neocortex: Insights from the successes and failures of connectionist models of learning and memory. *Psychological Review*, *102*, 419–457.

Munakata, Y., McClelland, J.L., Johnson, M.H., & Siegler, R.S. (1997). Rethinking infant knowledge: Toward an adaptive process account of successes and failures in object permanence tasks. *Psychological Review*, *10*(4), 686–713.

Nissen, M.J., & Bullemer, P. (1987). Attentional requirement of learning: Evidence from performance measures. *Cognitive Psychology*, *19*, 1–32.

O'Brien, G., & Opie, J. (1999). A connectionist theory of phenomenal experience. *Behavioral and Brain Sciences*, *22*, 175–196.

O'Reilly, R.C., & Munakata, Y. (2000). *Computational explorations in cognitive neuroscience: Understanding the mind by simulating the brain*. Cambridge, MA: MIT Press.

Perruchet, P., & Vinter, A. (1998). Learning and development: The implicit knowledge assumption reconsidered. In M.A. Stadler & P.A. Frensch (Eds.), *Handbook of implicit learning* (Vol. 15, pp. 495–531). Thousand Oaks, CA: Sage Publications.

Perruchet, P., Vinter, A., & Gallego, J. (1997). Implicit learning shapes new conscious percepts and representations. *Psychonomic Bulletin and Review*, *4*, 43–48.

Posner, M.I., & Rothbart, M.K. (1998). Attention, self-regulation, and consciousness. *Philosophical Transactions of the Royal Society B*, *353*, 1915–1927.

Reed, J., & Johnson, P. (1994). Assessing implicit learning with indirect tests: Determining what is learned about sequence structure. *Journal of Experimental Psychology: Learning, Memory and Cognition*, *20*, 585–594.

Rosenthal, D. (1986). Two concepts of consciousness. *Philosophical Studies*, *94*, 329–359.

Rosenthal, D. (1997). A theory of consciousness. In N. Block, O. Flanagan, & G. Güzeldere (Eds.), *The nature of consciousness: Philosophical debates*. Cambridge, MA: MIT Press.

Rumelhart, D.E., & McClelland, J.L. (1986). *Parallel distributed processing: Explorations in the microstructure of cognition. Volume 1: Foundations*. Cambridge, MA: MIT Press.

Schacter, D.L. (1989). On the relations between memory and consciousness: Dissociable interactions and conscious experience. In H.L. Roediger & F.I.M. Craik (Eds.), *Varieties of memory and consciousness: Essays in honour of Endel Tulving* (pp. 355–389). Mahwah, NJ: Lawrence Erlbaum Associates Inc.

Searle, J.R. (1980). Minds, brains, and programs. *Behavioral and Brain Sciences*, *3*, 417–457.

Searle, J.R. (1992). *The rediscovery of the mind*. Cambridge, MA: MIT Press.

Searle, J.R. (1999). Chinese room argument. In R.A. Wilson & F.C. Keil (Eds.), *The MIT encyclopedia of the cognitive sciences* (pp. 115–116). Cambridge, MA: The MIT Press.

Shanks, D.R., & St John, M.F. (1994). Characteristics of dissociable human learning systems. *Behavioral and Brain Sciences*, *17*, 367–447.

Smith, M.C., Theodor, L., & Franklin, P.E. (1983). The relationship between contextual facilitation and depth of processing. *Journal of Experimental Psychology: Learning, Memory, and Cognition*, *9*, 697–712.

Tarpy, R.M. (1997). *Contemporary learning theory and research*. New York: McGraw Hill.

Tononi, G., & Edelman, G.M. (1998). Consciousness and complexity. *Science*, *282*(5395), 1846–1851.

Tzelgov, J. (1997). Automatic but conscious: That is how we act most of the time. In R.S. Wyer (Ed.), *The automaticity of everyday life* (Vol. X, pp. 217–230). Mahwah, NJ: Lawrence Erlbaum Associates Inc.

Willingham, D.B., Nissen, M.J., & Bullemer, P. (1989). On the development of procedural knowledge. *Journal of Experimental Psychology: Learning, Memory and Cognition*, *15*, 1047–1060.

CHAPTER TWO

The Self-organising Consciousness: A framework for implicit learning

Pierre Perruchet and Annie Vinter
Universite de Bourgogne, France

The prevalent models of implicit learning have difficulty in accounting for the critical importance of the attention paid to the study material during the familiarisation phase of a learning session. In this chapter, we show that a close examination of the on-line content of successive attentional focuses, which form subjects' phenomenal experience, suggests a new interpretation of implicit learning. This interpretation is based on the fact that conscious contents are self-organising. We first present the notion of Self-organising Consciousness in the context of the discovery of words in artificial languages, and then generalise it to the formation of other forms of conscious representations. We then discuss how the concept of Self-organising Consciousness allows us to think in a non-standard way about the processes occurring in implicit learning situations, and even in situations involving some form of abstraction with regard to the surface features of the material. Finally, we discuss the meaning and the validity of introducing consciousness into a causal, computationally implementable framework.

ATTENTION IS A CONDITION FOR LEARNING

Most overviews of the literature (e.g. Cleeremans, Destrebecq, & Boyer, 1998) distinguish between three main situations in which implicit learning has been studied. In all three cases, subjects have to deal with a situation

41

governed by complex, arbitrary rules, without being prompted for an explicit analysis of the task.

In artificial grammar learning (e.g. Reber, 1976), the material is usually composed of a set of consonants, the nature and the ordering of which are defined by a finite-state grammar. Subjects have to learn by rote the letter strings generated by this grammar. After the training session, they are asked to judge the grammaticality of new sequences, half of which obey the rules of the grammar and half of which violate them.

In the dynamic system control tasks (e.g. Berry & Broadbent, 1988), subjects have to control a dynamic system simulated on a computer, such as a sugar production factory or a city transport system. They are required to reach and maintain specified target values of an output variable by varying one or two input variables. The output and input variables are linked by a linear equation including the current state of the system as one term.

Finally, in sequential reaction time tasks (e.g. Nissen & Bullemer, 1987), subjects have to respond to targets located at several places on a computer screen. In most cases, the underlying rule is simply that one and the same sequence is continuously repeated. Performance is assessed through choice reaction times to these targets.

There are many variants of these prototypical situations, and other situations have received increasing attention in recent years (for instance the implicit learning of invariant characteristics in the McGeorge & Burton [1990] paradigm). Whatever the paradigm, however, the same two results have emerged. Firstly, subjects are shown to perform above chance levels in such situations; secondly, most aspects of this behavioural adaptation to the structural features of the situation are not due to the intentional exploitation of subjects' explicit knowledge about these features (see Chapter 1 for a more detailed presentation of this literature).

A question of major interest is whether performance improvement depends on the amount of attention paid to the study material during the familiarisation phase. This question has not received the same amount of interest in the different subareas of the field, but, in each case, the same methodology has been applied. The principle consists in adding a concurrent secondary task during the training session, then observing whether performance improvement is equivalent to that observed in a single-task, standard procedure. Regarding artificial grammars, Reber (e.g. 1993) has acknowledged that attention to the study material is necessary for learning to occur, although the point has rarely been addressed in empirical investigations. In support of this claim, Dienes, Broadbent, and Berry (1991) have shown that the accuracy of grammaticality judgements was lowered when subjects had to perform a concurrent random number generation task during the familiarisation phase.

The studies carried out on dynamic system control tasks provide a more contrasted picture. The theory surrounding the early studies on these tasks posited a distinction between two forms of learning: Selective (i.e. with attention) and unselective (i.e. without attention; e.g. Berry & Broadbent, 1988). Unselective learning was assumed to occur when the situation was too complex to be solved by attention-based mechanisms. In support of this conception, Hayes and Broadbent (1988) reported that adding a secondary task of letter or digit generation interfered with learning a simple system control task, but facilitated learning in a more complex version of the same task. However, these results have been criticised for the lack of power of the statistical tests (Dienes et al., 1991). Moreover, both Dulany and Wilson (unpublished data) and Green and Shanks (1993) failed to replicate these results (despite extensive attempts to do so), and observed that, as a rule, the secondary task impaired performance irrespective of the complexity of the task. To the best of our knowledge, the notion of unselective learning, as initially discussed in the studies conducted by Broadbent and colleagues, is no longer advocated.

The idea of two forms of learning, differing according to whether attention is required or not, has also been proposed in the context of repeated sequence learning, although the proposal is diametrically opposed to the position adopted by Broadbent and co-workers. Indeed, the hypothesis was that attention is required for learning complex sequences, while non-attentional learning is efficient for the simplest forms of sequential dependencies. The secondary task typically used in this context is a tone-counting task, in which a high- or low-pitched tone sound is emitted after each trial and subjects are required to keep a running count of one of them (e.g. high-pitched tones). According to Cohen, Ivry, and Keele (1990), introducing this secondary task impaired learning of complex sequences, while failing to affect the learning of sequences incorporating only first-order contingencies.

However, again, this view no longer appears to be tenable. Observing performance improvement under dual-task conditions does not imply the existence of a non-attentional form of learning, because the secondary task might not deplete the attentional resources completely. As claimed by Stadler (1995, p. 683) "Even when implicit serial learning is observed in conjunction with the tone-counting task, . . ., it cannot be said that learning occurred without attentional capacity—the participants certainly devoted attention to the serial reaction time task". Evidence favouring attentional involvement stems notably from the fact that, as a rule, normal subjects have acquired explicit knowledge of the sequence after the training session, even when training was performed under dual-task conditions (e.g. Perruchet & Amorim, 1992; Shanks & Johnstone, 1999). The logic here is that because explicit memories require attentional processes, recall or recognition of a stimulus can be used as a measure of prior stimulus attendedness (e.g. Schmidt & Dark, 1998, p. 228). Closing their recent survey of the role of attention in implicit sequence learning, Hsiao and Reber (1998, p. 487) concluded: "We view sequence learning as occurring in the background of the residual attention after the cost of the tone-counting task and the key-pressing task. If there is still sufficient attention available to the encoding of the sequence, learning will be successful; otherwise, failure will result"; for other approaches that emphasise the role of attention, see Frensch, Buchner, and Lin (1994) and Jiménez and Mendez (1999). Note that this conclusion does not imply that performance is systematically impaired in dual-task conditions. Indeed, in a few cases, performance has been found to be insensitive to capacity load (Jiménez & Mendez, 1999; Stadler, 1995), a result that can be easily accounted for by some kind of floor or ceiling effect.

Thus, recent studies strongly challenge the claims that two forms of learning can be distinguished, with a non-attentional form emerging when the situation is very complex (e.g. Berry & Broadbent, 1988) or very simple (Cohen et al., 1990). Most probably, improved performance in any implicit learning situation implies at least minimal attentional involvement. This conclusion comes as no surprise, because the major role played by selective attention in acquisition processes is an old and robust empirical finding. This role has been identified, for instance, in the literature on animal conditioning (Mackintosh, 1975), automatisms (Fisk & Schneider, 1994), perception (Rock & Gutman, 1981), and memory (Roediger, 1990). This contention holds even for the so-called implicit memory phenomena, in which performance does not involve the recollection of the initial episodes. There is now overwhelming evidence that attention to the material at the time of encoding is a necessary condition for the observation of improved performance in subsequent implicit memory tests, such as word completion and perceptual identification tasks (Crabb & Dark, 1999), reading tasks (MacDonald & MacLeod, 1998), or object decision tasks (Ganor-Stern, Seamon, & Carrasco, 1998).

FROM ATTENTIONAL RESOURCES TO PHENOMENAL CONSCIOUSNESS

Attention is generally construed in terms of mental resources or capacity. The usual way of manipulating attention in implicit learning settings (namely, the dual task paradigm) and the aim of examining whether performance is impaired when attention is shared between different sources of information, are in keeping with this energetic, quantitative view of attention. Within this perspective, the need for a certain amount of mental resources for learning in the complex learning settings appears to be anything but surprising.

However, a closer look at this issue reveals a striking paradox. The general view of most contributors to the implicit learning literature is that implicit learning relies on powerful unconscious mechanisms, the main property of which is, precisely, their freedom from capacity limitations. Thus the idea that the involvement of attention is necessary for the recruitment of mechanisms that are thought to be free of attentional limitations is somewhat awkward.

This paradox appears still more pronounced if, instead of considering attention as a pool of processing capacities, we consider its content, which is generally identified with subjects' phenomenal consciousness (e.g. Cowan, 1995; Mandler, 1975; Miller, 1962; Posner & Boies, 1971).[1] Indeed, it turns out that, whatever this content might be, it certainly does not match the cognitive operations that most researchers hypothesise. Even a rough post-experimental interview is sufficient to make it clear that attention is not devoted to abstracting the rules that the advocates of abstractionist positions (e.g. Marcus, Vijayan, Rao, & Vishton, 1999; Reber, 1993) consider essential. Likewise, attention is certainly not devoted to the statistical analysis of the raw data that other authors claim to be the source of performance improvement in implicit learning settings (e.g. Cleeremans, 1993). Attention, presumably, is centred on the on-line processing of the sensory data. Thus, considering the object of attention actually makes the necessity of attention in implicit learning still more puzzling than considering attention only as an unspecified pool of capacity. Indeed, it looks quite mysterious why the initial coding of the sensory data should need attention, while all the subsequent operations performed on these data could be run without any attentional engagement and conscious counterparts.

To summarise: (1) empirical data provide evidence of a close link between improved performance in implicit learning settings and the amount of attention devoted to the material during the familiarisation phase of the task;

---

[1] Some authors (e.g. Velmans, 1999) have argued that phenomenal consciousness and attention ought to be distinguished, because attention is selective whereas "consciousness incorporates both a central focus, and a rich polymodal periphery", to borrow the expression used by O'Brien and Opie (1999). This argument amounts to defining attention as the conceptually driven mechanisms that are directed towards a specific source of information in response to task instructions. This view defines what Schmidt and Dark (1998) call the intention-equals-attention view, according to which participants' intention to attend exclusively to a target is sufficient to restrict attentional processing to this target. However, the fact that the instructions ask participants to pay attention to a target does not prevent them from making quick attentional shifts toward non-attended information. Therefore, unless one endorses a highly restrictive definition of attended information as the informational content on which subjects are asked to focus, we see no reason to dissociate attention and consciousness on the basis of their relative selectivity.

and (2) prevalent theories of implicit learning fail to incorporate this finding. Indeed, the dependence of implicit learning on limited attentional capacity is contradictory to the postulate (central to such theories) of a powerful unconscious processor, and this contradiction is exacerbated if one considers the mismatch between the content of attention such as it is revealed through verbal reports and the hypothesised mental operations. Overall, the hypothesised machinery would appear to be particularly ill adapted. If evolution has endowed human minds with the powerful and unlimited analytical capabilities that most theoreticians of implicit learning attribute to the unconscious mind, it appears especially inefficient that the expression of these capabilities should be dependent on an attentional bottleneck acting on the presumably simpler perceptual processing of the information.

Before taxing evolution for having missed its shot, however, we should perhaps examine whether the error might lie with the theories of implicit learning. The present chapter is intended to show that if learning needs attention, then this is simply because learning is a natural by-product of the attentional, on-line perceptual processing of the incoming information. The powerful processors whose existence is postulated by researchers, whether they are thought to be in the service of rule abstraction or statistical analysis, are devoid of any object. The subsequent sections are aimed at explaining why the close scrutiny of conscious contents in a dynamic perspective provides us with a new explanation for performance improvement in implicit learning. This is because this conscious content, as we will shortly show, has the astonishing property of being capable of self-organisation.[2]

THE SELF-ORGANISATION OF PERCEPTUAL EXPERIENCE IN WORD DISCOVERY

We introduce the notion of Self-organising Consciousness (SOC) by starting from the discovery of the words that form oral language as an

---

[2] At this point, it is crucial to avoid a deep misunderstanding of our proposal. In the implicit learning area, the term "consciousness" is regularly associated with the explicit knowledge that subjects might have gained about the study material during the study phase. As a rule, studies in which the measures of explicit knowledge fulfill both Shanks and St John's (1994) information and sensitivity criteria show that performance improvement is accompanied by the explicit knowledge of the relevant aspects of the procedure. In this context, our conception could be expected to be a variant of the view that subjects exploit their explicit knowledge about the structure of the situation with the powerful analytical tools of conscious thought in order to anticipate the next event or to select the right response in each situation. Our conception is, in fact, radically different. In the present chapter, the term "consciousness" designates the on-line content of the attentional focus, and not the explicit knowledge that subjects might have developed about the material, such as it might be revealed in post-experimental tests.

example of implicit learning. The reason we do not take one of the three major paradigms discussed above as our starting point is convenience of presentation, and it is worth stressing from the outset that the argument below is also relevant to these classical paradigms, in a way that will be made clear in a subsequent section.

Language acquisition initially proceeds from auditory input, and linguistic utterances usually consist of sentences linking several words without clear physical boundaries. The question thus arises: How do infants become able to segment a continuous speech stream into words? Recent psycho-linguistic research has identified a number of prosodic and phonological cues that could potentially help infants, but they provide only probabilistic information. The importance of prosodic and phonological cues in word discovery is further questioned by recent experimental studies showing that these cues are not necessary. For instance, Saffran, Newport, and Aslin (1996a) used an artificial language consisting of six trisyllabic words, such as *babupu* and *bupada*. The words were read by a speech synthesiser in random order in immediate succession, without pauses or any other prosodic cues. Thus the participants heard a continuous series of syllables without any word boundary cues. In the following phase, they were asked to perform a forced choice test in which they had to indicate which of two items sounded more like a word from the artificial language. One of the items was a word from the artificial language, whereas the other was a new combination of three syllables belonging to the language. Participants performed significantly better than would be expected by chance. This and other studies (Saffran, Aslin, & Newport, 1996b; Saffran, Newport, Aslin, Tunick, & Barrueco, 1997) offer impressive support for the hypothesis that people are able to learn the words forming a continuous speech stream without any prosodic or phonological cues for word boundaries. Our aim in this section is to show that word extraction can be explained by the action of elementary, associative-like processes acting on the initial conscious percepts, the result of which is to modify the conscious experience we have of the linguistic input.

What is the phenomenal experience of the listener of a new language such as the one used in the Saffran et al. experiments, at the beginning and end of training respectively? When people are confronted with material consisting of a succession of elements, each of them matching some of their processing primitives, they segment this material into small and disjunctive parts comprising a small number of primitives. As adults, we have direct evidence of the phenomenon. For instance, when asked to read nonsense consonant strings, we read the material not on a regular, rhythmic, letter-by-letter basis, but rather by chunking a few letters together. The same phenomenon presumably occurs when a listener is faced with an unknown spoken language, with the syllables or other phonological units forming the subjective processing primitives instead of the letters. Chunking, we contend, is a ubiquitous phenomenon, due to the intrinsic constraints of attentional processing, with each chunk corresponding to one attentional focus. Importantly, however, the listener's initial conscious experience consists of a succession of chunks that have only a weak probability of matching the words of the language.

After extensive exposure to the language, the listener's phenomenal experience is presumably the experience each of us has of our mother tongue, that is the experience of perceiving a sequence of words. Our proposal is that the final phenomenal experience of perceiving words emerges through the progressive transformation of the primitives guiding the initial perception of the language, and that this transformation is due to the self-organising property of the content of phenomenal experience. The basic principle is fairly simple. The primitives forming a chunk, that is, those that are perceived within one attentional focus as a consequence of their experienced temporal proximity, tend to pool together and form a new primitive for the system. As a consequence, they can enter as a unitary component into a new chunk in a further processing step. This explains why the phenomenal experience changes with practice. But why do the initial primitives evolve into a small number of words instead of innumerable irrelevant processing units?

The reason lies in the combined consideration of two phenomena. The first depends on the properties of the human processing system. The future of the chunk that forms a conscious episode depends on ubiquitous laws of associative learning and memory. If the same experience does not re-occur within some temporal lag, the possibility of a chunk acting as a processing primitive vanishes rapidly, as a consequence both of natural decay and of interference with the processing of similar material. The chunks evolve into primitives only if they are repeated. Thus some primitives emerge through a natural selection process, because forgetting and interference lead the human processing system to select the repeated parts from all of those generated by the initial, presumably mostly irrelevant, chunking of the material. The relevance of this phenomenon becomes clear when viewed in relation to a property inherent to any language. If the speech signal is segmented into small parts on a random basis, these parts have more chance of being repeated if they match a word, or a part of a word, than if they straddle word boundaries (for instance, in the prior sentence, "random" or "basis" have more chance of being repeated elsewhere in the text than "domba"). In consequence, the primitives that emerge from the natural selection due to forgetting and interference are more likely to match a word, or a part of a word, than a between-word segment.

This account has been implemented in a computer program, PARSER (see the Appendix on page 67) and applied to the artificial languages used by Saffran and colleagues. Simulations revealed that PARSER extracted the words of the language well before exhausting the material presented to participants in the Saffran et al. (1996b) experiments. In addition, PARSER was able to simulate the results obtained under attention-disturbing conditions (Saffran et al., 1997) and those collected from 8-month-old infants (Saffran et al., 1996a). Finally, the good performance of PARSER was not limited to the trisyllabic words used by Saffran et al., but also extended to a language consisting of one- to five-syllable words (Perruchet & Vinter, 1998a).

To summarise, we suggest that the discovery of the words results from the interaction between one property of language—essentially that the probability of repeatedly selecting the same group of syllables by chance is higher if these syllables form intra-word rather than between-words components—and the properties of the processing systems—essentially that repeated perceptual chunks evolve into processing primitives, which in turn determine the way further material is perceived.

GENERALISATION

We have spent a long time considering word discovery in artificial languages because we believe that the basic principles of the explanation proposed in this context extend to the formation of any perceptual and representational units regardless of the domain, the complexity of the material, and the timescale of the learning process. As we have mentioned, PARSER works thanks to the interaction between one property of the language and a few properties of the human processing system. There is no reason to believe that this interaction occurs only with artificial, simplistic languages.

On the one hand, the target property of artificial languages, namely that the probability of repeatedly selecting the same group of syllables by chance is higher if these syllables form intra-word rather than between-words components, is obviously shared by any natural language. Moreover, providing a change from phonological primitives to visual features, the same property is also true for the objects of the real world. For instance, the probability of repeatedly selecting two parts in the environment is stronger if these parts belong to the same object than if they belong to different objects. On the other hand, the properties of the processing system on which PARSER relies are very general.

Note that our solution to the word extraction issue does not involve any new and specialised learning devices. The unitisation of a few primitives, due to their processing within the same attentional focus, is one of the basic tenets of associative learning (Mackintosh, 1975). Besides being necessary, attention is also sufficient for memory and learning to occur. This means that no superimposed operations—such as some forms of intentional orientation towards learning—are required. The resulting picture is that most authors, under different terminology, would acknowledge that learning is an automatic associative process that would associate all the components that are present in the attentional focus at a given point (Frensch & Miner, 1994; Jiménez & Mendez, 1999; Logan & Etherton, 1994; Stadler, 1995; Wagner, 1981). Learning and memory are nothing other than the by-product of attentional processing.

Likewise, the laws of forgetting and the effects of repetition are ubiquitous phenomena. For instance, one fundamental assumption of the model is that a cognitive unit is forgotten when not repeated and strengthened with repetition. This assumption can be taken for granted irrespective of whether the process occurs in the few minutes of an experimental session or across larger timescales, in keeping with a long-standing tradition of research into the laws of memory and associative learning. Moreover, the interdependence of processing units and incoming information—the nature of the processing primitives determines how the material is perceived and the nature of the material determines the transformation of the processing primitives, and so on recursively—is consistent with a developmental principle initially described by Piaget's concepts of assimilation and accommodation (Piaget, 1985). Most current theories of development, although they use different terminology, also rely on the constructive interplay between assimilation-like and accommodation-like processes.

In consequence, PARSER's principles seem to be relevant to finding correct units in natural language and in the other naturalistic domains. Briefly stated, the generality of PARSER is ensured by both the generality of the world property (the most-repeated units are the relevant units of the world) and the generality of the behavioural laws (e.g. only repeated units shape long-lasting representations) on which it relies.

To summarise, the fact that conscious percepts are capable of self-organisation, initially applied to the word extraction issue in laboratory situations, suggests a new account of the human ability to build internal representations isomorphic to the actual world units.[3] In this account,

---

[3] Of course, this isomorphism is not perfect. Firstly, the representations we create are limited by sensory constraints. For instance, we do not have any perception about the sounds outside the 20–20,000 Hz range, or about the light sources in the infrared or ultraviolet wavelength range. Likewise, phenomenal experience does not provide us with any direct representation of the structure of the physical world at other scales, such as the atomic microstructure or galactic organisation. Secondly, even the parts of the world directly available to our sensory equipment can be misrepresented. For instance, in the perceptual illusions, perceptual processes generally well suited in natural situations cease doing their job reliably when faced with very special patterns. However, for the sake of brevity, we go on speaking hereafter about the isomorphism between subject's representations and world structure, even though the very phenomenon the expression recovers cannot be described as a simple term-to-term matching.

conscious representations participate in their own development. Basic principles of associative learning and memory allow conscious representations to reach their high degree of organisation and adaptiveness, provided we consider that associations occur between the rich content of conscious experiences. The notion of self-organisation excludes any organising cognitive systems or principles that would be superimposed on the phenomenal consciousness. The phenomenal consciousness itself ensures its own improvement in representational power, thanks to the propensity of conscious representations to evolve in accordance with basic associative learning principles.

RETHINKING IMPLICIT LEARNING

Even if one admits that the above account works well for the formation of conscious representations of parts of the world, such as words and objects, it turns out that those aspects are not usually conceived of as directly related to implicit learning. More generally, the existence of linguistically or physically relevant representations is not commonly considered as sufficient for accounting for human mental activities. Representations are generally construed as the elementary building blocks of thought, and mind activities are assumed to include the formation of knowledge in which the blocks are combined on the basis of some organising (e.g. logical, syntactical, or statistical) principles.

Our proposal is that the notion of self-organising consciousness offers a way of thinking about these complex aspects of behaviour without having recourse to the notion of unconscious rule abstraction or unconscious statistical computation. The idea is that the separation between basic units on the one hand, and rules governing those units on the other, or between lexicon and syntax in linguistic terminology, is warranted in a scientific approach (i.e. from the observer's viewpoint) but, at least on some occasions, might be irrelevant for the processing system. The purpose of the processing system is to generate a representation of the world that integrates the whole ongoing information (internal and external) into a coherent and meaningful event. This complex and integrative representation, we argue, makes any other forms of knowledge or computation devoid of any object. This thesis relies heavily on the idea that neural systems "trade representation against computation", to borrow the expression coined by Clark and Thornton (1997).

In Perruchet and Vinter (unpublished manuscript), we discuss at length how conscious representations can account for improved performances in various rule-governed situations. We argue that all the cases in which analytical operations, such as hypothesis testing, are apparently performed by the mind in the absence of any form of conscious awareness can be encompassed within the notion of self-organising consciousness. We saw earlier how the notion of self-organising consciousness allows us to account for the formation of internal representations that are increasingly congruent with the world structure. If we expand the scope of these representations to the various dimensions involved in a given problem, it becomes conceivable that a representation contains, in some sense, both the data and the solution of the problem. The solution pops up in the mind because it is a part of the model of the world that people have built through automatic associative processes. Let us take a simple example, one relating to the notion of transitivity. In the linear ordering tasks, two premises are presented, the formal expression of them being: A is longer than B and B is longer than C. Participants have to judge whether an expression such as: A is longer than C is correct. It can be assumed that people solve this task because they have some formal notion about the transitivity of the expression "larger than", and that they apply the transitivity rule to the problem at hand. However, people could also have built an integrative representation of the premises in the form of a linear array, and then read the response to the question directly from this representation. There is now a consensus about the idea that people proceed in this way (Evans, Newstead, & Byrne, 1993). This illustrates how a representation which is isomorphic to the world structure makes rule knowledge unnecessary.

How does our account apply to traditional situations of implicit learning? Our re-interpretation (e.g. Perruchet & Vinter, 1998b; Perruchet, Vinter, & Gallego, 1997) is that the training phase modifies the way the data are consciously coded and perceived. Let us consider artificial grammar learning as an illustration. Assuming that, say, XRX is a frequent recursion in the set of strings generated by a finite-state grammar, participants no longer perceive X and R as two familiar but separate entities, but perceive XRX as an increasingly familiar unit. One possible explanation for the above-chance grammaticality judgements of a new string including XRX is that participants interpret, more or less automatically, the level of perceptual fluency as an indicator of grammaticality. Strings that can be read easily because chunks of letters are directly perceived as familiar units would tend to be judged as grammatical. In short, in our re-appraisal, the formation of the conscious unit XRX replaces the unconscious extraction, retention, and use of a rule such as: If XR, then X.

It might seem, at first glance, that any fragment of a grammatical utterance is itself grammatical, and can be recombined with another fragment to form a new grammatical string. Given this logic, the initial chunking of the material would not matter. And indeed, the notion of "fragmentary knowledge" conveys the tacit implication that it is a quite impoverished form of knowledge. This view is faulty, as can be illustrated using the example of natural language. For instance, in the preceding sentence, the segments: "this view", or "natural language" form structurally relevant sequences, in the sense that they can be recombined with a large number of other sequences, whereas "faulty, as can" cannot be easily integrated as a component in another linguistic context, although it is a component of a legal sentence. It is obvious that it is preferable to become familiar with the former segments than with the latter. Likewise, in the letter strings generated by a finite-state grammar, it is preferable to become familiar with a subset of fragments—for instance, those that are generated by a recursive loop—than with other, randomly selected, fragments. We (Perruchet, Vinter, Pacteau, & Gallego, in press) have shown that participants in an artificial grammar learning setting indeed formed the structurally relevant units. They were asked to read each string generated by a finite-state grammar and, immediately after reading, to mark with a slash bar (/) the natural segmentation positions. The participants repeated this task after a phase of familiarisation with the material, which consisted of learning items by rote, performing a short-term matching task, or searching for rules. The same number of total units was observed before and after the training phase, thus indicating that participants did not tend to form increasingly larger units. However, the number of different units reliably decreased, whatever the task during training. This result was taken as evidence that participants' processing units became increasingly relevant as training progressed (see also Servan-Schreiber & Anderson, 1990). Perruchet et al. (in press) also showed that PARSER, the computer model that was used previously to account for the discovery of words in an unsegmented speech flow (Perruchet & Vinter, 1998a; see p. 67), also accounted for participants' actual performance. Thus the principles that make it possible to discover the lexical units of an artificial language built from the random concatenation of words also proved to be efficient in the discovery of the syntactically relevant units of an artificial language built from a finite-state grammar.

It is worth examining why such simple principles work well in a situation that was once thought of as involving grammatical rule abstraction. It is because first-order and second-order dependency rules capture virtually all the structural constraints of the standard finite-state grammars. For instance, Perruchet and Gallego (1997) have demonstrated that consideration of only the first-order dependency rules is sufficient to account for the performance of the participants in the Reber (1976) experiments and many others that use the same material.

The same demonstration can be repeated for other standard situations of implicit learning. Regarding the repeated sequence tasks, the situation is still simpler. Indeed, because the same sequence is repeated continuously, the way this sequence is segmented is of no consequence: no chunk is any more relevant than any other. There is a prerequisite, nevertheless: Namely, that the same parsing occurs throughout the session. Empirical data support the point. Of special interest in this context is the Stadler (1995) study. Stadler noted that the tone-counting task used in sequence learning paradigms can alter performance by dividing a pool of limited resources—the conventional interpretation of attentional effects—but also by disrupting the organisation of the sequence. Indeed, although a tone occurs after each trial, only some tones (e.g. high-speech tones) trigger the update of the running count. These tones, presumably, serve as boundaries for successive perceptual chunks. If these tones are introduced randomly then the content of the perceptual chunks changes continuously throughout the session, a circumstance that might impair learning. Stadler has shown that this hypothesis is correct: a task preventing the repeated processing of the same chunks is detrimental for learning, even though overall resources are left intact, whereas a task with additional attentional demands respecting the perceptual organisation has no effect. Stadler's study provides a strong indication that the function of attention must not be understood only as a pool of unspecific resources, and that the content of successive attentional focuses, or in other words the subjects' phenomenal experience of the task, is a determinant of performance improvement.

ABSTRACTING AWAY FROM THE SENSORY CONTENT

In the preceding section, we claimed that the changes in the way we consciously perceive and represent our environment might underlie some apparent phenomena of syntax sensitivity. In some cases, it is easy to see how a simple representation could replace genuine rule knowledge. For instance, it is easy to see how perceiving XRX as a unit could replace the rule: "If XR then X". However, adaptation to other situations does not seem reducible to the same approach. An especially striking example is provided by the studies that reveal participants' ability to abstract away from the sensory content of the training situation, an ability that cannot seemingly be explained by any association-based account.

Experimental evidence for abstraction

As a case in point, let us consider the recent experiments by Marcus, Vijayan, Rao, and Vishton (1999). Seven-month-old infants were exposed to a simplified, artificial language during a training phase. Then they were presented with a few test items, some of which belonged to the same language whereas others introduced some structural novelty. The infants controlled the exposure duration of the stimuli by their visual fixation on a light. Their discrimination was assessed through their longer fixation (and hence listening) times for items introducing structural novelty.

The point of interest is that Marcus and co-workers introduced a change in the sensory content of the material between the training and the test phases. For instance, in one experiment, infants heard 16 three-word sentences such as *gatiti*, *linana*, or *tanana*, during the training phase. All of these sentences were constructed on the basis of an ABB grammar. The infants were then presented with 12 other three-word sentences, such as *wofefe* and *wofewo*. The crucial point is that although all of the test items were composed of new words, only half of them were constructed from the grammar with which the infants had been familiarised. In the selected example, the grammatical item was *wofefe*. *Wofewo* introduces a structural novelty in that it is generated from a concurrent ABA grammar. The infants tended to listen more to the sentences generated by the ABA grammar, thus indicating their sensitivity to the structural novelty. In another experiment, infants were shown to be able to discriminate sentences generated by an AAB grammar.

Similar studies using more complex material have been performed with 11-month-old infants (Gomez & Gerken, 1999) and with adults. In some studies involving artificial grammar, the letters forming the study items are changed in a consistent way for the test of grammaticality (e.g. C is always replaced by X, B by L, and so on). Reber (1969), and several subsequent studies (Dienes & Altman, 1997; Manza & Reber, 1997; Mathews et al. 1989; Shanks, Johnstone, & Staggs, 1997; Whittlesea & Wright, 1997) have shown that participants still outperform chance level under these conditions. The principle underlying the transfer in the so-called "changed letter procedure" has been extended to other surface changes. For instance, the training items and the test items might be, respectively, auditory items and visual items (Manza & Reber, 1997), colour and colour names, sounds and letters (Dienes & Altman, 1997), or vice versa. Successful transfer was observed in each case. Reber claimed that these results testify to the fact that participants are able to abstract the "syntax" of the displayed material, independently of the "vocabulary".

At first glance, evidence for transfer between event patterns cutting across their sensory contents cannot be accounted for by our model of implicit learning. Indeed, the formation of an associative link between, say, *ga*, *ti*, and *ti*, whatever its strength, seems fundamentally unable to explain transfer to *wo*, *fe*, and *fe*, as observed in the Marcus et al. (1999) experiments. Accordingly, Marcus et al. concluded that infants have the capacity to represent algebra-like rules and, in addition, "have the ability to extract those rules rapidly from small amounts of input and to generalise those rules to novel instances" (p. 79). Likewise, Reber (1993), talking about performance in the transfer letter paradigm in artificial grammar learning studies, claimed that "the abstractive perspective is the only model of mental representation that can deal with the existence of transfer of knowledge across stimulus domains" (Reber, 1993, p. 121).

The outline of a re-appraisal

We have no problem with the claim that the evidence of transfer reviewed above is indicative of abstraction. However, we challenge the view that abstraction is indicative of rule formation and rule use. Our claim is that transfer is a natural implication of the SOC model.

Let us return to PARSER. PARSER shows how the initial conscious percept, which is generally irrelevant to the material structure, becomes increasingly isomorphic with the structurally relevant units, thanks to the elementary principles of associative learning and memory. On pages 46–49, we considered that the initial percept exactly matched the content of the perceived stimuli. For instance, given the auditory string *badubatibu*, we assume that participants first form the auditory units *baduba*, *tibu*, and so on, by chunking together the auditory primitives *ba*, *du*, *ti*, and *bu*, and this assumption was sufficient to account for the data. However, it is worth stressing that this assumption is notoriously restrictive. Indeed, the primitives that enter into the associations are internal representations that only partially match the external stimuli that trigger these representations. For instance, as a result of earlier associations, the representations of *ba*, *du*, *ti*, and *bu*, involve a written component in literate people. Thus, when a new association is built between, say, the components of the auditory percept *baduba*, the new unit is not limited to the auditory domain, but naturally extends to the area of generalisation of the primitive components, and especially to the visual domain. More generally, many examples of transfer originate in the fact that conscious primitives entering into the new associations are not tied to a fixed, domain-specific format of representation, but are instead often amodal, flexible, and domain-general. Conscious knowledge is represented into a cross-system code (e.g. Fodor, 1983), a property that ensures that any conscious content possesses a certain abstractness.

Going a step further, it can also be argued that when a few syllables are perceived within one attentional focus, the resulting conscious experience is not necessarily limited to the sum of these syllables (even considering that they are represented into a cross-system code) but instead could embed some direct perception of the overall structure. For instance, *baduti* will not be perceived as *bababa* or *baduba*. The obvious difference lies in the number of repetition of the same primitives. There is no doubt that a part of the representation of *bababa* is that it consists in the repetition of the same syllable (a "run"), and that a part of the representation of *baduba* is that the same syllable is repeated with an intervening syllable (a "trill"). Coding a pattern as a run or a trill entails some form of relational coding, the relation involved here being the same–different relationship. Thus, our assumption is that the sensory input processed within one attentional focus can also integrate some relational information.

If we take it for granted that such abstract and relational features are parts of conscious representations, then there is no reason not to apply to these features the same reasoning that we applied to PARSER's primitives. Abstract features, if they are frequently involved in the conscious perception of a given material, can emerge from noise on the basis of a selection process analogous to the one that we showed to be responsible for the formation of specific representations. As is the case for specific representations, the extraction of regularities is facilitated by the fact that, in its turn, the initial perception determines the way further material is perceived. Thus, when some abstract relations have been perceived frequently enough to become perceptual primitives, they are automatically detected in the new material whenever present. However, in this case, the end-product of the process will be the emergence of representations coding the deep structure of the situation at hand, which makes transfer to other surface features natural. To oversimplify the matter for the sake of understanding, one could say that, in the conventional account, perception provides the system with a database composed of elementary, specific primitives, from which the unconscious processor abstracts the deep underpinning rules. In our account, the primitives are a little more abstract and complex features. However, with these new primitive units, no further conceptual operations are needed to account for transfer.

It is worthy of note that this interpretation is viable only if the coding of the incoming information in an abstract and relational format remains simple enough to be attributed to low-level perceptual processes. Admittedly, if it turns out that the perceptual primitives needed to account for the available data are, say, nested high-level order dependency rules, it would be unrealistic to claim that these primitives are directly coded by elementary perceptual mechanisms. Thus it is important to show that the available evidence of transfer can be explained in terms of the coding of fairly simple relations. In the following section, we examine the form of abstract and relational coding needed to account for the available findings on transfer. We will show that only surprisingly simple forms of coding are required.

Perceptual primitives can be abstract and relational

To begin with the most simple case, let us consider the Manza and Reber (1997) results, showing a transfer between auditory and visual modalities in the artificial grammar learning area. These authors interpret their findings as providing support for their abstractionist, rule-based view. Although the authors do not make their interpretation more explicit, we assume that their line of reasoning could be as follows. If, for instance, subjects perceive the visual sequence XMX, they abstract the knowledge that the letter X can be repeated with a lag of one letter. When they again perceive XMX, but in the auditory modality, they might experience some familiarity with the display, because the same rule applies. This interpretation undoubtedly works well. However, the phenomenon can be explained easily without having recourse to rules. It suffices to consider that there is a direct correspondence between the visual and the auditory format of the letters X and M. It is worth stressing the differences between the two approaches. In the former case, a rule-governed pattern needs to be extracted from the visual stimuli, before being transferred to the auditory stimuli. In the latter case, matching is direct and independent of the structure of the material. A simple thought experiment can help to clarify the differences and, by the same token, demonstrates the irrelevance of a rule-based account. Suppose that the material is generated randomly, instead of by a finite-state grammar, and thus presents no rule-governed, salient pattern. For the sake of illustration, suppose that a string such as XMT is presented. In a rule-based interpretation, transfer should not occur, because a structure cannot be abstracted. Now, it is quite obvious that the prior auditory presentation of XMT increases familiarity with the visual display XMT even though there is no common salient structure.

The same comment can be applied to some other studies. For example, Dienes and Altman (1997) observed a positive transfer between colours and the name of colours, which can also be accounted for by the natural mapping between the primitives involved in the experiment. Again, transfer would probably occur even with randomly generated stimulus sequences, thus demonstrating the irrelevance of a rule-based interpretation. However, not all studies of transfer can be explained using so simple an argument. As a case in point, the above explanation does not apply to the Marcus et al. study in which transfer is observed between, say, *gatiti* and *wofefe*, because there is no natural mapping between *ga* and *wo*, or *ti* and *fe*.

Re-interpretation of the Marcus et al. data demands recourse to another property of conscious percepts, namely the direct coding of simple relations between the components of one percept. The relation that needs to be coded is the relation "same–different", or, in other words, the only ability that infants need to exhibit is that of coding the repetition of an event. If one postulates that infants are able to detect whether two successive stimuli are the same or not, the Marcus et al. results are easily explained. Indeed, as pointed out by McClelland and Plaut (1999), *gatiti*, *wofefe*, and, more generally, all the ABB items, can be coded as different–same, whereas none of the other items can be coded using the same schema. AAB items are coded as same–different; ABA items instantiate a slightly more sophisticated pattern. Note that there is no indication in the data that this pattern is actually perceived as special: Considering that ABA items do not match the pattern of the other items is sufficient to account for the data. However, it does not seem to be unrealistic to assume that a trill pattern is also directly perceived when the components of this pattern can be processed within a single attentional focus. The numerous studies showing infants' early sensitivity to symmetrical displays support this assumption.

At first glance, the demonstrations of transfer stemming from the more complex situations of artificial grammar learning in adults imply the coding of far more complex relations. We now argue that in fact, as surprising as this conclusion might be, the very same abilities that we have invoked up to now are sufficient. Indeed, although finite-state grammars embed complex relations, the coding of fairly simple patterns appears sufficient to account for improved performance in transfer situations. For instance, Whittlesea and Wright (1997, Experiment 4) reported successful transfer between letters and colours in artificial grammar learning. In their experiment 4, 5 out of the 20 training items begin with a salient alternation ("RMR"). Now, it turned out that colour alternation at the beginning of a string appeared in legal test items but never in illegal test items. It is enough to assume that participants consider the test items beginning with an alternation to be grammatical, and respond at random on the others, to simulate observed performance. If we take this interpretation for granted then transfer is easy to account for. Indeed, although there is no natural link between, for instance, R and a red square, a natural mapping may be established between the subjective unit "RMR" and "RED/YELLOW/RED", or any other colour alternation. Again, the observation of a positive transfer is irrelevant as to whether subjects have abstracted the complex grammar used to generate the material. It can be accounted for more parsimoniously by assuming that subjective units are at least partially represented into a relational code.

For a still more complex illustration, let us consider one of the recent studies by Shanks et al. (1997), which concluded that transfer in artificial grammar learning is mediated at least to some extent by abstract knowledge. Experiment 1 used a standard changed-letter procedure, in which the letters used during study—M, R, T, V, and X—were replaced by C, H, J, L, and N, respectively, for the test. Shanks et al. introduced five types of violation in their ungrammatical transfer strings. The only violation that led participants to reject the strings in a forced choice grammaticality test was illegal letter repetitions. In the original grammar, only R, T, and V could be repeated. Thus, in legal transfer items, H, J, and L could also be repeated, but C and N could not. Shanks et al. showed that participants rejected transfer items including a repetition of one of these two letters at a significant level. Such a result suggests that subjects were able to perform a quite sophisticated analysis, including at least two steps. They first have to identify the fact that M and X were never repeated in the original set, then to establish a correct mapping between M and C, on the one hand, and X and N on the other.

It can be shown that correct responses imply neither of these steps. Let us assume that participants have formed subjective units, each composed of a few letters. An examination of the training strings shows that these subjective units include far fewer repetitions than if letters had been selected at random. The training strings included nine repetitions, whereas we assessed (through a computational simulation) the number of repetitions expected by chance at about 22. Now, looking at the five pairs of transfer strings testing the "illegal letter repetition" feature, it appears that ungrammatical test strings always include more letter repetitions than grammatical test strings. It is enough for the participants to feel the encoding units including a letter repetition to be unfamiliar for them to choose the grammatical item from each pair. The point is that there is strictly no need to infer what letter repetitions were legal in the study strings, or to establish a letter-to-letter mapping: it suffices to be sensitive to the fact that subjective units rarely include a letter repetition, whatever the nature of these letters. Transfer originates in the fact that a unit's feature, such as "including a letter repetition", can be captured naturally, and not in the abstraction of the rules of the finite-state grammar used to generate the letter strings (for other analyses pointing out to the primary importance of repetition structure to account for transfer in artificial grammar learning, see Gomez, Gerken, & Schvaneveldt, 2000; Tunney & Altmann, 1999).

Is our account of transfer more parsimonious?

To recapitulate, in the conventional models, the data made available to the central processor are the individual sensory-based events. The task of finding analogies between events that differ in their surface appearance is the job of some further inferential processes. These processes belong to the domain of cognition and, more precisely (because we are not aware of them), to the realm of the sophisticated cognitive unconscious. In our alternative conception, unconscious (but elementary) processes provide a conscious representation of the sensory input that is framed directly in some abstract and relational way, as any conscious content is. With this modified input, the performance observed in transfer situations no longer needs to be explained in terms of a sophisticated unconscious processor. The ubiquitous learning and memory processes evoked in the previous sections are sufficient to explain the emergence of a reliable representation of the deep structure of the material. We have indicated how simple principles of associative learning and memory explain the emergence of conscious representations that are increasingly isomorphic to the world structure in cases where the sensory domain remains identical. When applied to more abstract primitives, the very same principles account for the discovery of the structure of the material in cases where the sensory domain is changed.

Opponents of this position might argue that our conception simply shadows or resituates the problem instead of solving it. The argument should be that positing that ongoing sensory information is directly coded into an abstract and relational code is akin to taking as a premise the to-be-explained phenomenon (i.e. the ability to transfer), and presumably further consideration of this initial stage of processing would indicate that it, in fact, involves the same kind of complex machinery that most authors include under the label of Cognitive Unconscious. This criticism is unsound, however, because the relationships we assume to be coded directly by low-level perceptual processes are considerably simpler than the abstract rules of the mainstream tradition. They are limited to a few aspects, including the same–different distinction, the properties of symmetry, repetition, and alternation, and relationships along some perceptual dimensions such as "smaller than" or "brighter than". It is not biologically implausible to assume that these relationships are coded at earlier stages of neural processing, although there is as yet no direct evidence (one exception is the direct coding of the relation "brighter than", that is at least partially coded at the retinal level by lateral interaction between concurrent stimulations).

In the absence of more extensive neuropsychological arguments, our hypothesis finds some support in the primacy of relational coding in phylogenetic evolution. It has long been shown that animals such as rats are able to perform tasks involving elementary forms of relational learning. For instance, if rats are trained with two stimuli differing in brightness in such a way that the choice of the brighter is rewarded and the choice of the darker is not rewarded, they subsequently choose the brighter of two new stimuli, even though the absolute brightness of the new rewarded stimulus might be identical to that of the old unrewarded stimuli. Thus rats appear to be sensitive to the relationship between stimuli rather than to their absolute properties. Such a demonstration has been replicated with various animal species and using a variety of simple relationships, such as "larger than". Primates and a number of birds also appear able to learn a discriminative response to pairs of stimuli, depending on whether they are identical or different and, once acquired, this ability can transfer to any new stimulus pair, irrespective of its nature. Within the perspective of evolutionary biology, these results are not at all surprising. In many cases, the raw information provided by an isolated event is only partially relevant. For instance, the retinal size of a perceived object or animal is uninformative, because it depends on the distance between the observer and the distal stimulus. Similarly, the absolute brightness provides incomplete information because perceived brightness depends on the ambient luminance. Considerably more reliable information is provided by a relational coding by means of which the size or brightness of a new stimulus is assessed by comparison with contextual stimuli.

CONSCIOUSNESS: FROM "NECESSITY" TO "SUFFICIENCY"

This chapter has proposed a new view of implicit learning, in which the phenomenon is conceived of as a transformation of conscious experiences through the action of elementary associative processes acting on the components of these experiences. To conclude, we would like to come back on the deep theoretical commitments of this view, and briefly to address some of the most common objections to it.

Our framework provides a specification of a meta-theory of the mind, partly rooted in the philosophical approach developed by Searle (1992), and, on the psychological side, in the work of Dulany (1997), who called it, for want of a better term, the "mentalistic" framework. The most salient feature of the mentalistic framework is the denial of the Cognitive Unconscious. The core of this position is the refutation of the notion of unconscious representations. Of course, this position also makes it necessary to reject the possibility of performing unconscious manipulations and transformations of these representations and, hence, the notions of unconscious rule abstraction, computation, analysis, reasoning, and inference, become meaningless. The only representations people create and manipulate are those that form the momentary phenomenal experience. To quote ourselves: "Processes and mechanisms responsible for the elaboration of knowledge are intrinsically unconscious, and the resulting mental representations and knowledge are intrinsically conscious. No other components are needed" (Perruchet et al., 1997, p. 44).

Several criticisms can be levelled at such a view. Some of them stress that there are several well-known empirical phenomena, such as the subliminal semantic activation effect, that provide direct demonstrations of the cognitive unconscious. The reliability of these alleged demonstrations has been questioned in earlier papers (Holender, 1986, Shanks & St John, 1994: see also Perruchet & Vinter, unpublished manuscript), and we do not deal further with this issue here. Other potential criticisms are directed more against the *a priori* interest or legitimacy of the approach than against its empirical likelihood. Arguments start from the idea that the main object of psychological science is the processing of information, such as it can be described in a program for a digital computer. Now, consciousness by itself is a property that is computationally irrelevant for information processing modelling. The functioning of any model does not depend in any way on the conscious/unconscious status we ascribe to the representations it manipulates and to the operations it performs. As a consequence, the question of knowing whether consciousness is necessary for any cognitive activity is not scientifically warranted, or, at best, needs to be postponed until substantial progress has been made regarding the "serious issues".

We acknowledge that consciousness, in itself, is computationally irrelevant. By the way, we also acknowledge that, because cognitive activities can be simulated on a machine, one is unable to prove the necessity of consciousness when cognitive activities are implemented in a brain. This does not mean that the issue of consciousness is irrelevant in a scientific approach. Indeed, positing that the model has to simulate conscious states while respecting the properties of conscious thought introduces considerable structural and functional constraints for the model. Attention and consciousness are linked to the notions of limited capacity, seriality and relative slowness of processing, as well as quick memory decay. These constraints are relevant for an information processing approach. They can be implemented in a computational model to address the following question: Is a model that is fulfilling these constraints sufficient to account for human thought and behaviour?

To illustrate, let us consider PARSER, the computational model of word segmentation that we present as supportive of our approach. Of course, PARSER is not conscious, nor are the computers on which it runs. The model would work as well whether the representations it manipulates are assigned a conscious or unconscious status. The relevance of PARSER with regard to our concern lies elsewhere. It lies in the fact that PARSER respects the striking constraints inherent to conscious thought. Thus the only representations included in the model closely match the conscious representations subjects might have when performing the task. The early coding of the material as a set of short and disjunctive units, as well as the final coding of the input as a sequence of words, are assumed to closely match the phenomenal perceptual experience of listeners. This correspondence also extends to the entire learning phase, thus permitting our model to perform word segmentation while mimicking the on-line conscious processing of incoming information. By doing so, PARSER demonstrates that conscious percepts and representations are sufficient for word extraction.

Generalising from word extraction along the lines set out in this chapter, our claim is that conscious percepts and representations are sufficient, from a computational standpoint, to account for the adaptive abilities described in the implicit learning literature, including those that seemingly point to rule abstraction. Here is, we believe, the ultimate interest of our approach: accounting for complex non-intentional learning phenomena without relying on the unlimited abilities of a putative cognitive unconscious.

ACKNOWLEDGEMENTS

This work has been supported by the Centre National de la Recherche Scientifique (CNRS, UMR SO22), the Universite de Bourgogne, and the Region de Bourgogne (AAFE).

REFERENCES

Berry, D.C., & Broadbent, D.E. (1988). Interactive tasks and the implicit–explicit distinction. *British Journal of Psychology, 79*, 251–272.

Clark, A., & Thornton, C. (1997). Trading spaces: Computation, representation and the limits of uninformed learning. *Behavioral and Brain Sciences, 20*, 57–90.

Cleeremans, A. (1993). *Mechanims of implicit learning: A connectionnist model of sequence processing*. Cambridge, MA: MIT Press/Bradford Books.

Cleeremans, A., Destrebecqz, A., & Boyer, M. (1998). Implicit learning: News from the front. *Trends in Cognitive Sciences, 2*, 406–416.

Cohen, A., Ivry, R.I., & Keele, S.W. (1990). Attention and structure in sequence learning, *Journal of Experimental Psychology: Learning, Memory, and Cognition, 16*, 17–30.

Cowan, N. (1995). *Attention and memory: An integrated framework*. New York: Oxford University Press.

Crabb, B.T., & Dark, V. (1999). Perceptual implicit memory requires attentional encoding. *Memory and Cognition, 27*, 267–275.

Dienes, Z., & Altmann, G. (1997). Transfer of implicit knowledge across domains: How implicit and how abstract? In D. Berry (Ed.), *How implicit is implicit learning?* Oxford: Oxford University Press.

Dienes, Z., Broadbent, D., & Berry, D. (1991). Implicit and explicit knowledge bases in artificial grammar learning. *Journal of Experimental Psychology: Learning, Memory, and Cognition, 17*, 875–887.

Dulany, D.E. (1997). Consciousness in the explicit (deliberative) and implicit (evocative). In J.D. Cohen & J.W. Schooler (Eds.), *Scientific approaches to the study of consciousness* (pp. 179–212). Mahwah, NJ: Lawrence Erlbaum Associates Inc.

Evans, J.St.B., Newstead, S.E., & Byrne, P. (1993). *Human reasoning*. Hillsdale, NJ: Lawrence Erlbaum Associates Inc.

Fisk, A.D., & Schneider, W. (1984). Memory as a function of attention, level of processing, and automatization. *Journal of Experimental Psychology: Learning, Memory and Cognition, 10*, 181–197.

Fodor, J. (1983). *The modularity of mind*. Cambridge, MA: MIT Press.

Frensch, P.A., Buchner, A., & Lin, J. (1994). Implicit learning of unique and ambiguous serial transitions in the presence and absence of a distractor task. *Journal of Experimental Psychology: Learning, Memory and Cognition, 20*, 567–584.

Frensch, P.A., & Miner, C.S. (1994). Effects of presentation rate and individual differences in short-term memory capacity on an indirect measure of serial learning. *Memory and Cognition, 22*, 95–110.

Ganor-Stern, D., Seamon, J.G., & Carrasco, M. (1998). The role of attention and study time in explicit and implicit memory for unfamiliar visual stimuli. *Memory and Cognition, 26*, 1187–1195.

Gomez, R.L., & Gerken, L.A. (1999). Artificial grammar learning by one-year-olds leads to specific and abstract knowledge. *Cognition, 70*, 109–135.

Gomez, R.L., Gerken, L.A., & Schvaneveldt, R.W. (2000). The basis of transfer in artificial grammar learning, *Memory and Cognition, 28*, 253–263.

Green, R.E.A., & Shanks, D. R. (1993). On the existence of independent learning systems: An examination of some evidence. *Memory and Cognition, 21*, 304–317.

Hayes, N.A., & Broadbent, D. (1988). Two models of learning for interactive tasks. *Cognition, 28*, 249–276.

Holender, D. (1986). Semantic activation without conscious identification in dichotic listening, parafoveal vision and visual masking: A survey and appraisal. *Behavioral and Brain Sciences, 9*, 1–23.

Hsiao, A.T., & Reber, A. (1998). The role of attention in implicit sequence learning: Exploring the limits of the cognitive unconscious. In M. Stadler & P. Frensch (Eds.), *Handbook of implicit learning* (pp. 495–531). Thousand Oaks, CA: Sage Publications.

Jiménez, L., & Mendez, C. (1999). Which attention is needed for implicit sequence learning? *Journal of Experimental Psychology: Learning, Memory, and Cognition, 25*, 236–259.

Logan, G.D., & Etherton, J.L. (1994). What is learned during automatization? The role of attention in constructing an instance. *Journal of Experimental Psychology: Learning, Memory, and Cognition, 20*, 1022–1050.

McClelland, J.L., & Plaut, D.C. (1999). Does generalization in infant learning implicate abstract algebra-like rules? *Trends in Cognitive Science, 3*, 166–168.

MacDonald, P., & MacLeod, C.M. (1998). The influence of attention at encoding on direct and indirect remembering. *Acta Psychologica, 98*, 298–310.

McGeorge, P., & Burton, M. (1990). Semantic processing in an incidental learning task. *Quarterly Journal of Experimental Psychology, 42*, 597–609.

Mackintosh, N.J. (1975). A theory of attention: Variations in the associability of stimuli with reinforcement. *Psychological Review, 82*, 276–298.

Mandler, G. (1975). Consciousness: Respectable, useful, and probably necessary. In R. Solso (Ed.), *Information processing and cognition: The Loyola symposium* (pp. 229–254). Hillsdale, NJ: Lawrence Erlbaum Associates Inc.

Manza, L., & Reber. A.S. (1997). Representing artificial grammar: Transfer across stimulus forms and modalities. In D. Berry (Ed.), *How implicit is implicit learning?* Oxford: Oxford University Press.

Marcus, G.F., Vijayan, S., Rao, S.B., & Vishton, P.M. (1999). Rule learning by seven-month-old infants. *Science, 283*, 77–80.

Mathews, R.C., Buss, R.R., Stanley, W.B., Blanchard-Fields, F., Cho, J.-R., & Druhan, B. (1989). Role of implicit and explicit processes in learning from examples: A synergistic effect. *Journal of Experimental Psychology: Learning, Memory, and Cognition, 15*, 1083–1100.

Miller, G.A. (1962). *Psychology: The science of mental life.* New York, Harper & Row.

Nissen, M.J., & Bullemer, P. (1987). Attentional requirements of learning: Evidence from performance measures. *Cognitive Psychology, 19*, 1–32.

O'Brien, G., & Opie, J. (1999). Putting content into a vehicle theory of consciousness. *Behavioral and Brain Sciences, 22*, 175–196.

Perruchet, P., & Amorim, M.A. (1992). Conscious knowledge and changes in performance in sequence learning: Evidence against dissociation. *Journal of Experimental Psychology: Learning, Memory, and Cognition, 18*, 785–800.

Perruchet, P., & Gallego, J. (1997). A subjective unit formation account of implicit learning. In D. Berry (Ed.), *How implicit is implicit learning?* (pp. 124–161). Oxford: Oxford University Press.

Perruchet, P., & Vinter, A. (1998a). PARSER: A model for word segmentation. *Journal of Memory and Language, 39*, 246–263.

Perruchet, P., & Vinter, A. (1998b) Learning and development: The implicit knowledge assumption reconsidered. In M. Stadler & P. Frensch (Eds.), *Handbook of implicit learning* (pp. 495–531). Thousand Oaks, CA: Sage Publications.

Perruchet, P., Vinter, A., & Gallego, J. (1997). Implicit learning shapes new conscious percepts and representations. *Psychonomic Bulletin and Review, 4*, 43–48.

Perruchet, P., Vinter, A., Pacteau, C., & Gallego, J. (in press). The formation of structurally relevant units in artificial grammar learning. *Quarterly Journal of Experimental Psychology.*

Piaget, J. (1985). *The equilibration of cognitive structures: The central problem of intellectual development.* Chicago: University of Chicago Press.

Posner, M.I., & Boies, S.J. (1971). Components of attention. *Psychological Review, 78*, 391–408.

Reber, A.S. (1969). Transfer of syntactic structure in synthetic languages. *Journal of Experimental Psychology, 81*, 115–119.

Reber, A.S. (1976). Implicit learning of synthetic languages: The role of instructional set. *Journal of Experimental Psychology: Human Learning and Memory, 2*, 88–94.

Reber, A.S. (1993). *Implicit learning and tacit knowledge: An essay on the cognitive unconscious.* New York: Oxford University Press.

Rock, I., & Gutman, D. (1981). The effect of inattention on form perception. *Journal of Experimental Psychology: Human Perception and Performance, 7*, 275–285.

Roediger, H.L., III (1990). Implicit memory: A commentary. *Bulletin of the Psychonomic Society, 28*, 373–380.

Saffran, J.R., Aslin, R.N., & Newport, E.L. (1996b). Statistical learning by 8-month-old infants. *Science, 274*, 1926–1928.

Saffran, J.R., Newport, E.L., & Aslin, R.N. (1996a). Word segmentation: The role of distributional cues. *Journal of Memory and Language, 35*, 606–621.

Saffran, J.R., Newport, E.L., Aslin, R.N., Tunick, R.A., & Barrueco, S. (1997). Incidental language learning. *Psychological Science, 8*, 101–105.

Schmidt, P.A., & Dark, V.J. (1998). Attentional processing of "unattended" flankers: Evidence for a failure of selective attention. *Perception and Psychophysics, 60*, 227–238.

Searle, J.R. (1992). *The rediscovery of the mind.* Cambridge, MA: MIT Press.

Servan-Schreiber, D., & Anderson, J.R. (1990). Learning artificial grammars with competitive chunking. *Journal of Experimental Psychology: Learning, Memory, and Cognition, 16*, 592–608.

Shanks, D.R., & Johnstone, T. (1999). Evaluating the relationship between explicit and implicit knowledge in a sequential reaction time task. *Journal of Experimental Psychology: Learning, Memory, and Cognition, 25*, 1435–1451.

Shanks, D.R., Johnstone, T., & Staggs, L. (1997). Abstraction processes in artificial grammar learning. *Quarterly Journal of Experimental Psychology, 50A*, 216–252.

Shanks, D.R., & St John, M.F. (1994). Characteristics of dissociable human learning systems. *Behavioral and Brain Sciences, 17*, 367–447.

Stadler, M.A. (1995). Role of attention in implicit learning. *Journal of Experimental Psychology: Learning, Memory, and Cognition, 21*, 674–685.

Tunney, R.J., & Altmann, G.T.M. (1999). The transfer effect in artificial grammar learning: Re-appraising the evidence of transfer of sequential dependencies. *Journal of Experimental Psychology: Learning, Memory, and Cognition, 25*, 1322–1333.

Velmans, M. (1999). Neural activation, information, and phenomenal consciousness. *Behavioral and Brain Sciences, 22*, 172–173.

Wagner, A.R. (1981). SOP: A model of automatic memory processing in animal behaviour. In N.E. Spear & R.R. Miller (Eds.), *Information processing in animals: Memory mechanisms* (pp. 5–47). Hillsdale, NJ: Lawrence Erlbaum Associates Inc.

Whittlesea, B.W.A., & Wright, R.L. (1997). Implicit (and explicit) learning: Acting adaptively without knowing the consequences. *Journal of Experimental Psychology: Learning, Memory and Cognition, 23*, 181–200.

APPENDIX: PARSER

PARSER is centred on a single vector, called Percept Shaper (PS). At the start, PS contains only the primitives composing the material, namely a few syllables. Learning proceeds through the iterative processing of small successive parts of the linguistic corpus. Each part is composed of one to three processing primitives (the number is determined randomly for each percept), thus simulating the successive attentional focuses of a human subject processing the same corpus. Each perceived part is added to PS, and can itself serve as a new primitive for the shaping of subsequent inputs, as the syllables did initially. This simulates the fact that perceptual contents are changing throughout the task. Finally, if learning has been successful, PS contains all the words, and only the words of the language.

Why does PS not become encumbered with an innumerable set of irrelevant and increasingly lengthy units? It is because the future of a unit depends on its weight, which represents trace strength. The weight of a given unit is incremented each time this unit is perceived (weight = +1), and decremented each time another unit is perceived (decrement = −0.05). Decrement simulates forgetting (in the original program there was also some interference, the computational details of which are irrelevant here). To fulfill its shaping function, any unit of PS needs to reach a threshold value (threshold = 1). As a consequence, a unit needs to be perceived repeatedly and regularly to persist on fulfilling a shaping function. In contrast, when the frequency of perception of a given element is not high enough to counteract the effects of forgetting and interference, this element is removed from PS when its weight becomes zero.

This simplistic algorithm is sufficient for PARSER to achieve the extraction of the words forming the artificial languages designed by Saffran and colleagues, with a much more limited amount of practice than real subjects need (Perruchet & Vinter, 1998a). However, it must be understood that the details of the functioning of the model are not intended to provide a realistic picture of the processes that are actually involved. As a case in point, forgetting is simulated through a linear decrement, whereas there is evidence that the forgetting curve fits only moderately well with a linear trend. A more recent version includes a more realistic power function.

More importantly, it can be argued that the general architecture of PARSER is not compatible with the meta-theory of the mind underlying this chapter. Indeed, PS can be thought of as a memory store or a mental lexicon, in which symbolic representations are assumed to be potentially active independently of the current phenomenal experience of the subject. This possibility is actually not allowed in our general framework. The contradiction is indeed patent, but, we believe, not detrimental to the demonstration provided by PARSER of the power of the general principles it implements. Indeed, the representations stored in PS play a role only when they match the external input. They perform no function apart from shaping the momentary percepts, that is to say when they enter as a component of the current phenomenal experience. As a consequence, the same result should have been obtained had the memory of the system been simulated as a capacity to build an on-line representation in the presence of a given input, without directly storing the representation itself. In fact, neural network modelling should certainly have been more in the spirit of our approach because it naturally implements the idea that the memory of the system is not necessarily a list of symbolic tokens. However, current connectionist models have fixed input units, whereas a learning principle constitutive of our approach is that percepts evolve throughout training. PARSER is indeed formal in nature, but this choice entails no allegiance to the principles usually found to underpin formal artificial intelligence.

CHAPTER THREE

A theory of the implicit nature of implicit learning

Zoltán Dienes
Experimental Psychology, University of Sussex, UK

Josef Perner
University of Salzburg, Austria

In this chapter we will establish what it is for something to be implicit. The approach to implicit knowledge is taken from Dienes and Perner (1999) and Perner and Dienes (1999), which relate the implicit–explicit distinction to knowledge representations. To be clear about exactly what our claims are, we will first discuss what a representation is. Then we will define what it is for a representation to represent something implicitly or explicitly and apply those concepts to knowledge. Next we will show how maximally explicit knowledge is naturally associated with consciousness, how some degree of explicitness is needed for voluntary control and thus how increasing explicitness is associated with increasing meta-cognitive abilities. We will then review evidence indicating the extent of people's implicit knowledge in a standard implicit learning paradigm, namely the artificial grammar learning paradigm. This review will indicate that people's relative lack of meta-knowledge justifies the claim that people have acquired genuinely implicit knowledge.

WHAT IS A REPRESENTATION?

Psychologists frequently talk about representations; indeed, it is difficult to find a theory in psychology, certainly in cognitive psychology, that does not postulate the existence of some type of representation. But what is a representation? This question sometimes takes psychologists by surprise, even though it is foundational (for an overview see Perner, 1991); it arouses considerable debate amongst philosophers, for whom the dust has not yet settled (see Dennett, 1987; Dretske, 1995; Fodor, 1990; Millikan, 1993). Consider an unambiguous case of a representation: A drawing of a house. In this case, and in general, a representation consists of something physical (the representational medium, for example, paper and ink) that is about something else (the representational content, for example, a house). But how is it that an object—paper and ink—can acquire meaning, a content? It might seem that the straightforward answer is: Because someone intends it to do so, they intend the drawing to mean a house. This does seem a good answer for many artifacts, like schematic drawings. But the mechanism is too restrictive in its scope. This answer—if it were the only answer—would restrict mental representations to only those a person intended to have. Further, the thought that provided the intention in such a case could not itself be a representation, paradoxically it could not itself be about anything (unless it was intended, and so on). Thus, most of modern psychology (which largely deals with representations not consciously intended to represent anything) would be undermined.

How could, say, a pattern of firing of a group of neurons in a person represent a cat? You might suggest—taking note of the way that neurophysiologists determine what a cell, or group of cells, code—that the pattern represents a cat if it is correlated with the presence of cats: Whenever you show a cat to the person, those neurons fire. Unfortunately, this does not quite do; it does not allow the person to misrepresent. If he saw a skunk on a dark night, the same neurons might fire. On the correlation story he has not misrepresented the skunk as a cat; he has just correctly detected a cat-OR-skunk-on-a-dark-night. But representations can misrepresent and any theory of representation must allow for that.

Correlations between patterns of neural activity and cats arise in people due to an evolutionary or learning history that has selected that pattern of activity because of the function it performs in dealing with cats. One might say the pattern has the function of indicating cats; or the function of producing further internal or behavioural reactions appropriate for dealing with real or imagined cats. According to one dominant (and we think persuasive) approach in philosophy, representations represent something precisely because of the functional role they play. Thus, on Dretske's (1988) approach, A represents B just in case A has the function of indicating B. For example, if a pattern of neuronal activity has the function of indicating cats, then it represents "cat". If it fires because of a skunk on a dark night, then it has misrepresented the skunk as a cat. Function can be produced by evolution or learning; but it can also be fixed by intention. Thus, representations produced by intentions are just a special case of representations whose meanings are fixed (to the degree that they are fixed) by function.

This approach to representation shows that the use of the word representation by psychologists, and cognitive scientists generally, is natural and appropriate. It indicates that monkeys' minds can represent the world, monkeys "thoughts" can have true meanings, even without the "intentions" of fully formed human minds; even fleas can represent the world in whatever way they do. Thus, this approach is consistent with the notion that minds—constituted of mental representations—are products of Darwinian evolution, which gradually over the aeons acquired the capacity to possess rich meanings and also endow artifacts (like words) with the rich meanings that they do (see Dennett, 1996, for a highly readable account, and Millikan, 1993, for a thorough account of the nature of representation).

It will be useful even at this early stage to indicate briefly the relation between representation and consciousness before coming back to this issue in more detail later (contrast our position with that of Searle, 1990). Is there any reason why all representations should be conscious? Not at all, as the previous reference to fleas implies. Drawings of houses are not conscious either. Imagine building a robot to interact with the world; the robot will be conscious of some aspects of its world. It might be useful to have the activity in some circuit have the function of indicating a particular internal or external state of affairs. There seems to be no *a priori* reason why the content of all such representations should constitute the content of the robot's conscious experience. Perhaps the representation was useful simply temporarily to inform another process downstream of processing; or the problems it is used to solve are "local" problems that do not need to concern the processing system generally. In any case, the extent to which people have interesting unconscious representations is by this approach an open question, and an empirical question given a theory of consciousness.

The relationship between consciousness and representation might be partly open but the relationship is not one of complete independence. In the nineteenth century Brentano (1874/1970) argued that what distinguished the mental from the physical was that the mental was always about something (e.g. a thought just has to be about something or it could not be a thought); physical objects typically just sit there not being about anything at all. Unless we have a materialist explanation of why mental states can be about things, then we are pushed towards dualism. Functional theories of representation show how a material object can become a representation without there being a mind to intend it so. By exactly the same token, it shows how consciousness can be consciousness *of* without invoking special non-physical mind-stuff. On these accounts, the content of our consciousness is just the content of some representation (Tye, 1995), the "aboutness" arising because of the function of the states involved. A question is raised by this answer: But what makes some representations conscious (when others are not)? We will provide an answer to this question later on.

Finally, note that the approach to representation we are advocating only requires that representations are defined by the ordinary English language use of the term: representations depict the world as being a certain way, that's all. We don't require that for something to be a representation it has to have other properties (necessary for at least some mental representations); for example, we don't require that for something to be a representation it has to be recombinable with other representations in a context-free way. Some representations have this property (English words and mental representations of concepts), and others do not. Activation patterns in a neural network can be representations. The weights in a neural network can also be representations: They have a function, defined by the fact that the neural network, including the learning algorithm by which it operates, evolved so that the weights would come to be brought into correspondence with relations in the environment. Thus, the weights represent, and can misrepresent, those relations.

We have put together different functional theories of representation as one class ignoring their differences. We are not committed to one particular account and the interested reader should refer to the cited papers to get a fuller understanding of the different approaches.

IMPLICIT VERSUS EXPLICIT REPRESENTATION

According to the approach we have just described, if it is the function of state A in a representational medium to indicate B, then A represents B. A has the function of indicating B partly because the state of A is used as information by the rest of the system to respond appropriately to B. Now, for A to indicate anything, for it to be used as information, requires that at a minimum the representational medium can go into two states. For example, if A represents "cat", then there should be one state for "cat" and another state for "not a cat" or "uncertain if cat or not-cat". We will define the explicit content of a representation in the following way: Distinctions (e.g. cat/not-cat) are explicitly represented only if there are corresponding distinctions in the representational medium. However, the explicit content of a representation rarely constitutes its entire content, as we will now begin to see.

A representation can express content that has a structure. But there is no reason why all the elements and relations in that structure must themselves be explicitly represented. Consider a device for distinguishing different animals. If you put a cat in front of its sensors, it goes into a "cat" state; if you put a dog there, it goes into a "dog" state, and so on. Thus, the distinction between cat and dog is explicitly represented, because differences in the device's representational medium correspond to the different animals placed before it. But the full content expressed by the representation when the device goes into its "cat" state is more than just "cat"; rather the device is indicating (and has the function to indicate) at least that "this is a cat". We could not say anything less, for example, than it only expresses knowledge of cat-ness, or of the concept of cat. The device can convey information that "this is a cat" or "this is a dog" by going into different states. Yet, what are made explicit within the vocabulary of this device are only the properties of being-a-cat, being-a-dog, and so on. That it is "this" rather than "that" object that is a cat is an element of the structure of the expressed content, an element that helps to constitute the meaning of the representation; it is, more generally, a necessary supporting fact for the representation to have the meaning it does. But there is no difference in the representational medium that corresponds to "this" rather than "that".

Based on the foregoing logic, we will distinguish explicit representation from something that is only implicitly represented in the following way: Any environmental feature or state of affairs that is not explicitly represented but forms part of the representational content is represented implicitly.

These definitions correspond in part to the everyday use of the terms explicit and implicit, as applied to linguistic expressions, but they are not synonymous with their everyday uses. Declaring that "Gerry is a bird" conveys explicitly that Gerry is a bird. If, for a community of people, being an animal is necessary to the meaning of being a bird, then Gerry's animal-hood has been conveyed implicitly. The implication is a necessary support-ing fact for the sentence to have the meaning it does. But there is nothing in the representation—the sentence—that has the function of indicating the precise distinction of animal versus not-animal. That is why the distinction is conveyed only implicitly. On the other hand, Euclid's axioms can imply many geometric theorems but, by our (stipulative) definition, those theor-ems are not implicitly represented by the axioms. The theorems are not part of the meaning of the axioms; geometers can believe a false theorem and not believe a true theorem without losing their right to claim they under-stand the meaning of the axioms. Declaring "Bill is a bachelor" explicitly represents that Bill is a bachelor; it implicitly represents that Bill is male (given that being a male is necessary to the meaning of being a bachelor). It does not implicitly represent that Bill is made of DNA, because a person can deny that Bill has any DNA in him without losing the right to say one understands the word bachelor.

Note that our definitions of implicit/explicit help motivate what follows in our story, but if you do not buy this approach to defining explicit/ implicit, the next part of our story can still be largely accepted, suitably adjusted. We believe, however, that our definitions are useful because they unify the multifarious uses of the implicit/explicit distinction in the psychological literature (see Dienes & Perner, 1999).

IMPLICIT AND EXPLICIT KNOWLEDGE

What is it to have knowledge? Firstly there is the content of the knowledge: A proposition, that is, something that can be true or false. This usually involves predicating a property (e.g. "is bald") to an individual (e.g. "the king of France").[1] Secondly, the content must be a fact at a given time. Thirdly, there is a person ("I") having an appropriate relationship to this proposition, that is, a relationship of knowing rather than, for example, wishing, guessing, considering, or dreaming.

A representation functioning as knowledge need not make all this structure explicit. The following does constitute a fully explicit representation of the knowledge that the present king of France is bald "I know (that it is a fact) that the present king of France is bald". We will now consider ways in which a person might not represent this state of affairs fully explicitly.

At one extreme, the person might explicitly represent only a property of a presented object or event. For example, when a person is flashed the word "butter", during perception of the event they might not form an explicit representation of the full proposition "The word in front of me has the meaning butter". Instead, the meaning butter is activated but it is not predicated of any particular individual (i.e. "the word in front of me"). The representational medium contains no distinction that indicates different individuals. So the full content of the proposition is not made explicit. But if the person acts appropriately towards the stimulus (in a certain context) the representation is functioning as knowledge. Thus, its status as knowledge, the fact that the feature applies to a particular individual (presented word) is represented implicitly, by our definition. This is maximally implicit knowledge on our scheme. Consider, for example, a blindsight patient presented with a square or a circle in their blind field. They can reliably indicate whether the object is a square or a circle but provide no evidence that anything more than "square" or "circle" has been explicitly represented about the fact that it is a square or circle presented to them (Weiskrantz, 1988).

We suggest that under subliminal conditions only the properties of a stimulus (the kind of stimulus) are represented explicitly (e.g. the word "butter"), not the fact that there is a particular stimulus event that is of that kind. This would be enough to influence indirect tests, in which no reference

---

[1] This is true, even of procedural knowledge. A procedure is of the general form "If condition X, then action Y". In a calculator, it may be: If "5 × 6" then show "30". The property of being 30 is predicated of the result of the operation 5 × 6. Note also that detailed perceptual properties can be predicated of individuals.

is made to the stimulus event (e.g. naming milk products), by raising the likelihood of responding with the subliminally presented stimulus ("butter" is listed as a milk product more often than without subliminal presentation). The stimulus word is not given as a response to a direct test (e.g. Which word did I just flash?) because there is no representation of any word having been flashed. Performance on a direct test can be improved with instructions to guess, because this gives leave to treat the direct test like an indirect test, just saying what comes to mind first.[2]

At the next stage of explicitness, the person represents the full content of the proposition (i.e. including the individual that the property is predicated to) and then represents the temporal context of the fact and whether indeed it is a fact or not. This extra representation of time and factuality might seem gratuitous but it is important for explicit memory rather than mere implicit memory (which can be based just on maximally implicit knowledge, where just a property is represented explicitly): To recollect the past one must represent the past events as having taken place in the past.

At the final stage of explicitness, one represents that one knows a particular proposition.[3] For example, in the case of perception, the knowledge is based on seeing and the perceptual process might yield the representation "I see that (it is a fact that) the word in front of me is butter". This representation would enable a person to report confidently on seeing the word butter; in other words it would enable conscious perception.

We are now in a position to show that the various distinctions associated with the implicit/explicit distinction differ in the amount of explicit representation required, and thus we will show how the implicit/explicit distinction is essentially related to meta-cognition. We will now show how our analysis of implicit/explicit knowledge clarifies why the implicit/explicit distinction has traditionally been brought into close contact with notions such as consciousness, procedural–declarative, verbalisability, and voluntariness–automaticity; then we will consider its relation to meta-cognition.

---

[2] It is the fact that the person can reliably identify the actually presented word (when e.g. given leave to guess) that entitles us to say the person has knowledge, and therefore allows us to talk about implicit knowledge. It is only in an appropriate supporting context that the representation functions as knowledge of a particular event. None the less, we will loosely refer to the representation as providing implicit knowledge in all contexts. In many cases (e.g. Bridgeman, 1991; Dienes & Perner, 1999), the visual system evolved the use of such (implicit) representations precisely because of their role in such supporting contexts, and so the proper function of the representation is indeed knowledge.

[3] In order to explicitly represent that one knows a fact, one must explicitly represent: that one has a representation of the fact, that the representation is accurate, that it is judged as accurate, and that it was caused by a generally reliable process.

CONSCIOUSNESS

Our analysis reveals why explicit knowledge is often equated with conscious knowledge. According to philosophers who subscribe to the higher-order thought theory (e.g. Rosenthal, 1986; see also Carruthers, 1992), a conscious mental state is conscious by virtue of having a thought about that mental state. This follows from the fact that a mental state is a conscious mental state if we are conscious of that mental state. And, according to Rosenthal, the relevant way of being conscious of the mental state is to have a thought about the mental state. For example, if the mental state is seeing that the banana in my hand is yellow, one becomes consciously aware of the banana being yellow by thinking "I *see* that the banana is yellow". That is, simply thinking "the banana is yellow" does not in itself make you conscious of the thought that the banana is yellow; you have to have a higher-order thought about the first-order mental state ("I am seeing that the banana is yellow"). It is this higher-order thought that enables you to behold that the banana is yellow with a conscious mental state; that is, that enables you to be consciously aware that the banana is yellow.

In general, according to these theories, it is a necessary and sufficient condition for conscious awareness of a fact that I entertain a second-order thought that represents the first-order mental state (in the example, the first-order mental state is seeing the banana; the second-order thought is representing that I am seeing the banana).[4] But this is just the same as our requirement for knowledge to be fully explicit: The person must represent that they know (e.g. by seeing) that the banana is yellow. We think this is consistent with the everyday notion of conscious knowledge: For knowledge to be conscious knowledge we must know that we know it. For example, imagine a blindsight patient who sincerely claims they are not conscious of anything, but if forced to guess they might correctly and reliably say "circle". It seems entirely congruent with the normal use of language to call such knowledge unconscious knowledge. The patient must have represented "circle" (making the property explicit) or even "the object is a circle" (making a proposition explicit), but that knowledge was not conscious because the higher-order representation "I see that the object is a circle" was not formed.

---

[4] Of course, there is philosophical controversy about whether this characterisation can capture the whole phenomenon of consciousness or just an aspect of it. The subjective feel of conscious experiences (phenomenal consciousness) is sometimes distinguished from access consciousness. Our concern, and that of most cognitive sciences, would be merely a case of "access consciousness" or "monitoring consciousness". There are, however, some interesting arguments to the effect that second-order mental states are necessary and sufficient for subjective feel (e.g. Carruthers, 1992, 2000; Rosenthal, 2000).

There is one caveat to identifying "knowing that one knows" with a higher-order thought of higher-order thought theory. Rosenthal requires the higher-order thought to be an occurrent thought. Thus, if by knowing we just meant a disposition of the right sort (which is how the word is often used), knowing that one knows p would not in itself produce a conscious mental state about p. But in our framework we require fully explicit knowledge to be occurrently represented "I know that p"; by Rosenthal's higher-order thought theory, the fully explicit representation does indeed imply consciousness of p.

Higher-order thought theory is not just a theory of "reflective consciousness". It might be thought that a theory of having thoughts about thoughts is just a theory about the sort of conscious experiences one has when one knowingly reflects on one's experiences; perhaps, in the absence of higher-order thoughts, there is a direct consciousness of events that is simply not reflective. By the same token, some could argue (e.g. compare Dulany, 1997) that implicit knowledge provides a direct consciousness or sense of a feature or event (e.g. a sense of a yellow banana), and having fully explicit knowledge of, for example, the banana being yellow just provides an extra "reflective consciousness" of the banana being yellow. In fact, higher-order thought theory is a theory of the conditions under which a person is consciously aware of anything, reflectively or otherwise. The second-order thought "I see that the banana is yellow" makes one consciously aware of the banana being yellow, but it does not make one aware of the second-order thought. To be aware of seeing that the banana is yellow (i.e. in order to have reflective consciousness of the banana being yellow) there must be a third-order thought, for example "I know that I see that the banana is yellow". In this case, the person is aware of the experience as a visual experience that they themselves have. So a second-order thought is always necessary for conscious awareness of an event; likewise, fully explicit knowledge is necessary for any knowledge to be conscious knowledge. For a person to knowingly reflect on their experiences, at least third-order thoughts are necessary.

PROCEDURAL VERSUS DECLARATIVE

The procedural–declarative distinction confounds two separate distinctions: A procedural–non-procedural one (knowledge that is or is not contained in a procedure) and declarative–non-declarative one. A declarative representation declares what is the case, that is, a declarative representation explicitly represents a property predicated of an individual and represents that this is a fact. A procedural representation need not (but could) represent the individual or the factuality of the knowledge.

Verbal communication proceeds by identifying an individual and then providing further information about this individual; it can also explicitly identify the status of the claim as knowledge, as a wish, and so on. For this reason, procedural non-declarative knowledge is non-verbalisable.

Our framework shows why declarative knowledge is often associated with conscious knowledge and procedural knowledge is often associated with unconscious knowledge. Declarative knowledge must, by definition explicitly represent factivity; procedural knowledge need not be so explicit. But although declarative knowledge must be explicit to the level of factivity, it need not be fully explicit. This raises the question whether there could be declarative knowledge that has not been made fully explicit and thus is not conscious. It might be that, as a matter of brute empirical fact, this does not happen: Whenever a proposition p has been represented as a fact for the system, it is automatically tokened as something the system knows (Gordon, 1995, calls this an "ascent routine"). But there might be ways by which this normal "ascent" can be inhibited, leading to possible unconscious declarative representations, discussed in the next section.

Conversely, could there be cases of conscious procedural knowledge? Tzelgov, Ganor, and Yehene (1999) argued that all automatic (procedural) processing results in conscious representations. For example, in a standard Stroop task in which a subject is shown a list of colour words in different colours and the task is to report the colour of the ink, the subject automatically perceives the meaning of the word (even if he does not want to) and is conscious of the word. This is indeed a case of procedural knowledge producing conscious experiences, by producing a fully explicit representation of the perception of the meaning of the word. As our framework makes clear, there can also be cases of automatic procedural knowledge producing unconscious representations: For example, the Stroop effects investigated by Cheesman and Merikle (1984) and Merikle and Joordens (1997). In Cheesman and Merikle's study, subjects declared that they were literally guessing about whether a word had been presented, but the word still produced Stroop effects. But regardless of whether people are conscious of the word, the issue is whether the procedural knowledge itself— that is, the connection between condition and action that it represents, rather than just the final representation it produces—is conscious, and clearly it is not in this case. The procedural knowledge itself represents only regularities of the relevant sort (perhaps binding values to variables and thereby making predication explicit) but it is not represented as something that could be a fact (or not) or as something towards which the person could have an attitude of knowing (or any other attitude). Thus, it is unconscious. To some, this would be an illustration of the old maxim that contents are conscious and processes are not (e.g. Nisbett & Wilson, 1977). However, if by contents the maxim means anything with representational content, then the maxim is false. Procedures are about things, and the procedure itself may represent regularities in the world. Thus, it has content but it is not a conscious content, and our framework shows how something with content (a representation) can be unconscious.

Are there any cases of procedural knowledge itself being conscious? An example might be intentions controlling an ongoing action (what Searle, 1983, called an intention-in-action). The intention could represent the input conditions, the action, and the outcome, and the link between all of them. Further, an intention is not like an inert declarative representation of the same information; it is actually part of the process by which something is done. A conscious intention-in-action is conscious procedural knowledge, itself relying on other unconscious procedures implementing actions at a lower level. Intention and voluntary control will be discussed in the next section.

Procedural knowledge is at least sometimes unconscious, and is capable at least sometimes of producing unconscious knowledge. Procedural knowledge can also operate on unconscious representations. For example, Reed, McLeod, and Dienes (unpublished data) found that people who use a type of perceptual information in a servo-mechanism to control their ball-catching behaviour consistently misdescribed the contents of that perceptual information; that is, the information available consciously contradicted the unconscious information used procedurally.

VOLUNTARY CONTROL

Voluntary or intentional control of knowledge means that one can use it intentionally. That is, one needs to represent that one wants to use that knowledge. One needs to reference the content as something to be desired and not, for example, as an existing fact. Thus, the factuality (or otherwise) of the content of the knowledge must be made explicit. This analysis shows why the common notion that voluntary control is associated with explicitness is justified.

Perner (1998, in press) presented a dual control model of action, in which there are two levels of control—content control and vehicle control. Control of action can occur at the level of representational content: An action schema comes to control behaviour because its goal has been represented as something desired; or an action schema is inhibited because the goal is represented as something not desired. In content control, the representation of the goal causes the relevant action schema to control behaviour, regardless of the existing strength of associative links between current actual conditions and particular actions. In contrast to content control, control of action can occur simply at the level of representational vehicle: An action schema comes to control behaviour simply because there are strong associative links between current actual conditions—the schema's triggering conditions—and the action. In this case, the action schema that controls behaviour is the one with most activation, and here activation is a property of the representational vehicle: The activation does not represent the goal of the schema, it just determines the probability with which it will control behaviour. For example, consider driving from work to the supermarket, the route taken being in part the same as the more normal route from work to back home. If one did not have active the goal of going to the supermarket at a crucial juncture (so content control fails) one would end up driving home (vehicle control determines behaviour; no explicit representation of a goal is needed).

Some tasks necessarily involve content control, for example, inhibiting normal reactions in order to do something novel in a situation. In such situations, good performance is possible only by representing the content of the goal as something that is needed and is therefore not actually a fact. So the goal state must be represented declaratively. Normally, there is an ascent from declarative knowledge to a relevant higher-order thought. Thus, content control is normally associated with conscious intentions. Conversely, vehicle control does not require conscious intentions. For example, Debner and Jacoby (1994) flashed a word to subjects and then asked them to complete a word stem with anything EXCEPT the word that had been flashed. The conscious intention to not use that word could inhibit the action schema responsible for completing with that word and allow other action schemata to control behaviour. Thus, for words flashed for a long enough duration, stems were completed with those words at below baseline levels. However, if words were flashed very quickly, they were not consciously perceived, no conscious intention could be formed that inhibited their normal use, and an action schema was chosen simply based on which became activated most strongly by the triggering stem. That is, only vehicle control was possible. In this situation, subjects completed stems with the flashed words at above baseline levels. (Of course, control occurs in the context of a hierarchy of goals; even vehicle control is relative to this context. Subjects would have had content control of the general action "complete the stem with *some* word".)

Content control only actually requires declarative representation; it does not require full explicitness, so it does not actually require conscious representations of goals. Hypnosis (and related psychopathological states like hysteria) provide a possible case where the ascent from representation of factivity to the representation of a mental state is inhibited, that is, hypnosis might be a case of unconscious declarative representations and unconscious content control. Sheehan and McConkey (1982) and Spanos (1986) have emphasised the strategic goal-directed nature of hypnotic responding. A subject can be given a suggestion to count but always miss out the number "4". The inhibition of normal associations is required, so content control is required. None the less, susceptible subjects will respond successfully to the suggestion (counting "1,2,3,5,6 . . ."), all the while affirming their ignorance that they are doing anything strange. Similarly, Spanos, Radtke, and Dubreuil (1982; cited in Spanos, 1986) found that when it was suggested to highly susceptible subjects that they forget certain words in any type of task given to them, they produced those words at a below baseline level in a word association test. This performance again calls for content control because the existing associations that would be produced by vehicle control must be suppressed. In general, virtually any arbitrary behaviour can be suggested hypnotically, despite the fact that such behaviour might be novel to the person; it is highly plausible that many hypnotic responses are under content control. Yet highly susceptible subjects claim that their actions do not feel like normal consciously controlled actions; they seem strangely involuntary. And indeed they would seem involuntary if one had not represented the relevant goals as things to which the "I" had a mental-state relation (Kihlstrom, 1997), that is, if ascent from explicit representation of factivity to full explicitness had been inhibited.[5]

IMPLICIT/EXPLICIT AND META-COGNITION

We can now see the relation between meta-cognition and implicit/explicit knowledge. Meta-cognition consists of monitoring and control (Nelson & Narens, 1990). In terms of monitoring implicit knowledge, the learning and perceptual processes producing implicit knowledge do not yield representations that a piece of knowledge is known or that something has been seen: The person lacks direct knowledge that these cognitive processes have produced particular knowledge contents. In terms of meta-cognition as control, control of implicit knowledge is also difficult. That is, implicit processes are essentially related to a lack of meta-cognition.

---

[5] Content control of actions might be easier if one kept in mind not just declarative representations of the content of goals, but also representations of the appropriate mental states "I wish that . . .". Conversely, a person particularly skilled at content control might find it easier to inhibit the normal ascent from explicit factivity (involved in content control) to full mental state explicitness, because the latter step is not needed. The prediction is that highly hypnotisable subjects should be better than low hypnotisables at tasks requiring content control. Indeed, there is a large body of evidence for this claim. For example, highs can generate random numbers with a greater degree of randomness than lows (Graham & Evans, 1977); and in selective attention tasks, highs can select on the basis of representational content (semantic selection, or "pigeon holing" [Broadbent, 1971]) to a greater degree than lows (Dienes, 1987).

Our capacity for meta-cognition is greatest for those processes that have a self-referential aspect to their representations. For example, consider looking at the word in front of you. If the only representation formed was "the word in front of me is butter" you would not have the experience of seeing that the word in front of you is butter. You would not be aware of seeing anything because the representation "the word in front of me is butter" does not constitute a higher-order thought about seeing. If, however, you are forced to guess, the representation that has been formed ("the word in front of me is butter"), although it is in itself unconscious, could under some conditions be engaged by the further processes brought into play by the attempt to guess. You might guess "butter"; that is, form the representation "I guess that the word in front of me was 'butter'", making the information conscious, but not conscious as a visual experience, just as a guess. You might then, as an explicit act of inference, conclude that you saw that the word was butter, and thereby gain some meta-cognitive awareness of the seeing process. But meta-cognition comes most directly when it is not experienced as an act of inference. The normal act of seeing the word butter creates not just the representation "the word in front of me is 'butter'". The act of seeing creates the representation "I know that ('butter' is the word in front of me and this knowledge comes directly from seeing the word in front of me)". This representation constitutes the experience of seeing, rather than simply guessing (Searle, 1983). Knowledge that it is seeing (i.e. a meta-cognitive awareness about seeing and its products) comes directly from the process of seeing itself.[6]

Similar considerations apply to memory (Searle, 1983). One might infer, on the basis of familiarity that a certain to-be-recognised word was on the list; as an act of inference one might represent "I know that the word 'butter' was on the list". Contrast this with recollective experience. To ensure a true episodic memory the encoding has to be self-referential: "I know that ('butter' was on the list and this knowledge comes directly from my past experience of the list)". In this case, knowledge that one is dealing with a memory comes not as an experience of inference but is a result of the memorial process itself.

In summary, people's meta-cognitive abilities are least for knowledge that is fully implicit; present in some degree when inferences are used (e.g. based on familiarity of terms in the test question); and fully present for those outputs automatically represented as coming from the process that produced them by the act of producing them.

---

[6] In a similar way, Rosenthal (1986) requires the higher-order thoughts to arise non-observationally and non-inferentially, e.g. to be conscious of seeing one must not consciously infer one is seeing.

IMPLICIT LEARNING

We will now see how to apply this notion of implicitness to the phenomenon of implicit learning. Implicit learning is a type of learning resulting in
knowledge that is not labelled as knowledge by the act of learning itself.
Implicit learning is associative learning of the sort carried out by first-order
connectionist networks. Explicit learning is carried out by mechanisms that
label the knowledge as knowledge by the very act of inducing it; a prototypical type of explicit learning is hypothesis testing. To test and confirm a
hypothesis is to realise why it is knowledge. Thus, explicit learning produces
conscious fully explicit knowledge; implicit learning is learning that
produces knowledge we do not know about.

Participants in an implicit learning experiment are quite capable of
analysing their responses and experiences, drawing inferences about what
knowledge they must have. These explicit learning mechanisms, when
applied to implicit knowledge, can lead to the induction of explicit knowledge, that is, some capacity for meta-cognition, for a feeling of knowing,
but only as an act of inference. The knowledge produced by the implicit
learning mechanisms is in itself unconscious.

The paradigm explored most thoroughly in the implicit learning
literature is artificial grammar learning (see Reber, 1989). In a typical study,
participants first memorise grammatical strings of letters generated by a
finite-state grammar. For example, subjects might see strings like
"MSVVX", "STVM", and so on. Then they are informed of the existence
of the complex set of rules that constrains letter order (but not what they
are), and are asked to classify grammatical and non-grammatical strings.
Typically, participants can classify novel strings significantly above chance
(60–70%). This basic finding has been replicated many times. So participants clearly acquire some knowledge of the grammar under these
incidental learning conditions, but is this knowledge implicit?

To clarify how explicitly participants can reflect on their knowledge it is
necessary to be clear about what piece of knowledge participants might be
reflecting on. We distinguish two different domains of knowledge. The first
we call grammar rules. These are the general rules of the grammar that the
participant has induced, for example, "M can be followed by T". The
second domain pertains to the ability to make grammaticality judgements.
This arises when the grammar rules are being applied to a particular string
and it pertains to the knowledge of whether one can judge the grammaticality of the given test string independently of any knowing that one
knows the rules one brings to bear for making this judgement.

Various relationships between the knowledge of rules and grammaticality judgements are possible. Reber (1989) showed that people do not use
the rules to respond deterministically. That is, when retested with the same

string, participants often respond with a different answer. Extending this argument, Dienes, Kurz, Bernhaupt, and Perner (1997) argued that the data best support the claim that participants match the probability of endorsing a string as grammatical to the extent to which the input string satisfies the learned grammatical constraints, and that this probability varies continuously between different strings. Learning increases the probability of saying "grammatical"" to some strings and decreases it for other strings, depending on the extent to which the string matches the subject's developing grammar. Furthermore, we will presume this happens because a learning mechanism (we suggest a connectionist one) has evolved in people that was selected precisely because under the conditions of use in its evolutionary environment the mechanism tended to produce correct responses. This means that the probabilities actually imply the epistemic status of the grammaticality judgement, ranging from a pure guess to reliable knowledge. However, the mechanism responsible for producing these probabilities need not explicitly represent that there is knowledge (i.e. explicitly represent that a representation of a regularity has been formed that is accurate, judged to be accurate, and caused by a generally reliable process).

One way to test whether participants can represent the epistemic status of their judgements explicitly is to ask them to state their confidence in each classification decision (e.g. on a scale which ranging from "guess", through degrees of being "somewhat confident", to "know"). Now imagine that we know with what probability a given subject responds "grammatical" to each item. Then we could plot "confidence that the string is grammatical" against the probability of saying "grammatical" to it. If the confidence rating increases with the probability of responding "grammatical" to each item, with random responding given a confidence of "guess", and deterministic responding given a confidence of "know", then the propositional attitudes implied by the probabilities have been used by the participant explicitly to represent the epistemic status of the grammaticality judgements. If confidence ratings are not so related to response probabilities, then epistemic status has been represented only implicitly. If a plot of confidence against probability is a monotonically increasing line going through ("know it's non-grammatical", 0) to (guess, 0.5) and on to ("know it's grammatical", 1.0) then participants have fully used the implications of the source of their response probabilities to infer an explicit representation of their state of knowledge (see Figure 3.1). If the line is horizontal, then their knowledge is represented purely implicitly. If the line has some slope, but participants perform above chance when they believe they are guessing, then some of the knowledge is explicit *and* some of the knowledge is implicit.

In artificial grammar learning experiments, participants typically make one or two responses to each test item, so it is not possible to plot the

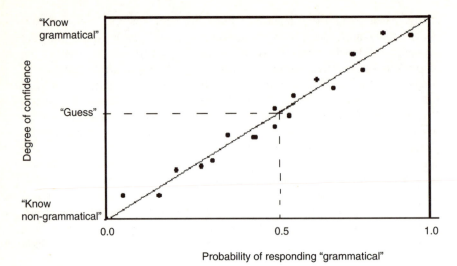

Figure 3.1. Theoretical graph indicating perfect explicit knowledge of the epistemic status of grammaticality judgements. The graph is over test items for one subject; it makes no assumptions about the experimenter knowing the subject's grammar.

confidence–probability graph just described, but we can get some way without all the information. We need to start by making an assumption: That the grammar induced by the participants happens to be the grammar specified by the experimenter, or is very highly correlated with it. Logically, there is no reason why this should be so (experimenters generally do not justify why they choose one grammar rather than another in terms of a learning theory); there are an infinite number of grammars that specify a finite number of strings, so how (short of extrasensory perception) could a participant know which grammar the experimenter happened to have in mind? Researchers in the area, ourselves included, have often fallen into the trap of talking about THE grammar, and wondering whether the participant has got this or that item "correct". Due to a remarkable coincidence, or insight on Reber's (1967) part, with exposure to a set of strings, subjects progressively classify more and more strings correctly according to the sort of grammar specified by the researchers in this area (at least when the set of non-grammatical test strings are created by typical procedures of researchers in the area, e.g. by randomly changing one or more letters—the ability to classify grammatical strings is always relative to the set of non-grammatical strings). Thus, a good approximation to the participant's grammar is the type of finite-state grammar typically used by the experimenter. But it is not perfect. Dienes et al. (1997) found that, for some grammatical items, training decreased the probability that they were called grammatical and, that for some non-grammatical items, training increased the probability with which they were called grammatical. This fact will produce some error in the procedure next described, because the procedure recognises as knowledge only those generalisations induced by the subject that classify test stimuli in the same way as the experimenter's grammar does.

Consider the case where the participant makes just one response to each test item. We divide the items into those with which the participant makes a correct decision ("correct items") and those with which the participant makes an incorrect decision ("incorrect items"). If accuracy is correlated with confidence, the correct items should be a selective sample of those given a higher average confidence rating than the incorrect items. Conversely, if participants do not assign greater confidence to correct than incorrect items, then that is evidence that the slope of the graph is zero, that is, they do not represent their state of knowledge of their ability to judge correctly. If participants give a greater confidence rating to correct than incorrect items, that is evidence of at least some explicitness. If, in this case, participants perform above chance when they believe they are literally guessing, that is evidence of some implicitness in addition to the explicitness.

Chan (1992) was the first to test whether participants explicitly represented knowing their grammaticality judgements. Chan initially asked one group of participants (the incidentally trained participants) to memorise a set of grammatical examples. In a subsequent test phase, participants gave a confidence rating for their accuracy after each classification decision. They were just as confident in their incorrect decisions as they were in their correct decisions, providing evidence that knowing was represented only implicitly. Chan asked another group of participants (the intentionally trained participants) to search for rules in the training phase. For these participants, confidence was strongly related to accuracy in the test phase, indicating that intentionally rather than incidentally trained participants represented their knowing more explicitly. Manza and Reber (1997), using stimuli different from Chan's, found that confidence was reliably higher for correct than incorrect decisions for incidentally trained participants. On the other hand, Dienes, Altman, Kwan, and Goode (1995) replicated the lack of correlation between confidence and accuracy, but only under some conditions: the correlation was low particularly when strings were longer than three letters and presented individually. Finally, Dienes and Altmann (1997) found that, when participants transferred their knowledge to a different domain, their confidence was not related to their accuracy.

In summary, there are conditions under which participants represent knowing grammaticality implicitly on most judgements, but there is generally also evidence of having an explicit attitude of knowing on other judgements. Even in the latter case, there is sometimes evidence of implicit knowledge: Both Dienes et al. (1995) and Dienes and Altmann (1997) found that even when participants believed they were literally guessing, they were still classifying substantially above chance.

Both the zero-correlation and guessing criteria have their problems as methodologies for indicating implicit knowledge. If the participant induces any explicit knowledge, then the zero-correlation criterion could show that the participant has at least some explicit knowledge; whether there is in addition any implicit knowledge is then unknown. Thus, although there might be much implicit knowledge induced, it is hard to determine that this is so simply because the participant has induced some explicit knowledge. None the less, differences between experimental conditions in the zero-correlation criterion can indicate differences in extent of meta-cognitive knowledge and hence differences in the amount of explicit knowledge and thus, by implication, differences in amount of implicit knowledge (assuming overall performance is equal between the conditions; i.e. implicit knowledge plus explicit knowledge is a constant).

The problem with the guessing criterion is power (in the statistical sense): Even if participants are using purely implicit knowledge, they might produce confidence ratings higher than guessing based on other considerations. Then the guessing criterion is computed on some fraction (typically one-third or less) of the total number of participants' responses and so can lack power. Frequently, studies will show no implicit knowledge by the guessing criterion, but the confidence interval on the amount of guessing knowledge is large. Allwood, Granhag, and Johansson (2000) and Johnstone (1999) both recommend looking at the full accuracy–confidence graph when assessing participants' realism in assessing their grammaticality judgements; we agree this should give a more sensitive assessment of degree of meta-knowledge. The guessing intercept could then be used to derive a type of guessing criterion estimate of implicit knowledge that uses more data than just the guessing responses themselves (Figure 3.2).

Another procedure for assessing meta-knowledge was used by Dienes et al (1995). The reliability with which participants gave the same confidence rating to the same string was assessed (for those cases where the participants gave a correct response). This reliability was found to be very low ($r_i = .16$). This indicates a lack of meta-knowledge. Whatever information led participants consistently to answer correctly to some strings rather than others was not being transmitted through their confidence ratings. (Note that these strings do have a reliable rank ordering in terms of participants' tendencies to give correct responses to them [Dienes, 1992].) For example, if familiarity of the string or its parts was driving the grammaticality judgements, that same function of familiarity could not have been driving the confidence judgements (contrast Koriat's 1993 theory of feeling of knowing,

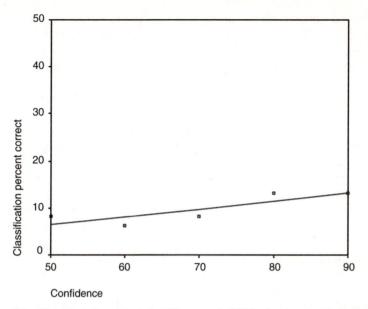

Figure 3.2.   Data from Experiment 5 of Dienes et al. (1995), showing the advantage in classification performance in the test phase of a group trained on grammatical strings (the informed group) over a group with no prior training (the control group) plotted against confidence (50 = guessing, 100 = certain). The graph shows a positive intercept (some implicit knowledge) and a positive slope (some explicit knowledge). The method assumes that the experimenter's grammar closely matches the grammar induced by the subject (in this case, the assumption is confirmed by the positive intercept and slope).

according to which feelings of knowing are based on the accessibility of relevant content).

To take a step back from the methodological details, it is important to note that all of these results bear on the extent to which subjects have meta-knowledge about the judgement process itself, that is, on the extent to which subjects know their judgements are based on induced knowledge. One reason why subjects might lack meta-knowledge about judgements is because they lack meta-knowledge of the induced rules. In fact, we take it that what most researchers find interesting about the implicitness of implicit learning is that subjects induce rules that are represented only implicitly. However, subjects might have induced rules represented implicitly but none the less learn to tell when their judgements are based on knowledge and when they are not. Allwood et al. (2000) found this pattern: In their first experiment subjects had little meta-knowledge about their grammaticality judgements; in their second experiment, subjects had considerably more experience with the task, and also had remarkably good meta-knowledge. In this case, it could be that the knowledge of the rules themselves is still implicit; and the real inferential basis of their grammatical decisions might still be implicit. But subjects could have come to notice feelings associated with the perception of different strings, feelings they could come to use in making confidence judgements by making explicit inferences regarding their relevance to the correctness of their judgements.

Koriat (2000) distinguished two ways of making meta-cognitive judgements: (1) information-based, in which the person is aware of the inferences they make in forming a conclusion about their knowledge state; and (2) feeling-based, in which the true inferential basis of the judgements is not explicit, the person is aware only of the result of the inference as a directly-experienced feeling (e.g. the tip of the tongue state). We suggest that, in artificial grammar learning, the knowledge of rules is often largely implicit and applied implicitly (i.e. their application is not represented as the application of knowledge, and the concomitant inferences are not represented as inferences). One common consequence of this state of affairs is that people often lack meta-knowledge about their judgements of grammaticality. Its fortunate that this is a consequence because this lack of meta-knowledge about judgements is easy to measure; measuring lack of meta-knowledge about the rules is a lot harder without us as experimenters knowing what the rules are. So, just as in the tip-of-the-tongue state, where the inferential basis is what is implicit, so it is in making judgements in artificial grammar learning: one judges the string as grammatical without representing the applied knowledge as knowledge and the process as an inference. None the less, in artificial grammar learning, subjects might learn to make information-based confidence judgements about the inferentially implicit grammaticality judgements. A methodological challenge for the future will be getting a good measure of the lack of meta-knowledge subjects have about rules; at the moment, we measure just one possible, but not necessary, symptom—the lack of meta-knowledge about judgements.

Finally, we note a common criticism of meta-cognitive measures of implicit knowledge or, in other words, what are called subjective threshold measures of consciousness (Reingold & Merikle, 1993). The argument is that these measures are flawed because they simply shift the responsibility for determining the participants' awareness of knowledge from the experimenter to the participants; and the participants might be responding according to whatever idiosyncratic theory they please. For example, whether participants give a guess response is up to the participants' theory of what guessing is, or just their criterion for responding. The implication usually given when these arguments are mentioned is that this is all that needs to be said; it's about time we put our hats on and went home to think of different approaches to consciousness and implicit knowledge.

In response, we note, firstly, that we do inform our subjects that by guessing we mean the assessment that the answer could just as well be based on a flip of a coin; we do regard it as very important that the participants understand that guessing occurs in the absence of any useful information whatsoever. The second point is that this type of argument simply opens up an interesting avenue of empirical exploration. Twyman and Dienes (2001) investigated how the various estimates of meta-knowledge were changed by, for example, training subjects in probability, exhorting them to be more or less confident, taking confidence ratings after blocks or individual trials. They found that the meta-cognitive measures were influenced by the manipulations. Several questions then arise. Under what conditions do the measures appear to distinguish functionally different types of knowledge? Under what conditions are subjects least biased in converting their actual degree of meta-knowledge into a verbal report? What conditions actually change the amount of subjects' meta-knowledge, and hence the conscious and unconscious status of the corresponding mental states? These are interesting questions to explore. But for the time being, our hats remain firmly on the hat rack.

SUMMARY

In this chapter we initially established what it is for something to be implicit, using the approach of Dienes and Perner (1999; Perner & Dienes, 1999), which led naturally to the conclusion that a lack of meta-knowledge is an essential feature of implicit knowledge. We then reviewed evidence indicating the extent of people's meta-knowledge in a standard implicit learning paradigm, namely the artificial grammar learning paradigm. People can induce a grammar through a reliable learning mechanism yet, under certain conditions, be largely unaware that they have any knowledge. Inducing such knowledge by a mechanism that does not label the knowledge as knowledge we take to be the essence of implicit learning. Implicit learning enables representations of regularities in the world to be formed that can control action (at the level of vehicle control, not content control, as shown recently by Destrebecqz & Cleeremans, 2001) without constituting conscious knowledge. Our framework shows how in fact the world can be represented without those representations having to be like the fully explicated normal contents of our conscious thoughts.

REFERENCES

Allwood, C.M., Granhag, P.A., & Johansson, H. (2000). Realism in confidence judgements of performance based on implicit learning. *European Journal of Cognitive Psychology, 12*, 165–188.

Brentano, F. von (1874/1970). *Psychology from an empirical standpoint* (Edited by O. Kraus, translated by L.L. McAllister.) London: Routledge.

Bridgeman, B. (1991). Complementary cognitive and motor image processing. In G. Obrecht &

L.W. Starke (Eds.), *Presbyopia research: From molecular biology to visual adaptation* (pp. 189–198). London: Plenum Press.

Broadbent, D.E. (1971). *Decision and stress*. New York: Academic Press.

Carruthers, P. (1992). Consciousness and concepts. *Proceedings of the Aristotelian Society, Supplementary vol., LXVI*, 42–59.

Carruthers, P. (2000). *Phenomenal consciousness naturally*. Cambridge: Cambridge University Press.

Chan, C. (1992). *Implicit cognitive processes: Theoretical issues and applications in computer systems design*. Unpublished D.Phil thesis, University of Oxford.

Cheesman, J., & Merikle, P.M. (1984). Priming with and without awareness. *Perception and Psychophysics, 36*, 387–395.

Debner, J.A., & Jacoby, L.L. (1994). Unconscious perception: Attention, awareness, and control. *Journal of Experimental Psychology: Learning, Memory, and Cognition, 20*, 304–317.

Dennett, D.C. (1987). *The intentional stance*. Cambridge, MA: Bradford Books/MIT-Press.

Dennett, D.C. (1996). *Darwin's dangerous idea: Evolution and the meanings of life*. London: Allen Lane

Destrebecqz, A., & Cleeremans, A. (2001). Can sequence learning be implicit? New evidence with the process dissociation procedure. *Psychonomic Bulletin and Review, 8(2)*, 343–350.

Dienes, Z. (1987). *Selective attention: Relevance to hypnosis and hypnotizability*. Thesis submitted in partial fulfillment of the requirements for Master of Arts (Hons), School of Behavioural Sciences, Macquarie University, Australia.

Dienes, Z. (1992). Connectionist and memory array models of artificial grammar learning. *Cognitive Science, 16*, 41–79.

Dienes, Z., & Altmann, G. (1997). Transfer of implicit knowledge across domains? How implicit and how abstract? In D. Berry (Ed.), *How implicit is implicit learning?* (pp. 107–123). Oxford: Oxford University Press.

Dienes, Z., Altmann, G., Kwan, L., & Goode, A. (1995). Unconscious knowledge of artificial grammars is applied strategically. *Journal of Experimental Psychology: Learning, Memory, & Cognition, 21*, 1322–1338.

Dienes, Z., Kurz, A., Bernhaupt, R., & Perner, J. (1997). Application of implicit knowledge: Deterministic or probabilistic? *Psychologica Belgica, 37*, 89–112.

Dienes, Z., & Perner, J. (1999) A theory of implicit and explicit knowledge. *Behavioural and Brain Sciences, 22*, 735–755.

Dretske, F. (1988). *Explaining behavior: Reasons in a world of causes*. Cambridge, MA: MIT Press.

Dretske, F. (1995). *Naturalizing the mind*. Cambridge, MA: MIT Press.

Dulany, D.E. (1997). Consciousness in the explicit (deliberative) and implicit (evocative). In J.D. Cohen & J.W. Schooler (Eds.), *Scientific approaches to the study of consciousness* (pp. 179–212). Mahwah, NJ: Lawrence Erlbaum Associates Inc.

Fodor, J.A. (1990). *A theory of content and other essays*. Cambridge, MA: MIT Press.

Gordon, R.M. (1995). Simulation without introspection of inference from me to you. In M. Davies & T. Stone (Eds.), *Mental simulation: Evaluations and applications* (pp. 53–67). Oxford: Blackwell.

Graham, C., & Evans, F.J. (1977). Hypnotizability and the deployment of waking attention. *Journal of Abnormal Psychology, 86*, 631–638.

Johnstone, T. (1999). *Structural versus processing accounts of implicit learning*. Unpublished PhD thesis, University College London.

Kihlstrom, J.F. (1997). Consciousness and me-ness. In J.D. Cohen & J.W. Schooler (Eds.), *Scientific approaches to consciousness*. Mahweh, NJ: Lawrence Erlbaum Associates Inc.

Koriat, A. (1993). How do we know that we know? The accessiblity model of the feeling of knowing. *Psychological Review, 100*, 609–639.

Koriat, A. (2000). The feeling of knowing: Some metatheoretical implications for consciousness and control. *Consciousness and Cognition, 9(2)*, 149–176.

Manza, L., & Reber, A.S. (1997). *Representation of tacit knowledge: Transfer across stimulus forms and modalities*. Unpublished manuscript.

Merikle, P.M., & Joordens, S. (1997). Parallels between perception without attention and perception without awareness. *Consciousness and Cognition, 6*, 219–236.

Millikan, R.G. (1993). *White queen psychology and other essays for Alice*. Cambridge, MA: Bradford Books/MIT-Press.

Nelson, T.O., & Narens, L. (1990). Metamemory: A theoretical framework and new findings. In G. Bower (Ed.), *The psychology of learning and motivation: Advances in research and theory* (Vol 26, pp. 125–173). San Diego, CA: Academic Press.

Nisbett, R.E., & Wilson, T.D. (1977). Telling more than we know: Verbal reports on mental processes. *Psychological Review, 84*, 231–259.

Perner, J. (1991). *Understanding the representational mind*. Cambridge, MA: Bradford Books/ MIT-Press.

Perner, J. (1998). The meta-intentional nature of executive functions and theory of mind. In P. Carruthers & J. Boucher (Eds.), *Language and thought* (pp. 270–283). Cambridge: Cambridge University Press.

Perner, J. (in press). Dual control and the causal theory of action: The case of non-intentional action and causal self-reference. In N. Eilan & J. Roessler (Eds.), *Agency and self-awareness*. Oxford: Oxford University Press.

Perner, J., & Dienes, Z. (1999). Deconstructing RTK: How to explicate a theory of implicit knowledge. *Behavioural and Brain Sciences, 22*, 790–808.

Reber, A.S. (1967). Implicit learning of artificial grammars. *Journal of Verbal Learning and Verbal Behaviour, 6*, 855–863.

Reber, A.S. (1989). Implicit learning and tactic knowledge. *Journal of Experimental Psychology: General, 118*, 219–235.

Reingold, E.M., & Merikle, P.M. (1993). Theory and measurement in the study of unconscious processes. In M. Davies & G.W. Humphreys (Eds.), *Consciousness* (pp. 40–57). Oxford: Blackwell.

Rosenthal, D.M. (1986). Two concepts of consciousness. *Philosophical Studies, 49*, 329–359.

Rosenthal, D.M. (2000). *Sensory qualities, consciousness, and perception*. Paper presented at the Fourth Annual Conference of the Association for the Scientific Study of Consciousness, Brussels, 29 June–4 July 2000.

Searle, J.R. (1983). *Intentionality*. Cambridge: Cambridge University Press.

Searle, J.R. (1990). Consciousness, explanatory inversion, and cognitive science. *Behavioural and Brain Sciences, 13*, 585–642.

Sheehan, P.W., & McConkey, K.M. (1982). *Hypnosis and experience: The exploration of phenomena and process*. Hillsdale, NJ: Lawrence Erlbaum Associates Inc.

Spanos, N.P. (1986). Hypnotic behaviour: A social-psychological interpretation of amnesia, analgesia, and "trance logic". *The Behavioural and Brain Sciences, 9*, 449–502.

Twyman, M., & Dienes, Z. (2001). *Metacognitive measures of implicit knowledge*. Proceedings of the 2001 Convention of The Society for the Study of Artificial Intelligence and the Simulation of Behaviour (AISB): Nonconscious Intelligence, from Natural to Artificial, York, 21–24 March 2001 (pp. 63–71).

Tye, M. (1995). *Ten problems of consciousness: A representational theory of the phenomenal mind*. Cambridge, MA: MIT Press.

Tzelgor, J., Ganor, D., & Yehene, V. (1999). Automatic processing results in conscious representations. *Behavioural and Brain Sciences, 22*, 786–787.

Weiskrantz, L. (1988). Some contributions of neuropsychology of vision and memory to the problem of consciousness. In A.J. Marcel & E. Bisiach (Eds.), *Consciousness in contemporary science* (pp. 183–199). Oxford: Clarendon Press.

CHAPTER FOUR

Modularity and artificial grammar learning

David R. Shanks and Theresa Johnstone
University College, London, UK

Annette Kinder
Philipps-Universität, Marburg, Germany

People have an impressive capacity for storing information about particular events. This "episodic" memory allows us to recall the context of specific experiences, such as what we did on our last holiday, and is now fairly well understood both psychologically (Tulving, 1983) and at the neural level (McClelland, McNaughton, & O'Reilly, 1995). We also have an ability, however, to acquire knowledge about generalities, that is, properties of classes of objects or events. We can judge the grammaticality of a novel sentence, read a word in an unfamiliar script, perform arithmetic operations, and so on. These seem to require representations of abstract, general properties such as the rules of a grammar that transcend and are separate from knowledge of specific objects or events.

Cognitive psychology has traditionally dealt with this distinction by assuming separate processes for acquiring specific and general knowledge. Under various terms (e.g. episodic, explicit, declarative), knowledge of specific events is assumed to be distinct from knowledge about general properties (e.g. semantic, implicit, procedural, non-declarative). A puzzle, however, is to explain how we acquire general knowledge, as abstract properties themselves are never directly observed (see Whittlesea, 1997a, b). Instead, such properties must be induced from multiple experiences with specific objects or events. Hence, the separate-systems account assumes that there exists a mechanism for creating abstractions across specific experiences. Moreover, as we are not normally deliberately intending to perform such abstraction, it must be a largely incidental and unconscious process.

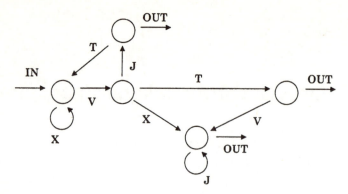

Figure 4.1.   One of the artificial grammars used by Knowlton et al. (1992).

The aim of this chapter is to evaluate this modular, separate-systems account in one particular branch of implicit learning research.

Undoubtedly, there is a wealth of evidence consistent with the separate-systems account with a good deal of that evidence coming from artificial grammar learning (AGL) research (see Chapter 6 for a review). For example, Knowlton, Ramus, and Squire (1992) trained normal participants and amnesic patients by asking them to memorise strings of letters generated from a finite-state grammar. One of the two grammars Knowlton et al. used is shown in Figure 4.1. This grammar specifies rules, similar to those that exist in natural languages, for ordering string elements. Grammatical strings are generated by entering the diagram at the leftmost node and moving along legal pathways, as indicated by the arrows, collecting letters, until an exit point is reached on the right-hand side. The letter string XXVXJJ is grammatical because it can be generated from the diagram, whereas TXXXVT is ungrammatical, because strings must begin with a V or an X.

Knowlton et al. (1992) tested specific knowledge by asking participants to recognise which letter strings they had seen during training using a set of test strings, half of which had been presented as training strings and half of which were novel. In contrast, general knowledge was tested by informing participants of the existence of a set of rules governing the structure of the training items—although they were not told what those rules were—and then asking them to classify novel letter strings as grammatical or ungrammatical depending on whether the letter strings appeared to conform to the rules or not. The fact that the amnesic patients were selectively impaired in making judgements about specific items, while their general knowledge of the grammar was intact, seems to support the idea of separate "implicit" (general) and "explicit" (specific) learning systems. We return to this particular piece of evidence later in the chapter.

Despite the wealth of evidence apparently supporting the dual-system account, we argue in the present chapter for a more parsimonious, unitary view of learning, which, we suggest, encompasses all of the key data from studies of artificial grammar learning. Our unitary account is applied to data from both normal and amnesic participants and makes a number of testable predictions that place it in opposition to the dual-system account. We review evidence indicating that these predictions are correct.

The dual-system theory of implicit learning is based on four major claims. Firstly, it is claimed that implicit knowledge is acquired when participants observe or memorise representative examples of a complex rule-governed concept, without being told that the examples conform to a set of rules (Knowlton & Squire, 1994, 1996; Meulemans & Van der Linden, 1997; Reber, 1967, 1989).

Secondly, in these incidental learning conditions, participants are passive "consumers" of stimulus-driven knowledge rather than active processors of knowledge (we elaborate more on this later).

Thirdly, it is claimed that an implicit learning system creates mental representations of abstracted knowledge, in parallel with an explicit system that creates representations of specific whole or partial training items in a separate episodic memory.

Finally, it is claimed that participants lack awareness of the knowledge they use to classify test items at above-chance levels because they cannot fully state the rules of the grammar (Reber & Lewis, 1977) and because accurate performance is accompanied by a subjective experience of guessing (Dienes, Altmann, Kwan, & Goode, 1995). In contrast, because participants are aware of observing or memorising whole or partial training examples, conscious recollection of "old" items and a sense of novelty for "new" items accompany (explicit) recognition performance.

In contrast to the dual-system theory, exemplar and fragment accounts are varieties of unitary theory, both of which assume that above-chance classification performance can be explained solely on the basis of episodic knowledge. The exemplar account claims that participants encode a collection of training examples (Brooks, 1978; Brooks & Vokey, 1991; McAndrews & Moscovitch, 1985; Neal & Hesketh, 1997; Vokey & Brooks, 1992) and that, at test, items that are highly similar to training items (e.g. differing by only one letter) are more likely to be called grammatical than dissimilar items. The letter-fragment account (Dulany, Carlson, & Dewey, 1984; Meulemans & Van der Linden, 1997; Perruchet, 1994; Perruchet & Pacteau, 1990; Redington & Chater, 1996) suggests that participants use specific knowledge of letter fragments seen in training strings to classify test items. In this case, participants are assumed to classify test items containing fragments seen in training as grammatical and test strings containing novel or less familiar fragments as ungrammatical.

Whereas the implicit rule abstraction, exemplar, and fragment accounts share an assumption that specific aspects of the structure of training examples (rules, exemplars, or letter-fragments) are acquired in a stimulus-driven manner, the episodic-processing account (Neal & Hesketh, 1997; Whittlesea, 1997a; Whittlesea & Dorken, 1993) suggests that knowledge acquisition is driven by processing. According to this account, participants actively process training strings in order to meet the demands of the training task and, in so doing, acquire knowledge of the specific aspects of training items (rules, exemplars, or letter fragments) necessary to meet those demands. As a result, episodic representations are created combining knowledge of both the processing carried out and the information used to satisfy the training instructions. At test, items that overlap with training items on the structural aspects encoded during training cue prior processing episodes and, as a result, are processed more fluently than dissimilar test items that do not cue prior episodes. The knowledge that induces fluency is neither implicit nor explicit. Instead, when participants are unaware of the relationship between fluency and the information they acquired during training, they will experience and respond on the basis of a feeling of familiarity and we will describe this as implicit; whereas when they are aware of the relationship, they will experience and respond on the basis of recollection and we will describe this as explicit.

The assumptions of the episodic-processing account can be illustrated using an AGL example in which a participant is asked to memorise a set of letter strings, such as MXRTMXR. In this example, the participant actively meets the demands of the memorisation task by mentally rehearsing each training string left to right as a series of two- and three-letter fragments. Using this strategy, MXRTMXR is rehearsed for example as the three letter fragments MXR, TM, and XR, and the episodic-processing system is assumed to create episodic representations of the mental rehearsal process applied to those specific fragments. By the end of the training phase, the participant will have acquired episodic representations by mentally rehears-ing a large number of letter fragments leading to an ability to process efficiently future letter strings containing the same letter fragments.

During a later classification test, the assumption is that test items that are similar to training items on the structural dimension used to process training items (letter fragments in this example) will cue episodic represen-tations of processing similar training items. Cueing prior episodes will result in similar test items being processed more efficiently (fluently) than dis-similar test items. Thus, continuing with the example, a test string con-taining previously seen letter fragments such as MXR, TM, and XR would cue episodic representations of processing those fragments, whereas a test string containing only novel fragments would not retrieve any episodic representations.

Finally, the suggestion that participants will respond on the basis of subjective feelings of familiarity if they are unaware, or on the basis of recollection if they are aware of the relationship between the information they acquired during training and test demands can be illustrated by comparing classification and recognition test performance (see also Buchner, 1994). When a participant is asked to classify novel test items as grammatical or ungrammatical, he or she will not understand the relationship between the letter-fragment knowledge gained in training and fluency of processing test items. Consequently, fluency in processing test items containing training fragments will unconsciously be attributed to grammaticality and accompanied by a subjective feeling of familiarity. In contrast, when the participant is asked to discriminate between fragments seen during training and novel fragments in a recognition test, old/new judgements could be based on the same unconscious attribution process or they could, alternatively, be based on conscious recollection of fragment knowledge. Recollection is a separate process involving retrieval of aspects of the context in which the item appeared.

There is therefore a similarity between the episodic-processing and rule-abstraction accounts as both accounts predict that knowledge can be applied implicitly in a classification test. However, these two accounts disagree about the form of knowledge (processing episodes versus rules) and whether knowledge is stored in an implicit form (Reber, 1967, 1989) or in a neutral form that can be expressed implicitly or explicitly depending on test instructions (Whittlesea & Dorken, 1997).

FORMS OF KNOWLEDGE

The first stage in evaluating the four accounts of implicit learning is to identify what knowledge is acquired during incidental memorisation conditions, as without reliable evidence about the information used to classify test items it is impossible to know whether that knowledge is implicit or explicit (see Shanks & St John, 1994).

Rule knowledge

Convincing evidence that participants classify on the basis of rules depends on having a clear definition of what a rule is and on unconfounding rule knowledge from other explanations of test performance. Unfortunately, researchers have been less than forthcoming on this issue. However, the general idea is that, at least in the case of finite-state grammars, learning the structure of the grammar entails forming some abstract mental representation that describes each of the states of the grammar (i.e. the nodes in Figure 4.1), together with the legal letter continuations from that state and the ensuing state. This mental representation is usually thought of as a symbolic or "algebraic" structure (Marcus, Vijayan, Bandi Rao, & Vishton, 1999) and is assumed to be quite independent of, and distinct from, a specification of the transitional probabilities or distributional statistics of the surface elements instantiating the grammar.[1] Test strings are classified as grammatical if they can be parsed by the grammar. Manza and Reber (1997, p. 75) wrote that:

> This position is based on the argument that the complex knowledge acquired during an AG learning task is represented in a general, abstract form. The representation is assumed to contain little, if any, information pertaining to specific stimulus features; the emphasis is on structural relationships among stimuli. The key here is the notion that the mental content consists, not of the representation of specific physical forms, but of abstract representations of those forms.

The strongest evidence for abstract rule knowledge is found in "transfer" tests where participants train on items in one letter-set or modality and successfully classify test items presented in a different letter-set or modality (e.g. Altmann, Dienes, & Goode, 1995). The only common factor between training and test items is their underlying abstract structure. For example, Altmann et al. (1995, Experiment 1) trained one group of participants on standard letter strings and a second group on sequences of tones, with both the letter strings and tone sequences conforming to the same rule structure. Thus each letter string had an equivalent tone sequence in which, for instance, the letter M was translated into a tone at the frequency of middle C. In the test phase, participants classified strings presented in the same modality as their training strings (letters/letters or tones/tones) or in the opposite modality (letters/tones or tones/letters). There were two types of control groups who either received no training or who were trained on randomly generated sequences. The results suggested that prior exposure to the grammar led to accurate classification performance (same modality 56% correct, changed modality 54% correct), whereas control groups performed at chance (50%).

---

[1] Cleeremans, Servan-Schreiber, and McClelland (1989, pp. 380–381) showed that a simple recurrent network (SRN; we describe such networks in more detail later) can effectively learn any finite-state grammar and can "develop internal representations that correspond to the nodes of the grammar, and closely approximates the corresponding minimal finite-state recognizer". However, because internal representations in an SRN are tied to specific input elements, are non-symbolic, and strongly code transitional probabilities, our understanding is that Manza and Reber (1997), Marcus et al. (1999), and other proponents of the abstract grammar-learning view would strongly dissociate themselves from the suggestion that an SRN can implement the type of true abstract grammar learning that they believe infants and adults can perform.

Although this experiment appears to provide evidence that changed modality groups used general, abstract, rule knowledge that goes beyond perceptual features, Redington and Chater (1996) demonstrated that participants could have used surface fragments of two or three letters to perform abstraction at test. Moreover, Gomez (1997) has presented convincing evidence that transfer is always accompanied by explicit knowledge: Participants who achieved above-chance transfer scores also scored above-chance on direct tests. Thus there is little evidence at present that transfer is mediated by implicit, abstract knowledge.

Exemplar knowledge

The exemplar account assumes that participants retrieve specific training examples from memory when they classify test items. For example, Vokey and Brooks (1992) trained participants on grammatical strings and tested them on novel strings, where half the test strings were grammatical and half ungrammatical. Orthogonal to grammaticality, half the test items were similar to one training item (differing by only one letter) while half were dissimilar to all training items (differing by two or more letters). Independent effects of grammaticality and similarity were found in both classification and recognition tests.

Vokey and Brooks (1992, p. 328) used instance models (Hintzman, 1986) to argue that independent effects of grammaticality and similarity are consistent with models that rely solely on retrieval of specific items. As new grammatical test items are likely to resemble a large number of grammatical training items, the difference between classification of grammatical versus ungrammatical test items can be explained by "retrieval time averaging". On the other hand, the difference between similar and dissimilar test items can be explained on the basis that a test item that is highly similar to an item in memory has a disproportionately large effect on test performance. Hence the grammaticality effect could arise because grammatical test items are moderately similar to many training items and the similarity effect could arise because each similar test item is highly similar to one training item. However, Vokey and Brooks (1994) conceded that their design did not allow them to falsify the abstract rule knowledge account.

Fragment knowledge

An opposing theory is that participants learn about the frequency of occurrence of fragments (i.e. two-letter bigrams, three-letter trigrams, etc.) in the training strings and classify novel test strings as grammatical to the extent that test strings contain fragments that were present in the training strings. Perruchet and Pacteau (1990) compared the performance of participants trained on grammatical letter strings with those trained on the bigrams used to construct the grammatical training strings. The finding that both groups were able to classify novel test strings at above-chance levels suggests that fragment knowledge alone is sufficient to account for accurate classification performance. In fact, Perruchet (1994) was able to explain both the grammaticality and similarity effects found by Vokey and Brooks (1992) solely on the basis of trigram knowledge.

However, Gomez and Schvaneveldt (1994) demonstrated that there are two types of bigram violation within ungrammatical strings and participants trained on bigrams were sensitive to only one violation type. Participants trained on grammatical strings could detect both illegal letter pairs and legal letter pairs in illegal positions within a string, while participants who memorised bigrams were able to detect only illegal letter pairs. But Redington and Chater (1996) added a further dimension to this debate by showing that Gomez and Schvaneveldt's results can be predicted by models that call a test string grammatical if all bigrams and trigrams have been seen in training items, and call a test string ungrammatical if it contains novel letter fragments. Overall, then, the evidence that grammaticality judgements are to some extent mediated by fragment knowledge is quite strong.

Combined rule and fragment knowledge

Knowlton and Squire (1994, Experiment 2b) challenged the exemplar account by using test stimuli that contained the same orthogonal grammaticality and whole-item similarity manipulations as Vokey and Brooks (1992) had used, but with an added manipulation where fragment similarity was held constant across similar and dissimilar test item types. The results showed that Vokey and Brooks' results were more likely to have been produced by rule and fragment knowledge than by rule and whole-item knowledge. However, these results leave open the debate about whether the grammaticality and fragment effects are derived from dual knowledge sources or from only one knowledge base.

Meulemans and Van der Linden (1997) have provided the most convincing rule and fragment account using test stimuli that balance rule knowledge orthogonally to fragment knowledge. They found that after training on 32 letter strings (Experiment 2a), participants classified test strings using fragment knowledge, whereas after training on 125 letter strings (Experiment 2b) they classified on the basis of rule knowledge. We evaluate this study in more detail below.

EVIDENCE FOR THE EPISODIC-PROCESSING ACCOUNT

The episodic-processing account challenges all of the above accounts by suggesting that, rather than focusing solely on stimulus-driven acquisition of structural aspects of training items (i.e. rules, exemplars, or letter-fragments): (1) processing knowledge is acquired in addition to structural knowledge; (2) training instructions dictate which aspects of the structure of training items are encoded; and (3) participants can apply the same knowledge explicitly or implicitly, depending on whether they understand the relationship between processing fluency and the knowledge they acquired by processing training items in particular ways.

Evidence that knowledge of both structure and processing is encoded during training was provided by Whittlesea and Dorken (1993). Participants memorised items (e.g. ENROLID) that were generated from a grammar, either by pronouncing or spelling them aloud, and then classified test items by pronouncing half of them and spelling the remainder. Test performance was reliably above chance only when the study and test processes were the same. When items were spelled in training and pronounced at test or pronounced during training and spelled at test, participants classified at chance levels. Thus, the knowledge gained during training included details of processing as well as structural aspects of stimuli, and test performance was successful to the extent that the test instructions cued prior processing episodes.

Evidence that training instructions dictate which aspects of the structure of training items are encoded was presented by Wright and Whittlesea (1998). In the study phase, participants were presented with digit strings, such as 1834, all of which conformed to an odd-even-odd-even rule. One group processed each digit by saying it aloud and immediately making a judgement about whether it was low (less than 5) or high (greater than 4). For example, 1834 would be processed as "1-low-8-high-3-low-4-low". A second group processed each string by pronouncing the two-digit pairs. In this case, 1834 would be processed by saying "eighteen thirty-four". At test, half the strings were created by reversing the order of the two familiar digit pairs in training items (e.g. 1834 became 3418) and half the test items comprised novel digit pairs.

Although all test strings were novel, participants were asked to discriminate between "old" items seen during training and "new" items. The group who said the training items as two-digit pairs were more likely than the group who read strings digit-by-digit to say that test items containing familiar digit pairs were old and test items containing unfamiliar digit pairs were new. Thus the manner in which training items were processed dictated which aspect of the structure of test items was encoded (single digits or digit pairs) and subsequent test performance. These results cast doubt on the idea that there is a "neutral" form of coding, whether it is of whole items, fragments, or rules. Instead, and consistent with the principles of transfer-appropriate processing (Morris, Bransford, & Franks, 1977), what is learned depends on the processing demands of the task.

Whittlesea and Williams (1998) put forward a discrepancy-attribution hypothesis that suggests that participants will apply knowledge explicitly or implicitly at test depending on whether they understand the relationship between processing particular test items fluently and the knowledge they acquired during training. During training, participants pronounced natural words (e.g. TABLE), orthographically regular, easily pronounced non-words (e.g. HENSION) and less regular and hence harder to pronounce non-words (e.g. LICTPUB). At test, participants were asked to pronounce old and novel versions of these three types of items and to indicate whether each item had been seen during training or not.

In one experiment, Whittlesea and Williams found that novel regular non-words were 21% more likely to be called old than novel words, and 28% more likely to be called old than novel irregular non-words. As the words were pronounced more rapidly than the regular non-words, with the irregular non-words being slowest to pronounce, it is clear that fluency *per se* is not the critical variable. Whittlesea and Williams suggested that participants did not expect non-words to be processed fluently and, as a result, unconsciously attributed the surprising fluency of reading the orthographically regular ones to those items having been presented during training. In contrast, there was no discrepancy between the first impression that a letter-string such as TABLE is a word and the subsequent fluency of processing. Participants were therefore able to discount fluency and use conscious recollection to make test responses for natural words.

Summary

Despite 30 years of AGL research there are still debates about whether participants who memorise representative examples of a complex rule-governed concept, without knowing that those examples conform to a set of rules, classify on the basis of implicit or explicit knowledge. However, before we can determine whether knowledge acquired in incidental learning situations is implicit or explicit, it is necessary to gain a better understanding of the form of knowledge (i.e. rules, exemplars, fragments, or processing episodes) used to classify test items. We will now discuss weaknesses in the standard finite-state grammars typically used to investigate implicit learning and suggest that the debate about forms of knowledge can be more successfully investigated using a biconditional grammar.

PROBLEMS WITH FINITE-STATE GRAMMARS

Johnstone and Shanks (1999) questioned the use of artificial grammars that are based on finite-state transition rules to investigate implicit learning, because these grammars do not provide a means of convincingly determining the contributions of rule and fragment knowledge in classification

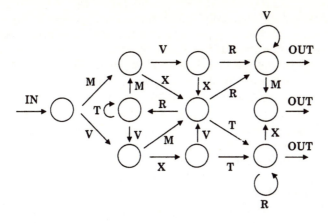

Figure 4.2. The artificial grammar used by Brooks and Vokey (1991).

performance. In short, it is very hard to create test items that unconfound grammaticality and fragment composition. The problem with transition-rule grammars is that they use a rule structure that dictates legal consecutive letters tied to particular letter string locations. For example, all legal strings generated from the grammar used by Meulemans and Van der Linden (created by Brooks & Vokey, 1991, and shown in Figure 4.2) start with MV, MX, VM, or VX. But, if participants classify test strings because they know what letters are legal in the first two positions, it is not clear what type of knowledge they are using to make this decision. They could be using rules (i.e. "all legal strings must begin with M or V"; "an initial M can be followed only by V or X"; and "an initial V can be followed only by M or X"), but they could also be using bigram knowledge (i.e. MV, MX, VM, and VX might just feel familiar).

In recent years there has been a trend to control for and quantify fragment statistics at increasing levels of detail. However, grammatical knowledge has remained a vague concept, quantified only in terms of two distinct categories (grammatical versus ungrammatical), that is assumed to exist whenever fragment statistics do not account for all of the variance in test performance. One way of clarifying matters is to quantify grammaticality, although we are not convinced that this will allow unequivocal conclusions (see Johnstone & Shanks, 1999, for a preliminary effort along these lines). A sounder way, which we describe below, is to use a different type of grammar that allows us to unconfound grammaticality, fragment similarity, and whole-item similarity more convincingly.

In their Experiments 2a and 2b (see page 100), Meulemans and Van der Linden made heroic efforts to unconfound grammaticality and fragment statistics. Half of the test items were grammatical and half were ungrammatical and, orthogonally, half of the test strings were highly associated with training strings (i.e. contained familiar letter fragments) and half were not. This created four sets of test items: grammatical and associated (GA), grammatical and not associated (GNA), ungrammatical and associated (NGA), and ungrammatical and not associated (NGNA). The degree to which test strings were associated to training strings was measured using a statistic called associative chunk strength (ACS). This measures the overlap of letter-fragments (chunks) of two (bigrams) and three (trigrams) letters between test and training strings weighted by the number of times a chunk occurred in the training strings. Meulemans and Van der Linden calculated mean ACS statistics for letter chunks that occurred in anchor positions (initial and terminal chunks) and in global positions (anywhere within a letter string). In both experiments, ACS varied between associated and non-associated items, but was balanced across grammatical and ungrammatical strings. Experiments 2a and 2b differed in two respects. Firstly, test items in Experiment 2b contained chunks that had been seen at least once during training, whereas the test items in Experiment 2a contained some novel chunks that had not been seen at all during training. However, the number of novel chunks was equivalent across grammatical and ungrammatical strings in Experiment 2a. Secondly, the two experiments differed in terms of the number of training strings (32 versus 125 respectively) and training trials (64 versus 125 respectively) experienced by participants.

Table 4.1 summarises the test string characteristics and Meulemans and Van der Linden's key findings. The row labelled "Classification" gives the percentages of strings of each type classified by participants as grammatical. On the basis of analyses of variance (ANOVA), Meulemans and Van der Linden concluded that after the short training phase (Experiment 2a) participants classified test strings on the basis of ACS, with no reliable effect of grammaticality: The classification rates closely parallel the ACS measures. However, when participants received extended training (Experiment 2b), they classified test strings on the basis of grammaticality, with no reliable effect of ACS. In this case, the classification rates do not parallel the ACS measures but instead tend to be higher for grammatical than ungrammatical strings. Meulemans and Van der Linden suggested that these results provide evidence of two independent learning mechanisms that are brought into operation depending on the number of items presented in the training phase. When fewer training strings are presented, classification judgements are based on chunk frequency and overlap with training items, whereas with longer training performance is based on knowledge of the rules of the grammar.

Meulemans and Van der Linden's findings were based on an assumption that the training strings provided participants with only two types of knowledge: (1) grammatical rules; and (2) chunk frequency information.

TABLE 4.1.
Mean string characteristics and percentage of test strings classified as grammatical by the experimental groups in Meulemans and Van der Linden's (1997) experiments 2a and 2b.

	Grammatical Associated	Grammatical Non-associated	Ungrammatical Associated	Ungrammatical Non-associated
Experiment 2a				
Anchor ACS	4.78	3.31	4.44	3.41
Global ACS	9.69	6.17	9.71	6.30
Novelty	0.00	1.25	0.00	1.50
NCP	0.63	1.75	1.38	2.13
Length	6.88	6.00	6.75	6.63
Classification	**65.31**	**42.81**	**67.50**	**45.00**
Experiment 2b				
Anchor ACS	18.00	13.38	18.25	12.25
Global ACS	35.44	23.43	34.80	23.80
Novelty	0.00	0.00	0.00	0.00
NCP	0.25	0.25	0.63	1.88
Length	6.50	6.50	6.75	6.63
Classification	**67.81**	**62.81**	**56.25**	**60.31**

ACS, associative chunk strength; NCP, novel chunk position.

Johnstone and Shanks (1999), however, suggested that the training strings also provided information about legal locations of chunks within training strings, and that this finer level of knowledge was not captured by the global ACS measure. Meulemans and Van der Linden balanced the number of novel chunks across grammatical and ungrammatical test strings in Experiment 2a (although not between associated and non-associated items) and ensured that test strings did not contain any novel chunks in Experiment 2b. But this measure is not sensitive to familiar training chunks in novel positions within test strings, and a number of researchers have suggested that participants could acquire knowledge of the legal positions of chunks within letter strings (e.g. Dienes, Broadbent, & Berry, 1991; Dulany et al., 1984). So there is a possibility that participants could become sensitive to chunks that they have seen in training being presented in novel locations in test strings.

Table 4.1 demonstrates that in Experiment 2b grammaticality was confounded with positional information. The rows labelled NCP in Table 4.1 refer to a measure of the frequency with which familiar chunks appeared in novel positions in test strings. It is clear that, in Experiment 2b, classification tends to be correlated with the NCP measure in that grammatical items have lower NCP scores and higher classification rates than ungrammatical items. Johnstone and Shanks (1999) went on to develop a multiple regression procedure that allows all of the potential variables, such as chunk strength, grammaticality, and NCP, to be evaluated as predictors of classification rates. The results were clear-cut: Grammaticality was a significant predictor in neither Experiment 2a or Experiment 2b, whereas NCP was a reliable predictor in both experiments.

The problem of unconfounding rule and fragment structure in traditional grammars is, we contend, insuperable. In the next section we describe a better approach, which employs a biconditional grammar.

THE BICONDITIONAL GRAMMAR

Shanks, Johnstone, and Staggs (1997, Experiment 4) constructed letter strings from a grammar originally designed by Mathews et al. (1989). This biconditional grammar generates strings of eight letters and has three rules governing the relationship between letters in positions 1 and 5, 2 and 6, 3 and 7, and 4 and 8, such that when one position contains a D, the other should be an F, where there is a G the other letter should be an L, and where there is a K the other letter should be an X (e.g. DFGX.FDLK is legal, whereas LFGK.KDLX is not; see Figure 4.3). This grammar has three advantages over transition-rule grammars. Firstly, each of the three rules can occur in any of the letter locations. For example, a D can be placed in any of the eight positions, as long as an F occurs in the associated letter location. Secondly, as the rule-related positions have three intervening letters, it is possible to unconfound rule and fragment knowledge. Finally, it is straightforward to quantify how grammatical test strings are. All grammatical strings contain four valid rules and, in our studies, all ungrammatical test strings contain three valid rules and one illegal letter pairing. The strings generated from this biconditional grammar allow whole-item and fragment information to be unconfounded from grammaticality far more successfully than has been achieved with finite-state grammars. The principal aim of our research, therefore, is to re-evaluate the key issues (What are the conditions of implicit learning? What is its content? To what extent is it consciously accessible?) that have driven AGL research in the last 30 years but which have yet to be settled.

We have used this grammar in conjunction with a match task, in which participants are told that they are being tested on how good their short-term memory is for strings of letters like DFGX.FDLK. On each of the study trials a string appears on the screen and the participant is asked to rehearse it mentally. The string stays on the screen for 7 s and then the screen goes blank for 2 s. A list of three strings is then displayed and the participant is asked to identify the string that matches the one they were rehearsing. Then, in the test phase, new strings are presented for classification. As is standard, half are grammatical and half ungrammatical.

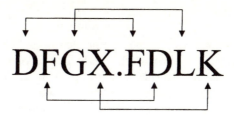

Biconditional rules: D $\leftrightarrow$ F

G $\leftrightarrow$ L

X $\leftrightarrow$ K

Figure 4.3. The biconditional grammar. Strings comprise eight letters, with a dot separating the first four from the last four. Letter positions 1 and 5, 2 and 6, 3 and 7, and 4 and 8 are linked (arrows) and there are three linkage rules, such that when one position contains a D the linked position must be an F, where there is a G the other letter must be an L, and where there is a K the other letter must be an X. Strings conforming to these linkages are grammatical, ones that do not (e.g. LFGK.KDLX) are ungrammatical.

Our results (Johnstone & Shanks, 2001) show quite unequivocally that participants cannot learn the biconditional rule structure under the implicit match training conditions (although as we argue later, the rule structure is learnable under other conditions): Participants are at chance in judging grammaticality. We believe that this result reinforces our interpretation of the data from studies using standard finite-state grammars and provides strong support for the anti-abstractionist view. A second finding is that, in contrast to the rule structure, participants do learn about the fragment structure of the study strings. If the test strings vary associative chunk strength orthogonally from grammaticality, the former reliably controls responding: Participants call a string "grammatical" if it is composed of familiar bigrams and trigrams, and they call it "ungrammatical" if it is composed of unfamiliar chunks. Indeed, it is even possible to obtain a "reverse" grammaticality effect, whereby participants endorse more ungrammatical than grammatical strings as being grammatical, if the former contain a greater proportion of familiar chunks.

Finally, whole-item similarity has no detectable effect on responding over and above chunk strength. Test strings that are highly similar to specific training strings are no more likely to be called "grammatical" than ones dissimilar from the training strings, if the two types are equated for associative chunk strength. In a nutshell, the results can be very satisfactorily accounted for by a single-system fragment-based model.

Rule learning

In addition to studying implicit rule learning, Shanks, Johnstone, and Staggs (1997) also looked at the performance of participants who consciously tried to learn the rules of a grammar. In most previous studies (e.g. Turner & Fischler, 1993), instructions aimed at encouraging rule learning were minimal (e.g. participants were simply informed prior to a standard study phase that the strings conformed to a set of rules and that discovering these rules might be helpful). However, Shanks et al. used an edit task, originally created by Mathews et al. (1989), that was designed to encourage rule learning. Participants were shown flawed examples of grammatical strings, asked to indicate which letters they thought created violations of the grammar, and then given feedback about their accuracy. Training strings contained one or two violations of the biconditional rules and participants adopted a hypothesis-testing strategy to determine the underlying rules used to generate grammatical strings. Like Mathews et al., Shanks et al. found a clear dissociation in classification test accuracy, with chance-level performance by some participants and almost perfect performance by others. Shanks et al. found that these latter participants showed a strong effect of grammaticality and no effect of whole-item similarity, suggesting that the mental representations underlying their performance were the abstract principles of the grammar. These results suggest that, as predicted by the episodic-processing approach, rule abstraction depends on active, conscious efforts to identify the rules of the grammar, leading to explicit knowledge.

In our more recent studies (Johnstone & Shanks, 2001), we have found not only that participants trained explicitly with the edit task learn the rules of the grammar, but that they: (1) have full awareness of these rules and can report them verbally; and (2) are much less sensitive than match participants to the chunk strength of test items. This latter result suggests that, when judging whether an item is grammatical or not, participants are relatively unconcerned with whether the string looks familiar or contains familiar components but are merely concerned with whether it conforms to the rules or not. It has been argued that this relative insensitivity to surface similarity is a hallmark of rule-based behaviour (Hahn & Chater, 1998; Shanks, 1997).

The combined results from the match (strongly sensitive to fragment familiarity, insensitive to rule structure) and edit (weakly sensitive to fragment familiarity, strongly sensitive to rule structure) groups are entirely consistent with the episodic-processing account. Participants learn about the aspects of the stimuli that are relevant to the task they are engaged in, with learning providing affordances for subsequent, related, tasks. If a particular attribute is irrelevant to the study task, it is not "implicitly" abstracted.

ARTIFICIAL GRAMMAR LEARNING IN AMNESIA

The most compelling evidence for the existence of two distinct and independent learning systems has been accumulated in studies with amnesic patients. Amnesics, whose declarative memory is poor, have been demonstrated to show intact learning in various tasks of non-declarative memory. Among these are speeded reading of repeated non-words, the resolving of random-dot stereograms, mirror reading, and performance in the serial reaction task. Priming, which is also thought to reflect non-declarative memory, has likewise been shown to be fully intact in amnesic patients (see Gabrieli, 1998; Squire, Knowlton, & Musen, 1993, for reviews).

Showing that amnesics perform normally in a non-declarative memory test while being impaired in a test of declarative memory supports the notion of two distinct memory systems. A significant problem, however, is that the two tests often differ in numerous ways. For example, the materials, instructions, and task demands are very different in a priming experiment than in a test of delayed story recall. As a result, memory might play more of a role in tests of declarative memory, whereas tests of non-declarative memory could to a large extent include processes not related to memory at all, for example, perceptual and motor processes. This assumption might be sufficient to explain some of the dissociations found between the two types of task.

But this problem is circumvented if tests of non-declarative and declarative memory are constructed to be as similar as possible, differing principally in the kind of instructions given at test. One domain in which this is achieved is in studies in which declarative memory is assessed by a recognition test whereas non-declarative memory is assessed by a classification test. Some experiments comparing classification and recognition performance in amnesics and controls were carried out by Knowlton and Squire (1993), who used dot patterns generated from a prototype via the classic statistical distortion methods of Posner and Keele (1968). In the classification task, amnesic patients and control participants first viewed a large number of distortions of a prototype. During the test, they were asked to categorise new patterns as belonging or not belonging to the same category as the training stimuli. This task is thought to be based upon an unconscious representation of the prototype and is therefore a typical test of non-declarative memory. In the study phase of the recognition task, participants at first viewed a small number of patterns, which were presented several times. In the test phase, they were presented with the training patterns as well as with new patterns, and were asked to judge them as old or new. This task is a typical test of declarative memory. As expected, the amnesic patients showed impaired performance on the recognition test but normal performance on the classification test. This result was interpreted by Knowlton and Squire as evidence that performance on the two tasks is indeed mediated by different memory systems, one of which is impaired and the other of which is spared in amnesia.

Recently, however, Nosofsky and Zaki (1998) seriously challenged this conclusion by demonstrating that a single-system model, the Generalised Context Model (GCM), accounts for the observed dissociation. According to the GCM, there is only a single memory system in which representations of entire training stimuli are stored. In a recognition task, the probability of a "yes" response to a test string is positively related to its mean similarity to all stored training exemplars. In classification, the similarity of the probe to the stored training exemplars is also thought to be crucial. However, in this case the probability of an item being judged a member of a particular category is both a positive function of its similarity to the exemplars of that category and a decreasing function of its similarity to exemplars of alternative categories. But if only a single category is involved in training and test, as in Knowlton and Squire's task, the process of classification becomes identical with the process of recognition. The GCM nevertheless predicts different outcomes for the two tasks administered in this experiment because different stimuli were used in classification and recognition both at training and at test.

In Nosofsky and Zaki's modelling approach, only a single parameter—the sensitivity parameter—was varied in order to account for a general difference between the two groups of participants. This parameter represents the ability to discriminate between distinct exemplars stored in memory. This capability is perhaps reduced in amnesics as a result of their deteriorated memory capacity. Nosofsky and Zaki showed that decreasing the value of this parameter considerably reduced recognition performance while only slightly reducing classification performance. Thus, the GCM successfully accounts for the dissociation between classification and recognition observed by Knowlton and Squire (1993). By showing that a single-system model can explain this dissociation, Nosofsky and Zaki made it clear that a dual-system interpretation is not compelled by the data.

The study by Knowlton and Squire, however, is only a single example in which amnesic patients show intact classification performance but are impaired in recognition tasks. Further studies have been conducted in the domain of artificial grammar learning (see Chapter 6). The overall aim of our research on this topic, like that of Nosofsky and Zaki (1998), is to show that dissociations between declarative tasks (e.g. recognition) and non-declarative ones (e.g. classification, repetition priming) can be explained on the basis of a unitary system with a single form of knowledge representation.

Classification and recognition in artificial grammar learning

We described earlier the fact that Knowlton et al. (1992) and Knowlton and Squire (1994, 1996) have reported several AGL experiments showing that classification performance in amnesic patients is similar to that in control participants, although further experiments showed the amnesic patients to be significantly impaired in recognition, both of whole training strings and of fragments of those strings. Thus, results of AGL experiments are consistent with those obtained in other tasks in supporting the notion of two distinct memory systems.

As we have shown, in "implicit" AGL, participants base their judgements on distributed information drawn from the entire set of training strings rather than on similarity to specific training exemplars (Kinder, 2000; Shanks et al., 1997). Therefore, the GCM (as well as other exemplar models) does not give an appropriate account of performance at test (see Dienes, 1992, for empirical support for this assertion). Thus, Nosofsky and Zaki's demonstration that an exemplar-based single-system model can reproduce the dissociation between recognition and classification observed with dot patterns does not directly challenge the evidence in support of separate memory systems found in studies of AGL.

We (Kinder & Shanks, 2001) therefore pursued an alternative to Nosofsky and Zaki's approach by exploring whether a connectionist model of AGL, the Simple Recurrent Network (SRN) model, can produce the dissociation between recognition and classification found in the AGL experiments reported by Knowlton and colleagues. Like Nosofsky and Zaki, we rely on varying only a single parameter to account for a general difference in memory efficiency between amnesic patients and control participants. Nosofsky and Zaki manipulated the sensitivity parameter that affects the GCM's ability to distinguish between different training exemplars stored in memory and assumed that this ability is impaired in amnesia. It is plausible that varying this parameter has a larger effect on recognition than on classification, because the former requires retrieval of specific training items whereas in the latter more "fuzzy" information is sufficient. The SRN model has no equivalent to the sensitivity parameter. However, unlike the GCM, it accounts not only for performance at test but also describes the process of learning. Therefore, amnesia can be simulated in a straightforward way by assuming the learning process, governed by a single rate parameter, to be less effective than normal. No further assumptions have to be made about the effect of this reduced efficiency on stored information.

At present, the SRN model appears to be the most successful computational model of AGL (see Redington & Chater, unpublished manuscript, for a comparison of computational models of AGL). It has been shown to reproduce several phenomena found in AGL, such as the effects of similarity to training strings and grammaticality reported by Vokey and Brooks (1992; and see Dienes, Altmann, & Gao, 1999), the effects of grammaticality and chunk strength found by Knowlton and Squire (1996; and Redington, unpublished manuscript), and the transfer of grammar knowledge to a new letter set (Shanks et al., 1997; and see Dienes et al., 1999). Other models of AGL, such as the competitive chunking model (Servan-Schreiber & Anderson, 1990) and the auto-associator model (Dienes, 1992), have been shown to be less successful in reproducing the rank-orderings of item difficulties (Redington & Chater, unpublished manuscript).

Kinder (2000) recently investigated whether the SRN and the auto-associator model correctly predict what kind of knowledge is acquired in AGL. Three types of knowledge were examined: (1) about the position of single letters in training strings; (2) about fragments of training strings; and (3) about entire training strings. Kinder found that participants primarily acquire knowledge about fragments of training strings. Her data showed that participants also acquire some knowledge about letter positions. However, knowledge about entire training strings did not seem to be important at all. Kinder then performed various simulations to investigate whether the SRN and the auto-associator could account for these findings. The study showed that the auto-associator failed to reproduce the correct pattern of results: It falsely predicted that knowledge about entire training strings should be important. The SRN, by contrast, successfully reproduced the experimental results. Thus, the SRN is superior in predicting what kind of knowledge is acquired in AGL. Furthermore, the model also accounts for the failure of participants to learn relations between non-adjacent letters (St John & Shanks, 1997). The following paragraphs will describe the model in detail.

The Simple Recurrent Network (SRN) Model

The SRN model of AGL (Figure 4.4) can be depicted as a multi-layered network that learns by error backpropagation. It is designed to be trained with a sequence of stimuli, with the target output at time t equalling the input at time $t + 1$. Thus, the model is trained always to predict the next stimulus in the sequence. Its architecture consists of an input layer (where the current stimulus is coded), a hidden layer (where an internal representation is generated), and an output layer (where the response is represented). The special feature of the model is the context layer, which contains a copy of the hidden layer's activation pattern on the last presentation. Because of this context layer, the network is capable of predicting a stimulus not only from its immediate predecessor but from several previous stimuli (Cleeremans, 1993; Cleeremans & McClelland, 1991; Elman, 1990).

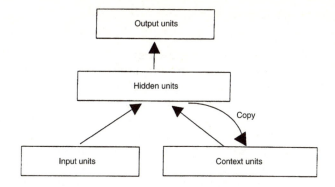

Figure 4.4. The architecture of the Simple Recurrent Network (SRN).

To simulate artificial grammar learning, the network is trained with the same stimuli as participants. The input layer consists of a number of units, each of which locally represents one letter from the grammar. Additionally, there are two units coding the beginnings and endings of the letter strings. The output layer contains the same number of units also representing all the letters and the beginning and ending of a string. Each string is presented letter-by-letter from left to right. A letter (or the beginning or ending of a letter string) is coded by setting the unit representing it to an activation of .9 while setting all other units to an activation of .1. On the presentation of each letter, the network's goal is to predict the next letter in the string. Before a new string is presented, activation values of all copy layer units are set to .5.

During testing, the model produces an endorsement rate for each test string. This endorsement rate is related to the accuracy with which the model predicts the letters comprising that string. To obtain a measure of prediction accuracy, first, all the output vectors, which represent the letters predicted by the network, are concatenated. The length of the resulting vector corresponds to the length of a single output vector times the length of the test string plus 1 (because the end of the string is predicted as well). The target vectors, which represent the correct predictions, are also concatenated. Next, the cosine of the angle θ between the global output vector and the global target vector is computed. The value of the cosine is translated into an endorsement rate by the logistic function:

$$p(g) = \frac{1}{1 + e^{-a\cos\theta - b}}$$

where a is a scaling parameter and b is the model's threshold for endorsing an item as grammatical or old.

Overview of the simulation study and general assumptions

We assume classification and recognition in AGL to be functionally equivalent. Firstly, we assume that, on both tasks, an identically structured system is used and that this can be depicted as an SRN. Secondly, we assume that the information stored in that system is used in identical ways independent of whether a classification or a recognition response is required. Thus, our simulations follow from the assumption that a single system mediates performance both in classification and in recognition of stimuli generated by an artificial grammar. In accord with this assumption, we varied only a single parameter, the learning rate, to account for a general difference in memory efficiency between amnesic patients and control participants. Identical parameter values were chosen in both tasks.

There are two different sets of free parameters in the SRN, one of which affects learning and the other of which exclusively influences performance at test. Parameters that affect learning are: (1) the learning rate parameter; (2) the momentum term; (3) the number of learning epochs; and (4) the number of hidden units. The learning rate and the momentum term enter directly into the backpropagation algorithm (see McClelland & Rumelhart, 1988). The number of learning epochs, that is, the frequency with which the whole set of learning stimuli is presented, is usually considerably higher than in the experiments (where it is regularly one or two) in order to yield an appropriate level of performance at test.

These parameters have to be varied to simulate any experimental variation concerning the training stage (such as the type of training procedure, the letter set, or the type of grammar). They also should be allowed to vary when performance of groups differing in age, intelligence or, as in the present case, memory ability, is simulated. Varying all these parameters has a rather similar effect. Thus, for example, instead of changing the number of learning cycles, the value of the momentum parameter could be changed.

In contrast to these parameters, the logistic function parameters exclusively change performance at test. The scaling parameter a has an impact on the model's sensitivity in discriminating between grammatical and ungrammatical items (or old and new items). This parameter might be changed as a function of different testing conditions, for instance. The threshold b has an impact on the percentage of test items classified as grammatical or old, and thus on the bias. This parameter can be varied to obtain an average of about 50% of items being classified as grammatical or old.

Simulation of Knowlton, Ramus, and Squire (1992)

Knowlton et al. (1992) report an artificial grammar learning experiment in which amnesic patients and control participants were tested on their performance both in recognition and in classification. In the classification task, participants had to judge whether letter strings adhered to a finite-state grammar after they had memorised strings generated from that grammar. The two groups did not differ significantly in classification performance, although, numerically, performance of the controls was higher (see Figure 4.5, top left). Both groups of participants performed above chance. In the second task, too, participants were trained on grammatical items. In this task, however, recognition judgements were required, with the stimuli being old grammatical items and new ungrammatical items. In this test, the amnesic patients performed significantly more poorly than the control participants (see Figure 4.5, top right).

We (Kinder & Shanks, 2001) trained and tested an SRN on the same stimuli as participants in the experiment. As in the experiment, two different grammars were used (see Figure 4.1). Half of the simulation used grammar A and the other half grammar B. Because Knowlton et al. used two different sets of letters in the two grammars, all letters of both grammars were coded. Each simulated network was tested on both tasks, recognition and classification. We averaged across 100 simulations to reproduce performance of each group and with each grammar. Parameters were set to identical values for both groups and for both tasks, except for the learning rate, which was set to a lower value (.05 versus .6) when the performance of the amnesics was simulated.

The simulation results (Figure 4.5) resemble the experimental data very closely. Whereas there was only a small difference in classification performance, recognition performance was considerably better when the learning rate had been set to a high value. Why does this effect occur? The reason is that in the recognition test participants had to discriminate between old grammatical and new ungrammatical items, whereas in the classification test they discriminated between new grammatical and new ungrammatical items, and the former is objectively an easier discrimination. This means that the asymptote of performance is much lower in classification than in recognition and, as the learning rate increases from zero, the asymptote is reached sooner in the former than in the latter. Consequently, an increase in learning rate from a low value (simulating amnesia) to a medium value (simulating normal performance) has little effect on classification but a larger effect on recognition.

Thus, in the simulations a dissociation between recognition and classification emerged merely as a result of the target test stimuli being different in the two tasks (old grammatical items in the recognition task and new grammatical items in the classification task). No differences in the mechanisms being used in these two tasks needed to be assumed in order to account for the pattern of results. We conclude that the apparent dissociation of classification and recognition in amnesia is not troubling for a

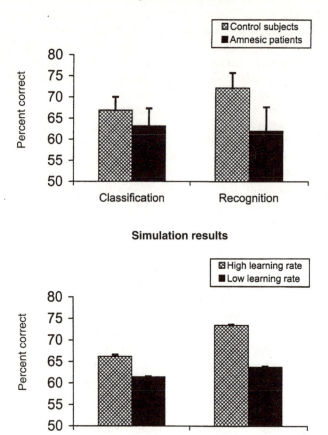

Figure 4.5. Top panel: Results from Knowlton et al. (1992). Classification and recognition performance (percentage of correct responses) in the amnesic patients and the control participants. Bottom panel: Percentage of correct responses with different learning rates for controls (.6) versus amnesics (.05) when the SRN was tested on either the recognition stimuli (old grammatical and new non-grammatical) or the classification stimuli (new grammatical and new non-grammatical). Error bars indicate the 95% confidence intervals.

single-system approach and is not attributable to the contributions of separate memory systems. Indeed, we would go further and argue that the data are in fact better accounted for by our single-system account. Recall that the SRN treats recognition and classification as functionally identical. In experiments with normal participants, we (Kinder & Shanks, 2001) have found support for this aspect of the model in that if the test items are the same in recognition and classification, participants respond to them identically. Instructions *per se* have no influence on performance in AGL. For example, we have found that participants call new grammatical test items "old" as frequently as they call them "grammatical". This is problematic for dual-system theories because these items are targets under grammaticality instructions but non-targets under recognition instructions, and this is precisely where such a theory would expect responding to be dissociated.

CONCLUSIONS

In the first part of this chapter, we presented evidence that artificial grammar learning can be understood from an episodic-processing perspective (Whittlesea & Dorken, 1993) in which the nature of processing itself (in addition to structural knowledge) is encoded, training instructions dictate which aspects of the structure of training items are encoded, and participants can apply the same knowledge explicitly or implicitly, depending on whether they understand the relationship between processing fluency and the knowledge they acquired by processing training items in particular ways. This account interprets classification under implicit learning instructions as depending on an attribution of fluent processing.

The combined results from the match (strongly sensitive to fragment familiarity, insensitive to rule structure) and edit (weakly sensitive to fragment familiarity, strongly sensitive to rule structure) groups provide further support for the episodic-processing account. Under "explicit" edit instructions, participants processed the rule structure but not the fragment structure of the training strings.

The episodic-processing account also interprets recognition under implicit learning instructions as depending on the attribution of fluent processing and, consistent with this, participants do not seem to differentiate classification and recognition instructions in AGL. An apparent counter-example, the selective impairment of recognition in amnesia, turns out to be essentially an artifact of the use of different test stimuli in the two cases (Knowlton et al., 1992) and is easily simulated by a single-system model (the SRN). This model is, of course, only a partial embodiment of the episodic-processing view: it simulates only standard "implicit" learning conditions and it does not explicitly represent variations in the nature of processing. Nevertheless, this single-system model—when combined with the broader framework provided by the episodic-processing view—currently provides the most complete account of artificial grammar learning.

ACKNOWLEDGEMENTS

The research described here was supported by grants from the United Kingdom Economic and Social Research Council (ESRC) and Medical Research Council. The work is part of the programme of the ESRC Centre for Economic Learning and Social Evolution, University College London. We thank Nick Chater and Richard Tunney for their helpful suggestions.

REFERENCES

Altmann, G.T.M., Dienes, Z., & Goode, A. (1995). Modality independence of implicitly learned grammatical knowledge. *Journal of Experimental Psychology: Learning, Memory, and Cognition, 21*, 899–912.

Brooks, L. (1978). Nonanalytic concept formation and memory for instances. In E. Rosch & B.B. Lloyd (Eds.), *Cognition and categorization* (pp. 169–211). Hillsdale, NJ: Lawrence Erlbaum Associates Inc.

Brooks, L.R. & Vokey, J.R. (1991). Abstract analogies and abstracted grammars: Comments on Reber (1989) and Mathews et al. (1989). *Journal of Experimental Psychology: General, 120*, 316–323.

Buchner, A. (1994). Indirect effects of synthetic grammar learning in an identification task. *Journal of Experimental Psychology: Learning, Memory, and Cognition, 20*, 550–566.

Cleeremans, A. (1993). *Mechanisms of implicit learning.* Cambridge, MA: MIT Press.

Cleeremans, A. & McClelland, J.L. (1991). Learning the structure of event sequences. *Journal of Experimental Psychology: General, 120*, 235–253.

Cleeremans, A., Servan-Schreiber, D., & McClelland, J.L. (1989). Finite state automata and simple recurrent networks. *Neural Computation, 1*, 372–381.

Dienes, Z. (1992). Connectionist and memory-array models of artificial grammar learning. *Cognitive Science, 16*, 41–79.

Dienes, Z., Altmann, G.T.M., & Gao, S.-J. (1999). Mapping across domains without feedback: A neural network model of transfer of implicit knowledge. *Cognitive Science, 23*, 53–82.

Dienes, Z., Altmann, G.T.M., Kwan, L., & Goode, A. (1995). Unconscious knowledge of artificial grammars is applied strategically. *Journal of Experimental Psychology: Learning, Memory, and Cognition, 21*, 1322–1338.

Dienes, Z., Broadbent, D.E., & Berry, D. (1991). Implicit and explicit knowledge bases in artificial grammar learning. *Journal of Experimental Psychology: Learning, Memory, and Cognition, 17*, 875–887.

Dulany, D.E., Carlson, R.A., & Dewey, G.I. (1984). A case of syntactical learning and judgment: How conscious and how abstract? *Journal of Experimental Psychology: General, 113*, 541–555.

Elman, J.L. (1990). Finding structure in time. *Cognitive Science, 14*, 179–212.

Gabrieli, J.D.E. (1998). Cognitive neuroscience of human memory. *Annual Review of Psychology, 49*, 87–115.

Gomez, R.L. (1997). Transfer and complexity in artificial grammar learning. *Cognitive Psychology, 33*, 154–207.

Gomez, R.L., & Schvaneveldt, R.W. (1994). What is learned from artificial grammars? Transfer tests of simple association. *Journal of Experimental Psychology: Learning, Memory, and Cognition, 20*, 396–410.

Hahn, U. & Chater, N. (1998). Similarity and rules: Distinct? exhaustive? empirically distinguishable? *Cognition, 65*, 197–230.

Hintzman, D.L. (1986). "Schema abstraction" in a multiple-trace memory model. *Psychological Review, 93*, 411–428.

Johnstone, T., & Shanks, D.R. (1999). Two mechanisms in implicit artificial grammar learning? Comment on Meulemans and Van der Linden (1997). *Journal of Experimental Psychology: Learning, Memory, and Cognition, 25*, 524–531.

Johnstone, T., & Shanks, D.R. (2001). Abstractionist and processing accounts of implicit learning. *Cognitive Psychology, 42*, 61–112.

Kinder, A. (2000). The knowledge acquired during artificial grammar learning: Testing the predictions of two connectionist models. *Psychological Research, 63,* 95–105.

Kinder, A., & Shanks, D.R. (2001). Amnesia and the declarative/nondeclarative distinction: A recurrent network model of classification, recognition, and repetition priming. *Journal of Cognitive Neuroscience, 13,* 648–669.

Knowlton, B.J., Ramus, S.J., & Squire, L.R. (1992). Intact artificial grammar learning in amnesia: Dissociation of classification learning and explicit memory for specific instances. *Psychological Science, 3,* 172–179.

Knowlton, B.J., & Squire, L.R. (1993). The learning of categories: Parallel brain systems for item memory and category knowledge. *Science, 262,* 1747–1749.

Knowlton, B.J., & Squire, L.R. (1994). The information acquired during artificial grammar learning. *Journal of Experimental Psychology: Learning, Memory, and Cognition, 20,* 79–91.

Knowlton, B.J., & Squire, L.R. (1996). Artificial grammar learning depends on implicit acquisition of both abstract and exemplar-specific information. *Journal of Experimental Psychology: Learning, Memory, and Cognition, 22,* 169–181.

Manza, L., & Reber, A.S. (1997). Representing artificial grammars: Transfer across stimulus forms and modalities. In D.C. Berry (Ed.), *How implicit is implicit learning?* (pp. 73–106). Oxford: Oxford University Press.

Marcus, G.F., Vijayan, S., Bandi Rao, S., & Vishton, P.M. (1999). Rule learning by seven-month-old infants. *Science, 283,* 77–80.

Mathews, R.C., Buss, R.R., Stanley, W.B., Blanchard-Fields, F., Cho, J.R., & Druhan, B. (1989). Role of implicit and explicit processes in learning from examples: A synergistic effect. *Journal of Experimental Psychology: Learning, Memory, and Cognition, 15,* 1083–1100.

McAndrews, M.P., & Moscovitch, M. (1985). Rule-based and exemplar-based classification in artificial grammar learning. *Memory & Cognition, 13,* 469–475.

McClelland, J.L., McNaughton, B.L., & O'Reilly, R.C. (1995). Why there are complementary learning systems in the hippocampus and neocortex: Insights from the successes and failures of connectionist models of learning and memory. *Psychological Review, 102,* 419–457.

McClelland, J.L., & Rumelhart, D.E. (1988). *Explorations in parallel distributed processing.* Cambridge, MA: MIT Press.

Meulemans, T., & Van der Linden, M. (1997). Associative chunk strength in artificial grammar learning. *Journal of Experimental Psychology: Learning, Memory, and Cognition, 23,* 1007–1028.

Morris, C.D., Bransford, J.D., & Franks, J.J. (1977). Levels of processing versus transfer appropriate processing. *Journal of Verbal Learning and Verbal Behavior, 16,* 519–533.

Neal, A., & Hesketh, B. (1997). Episodic knowledge and implicit learning. *Psychonomic Bulletin & Review, 4,* 24–37.

Nosofsky, R.M., & Zaki, S.R. (1998). Dissociations between categorization and recognition in amnesic and normal individuals: An exemplar-based interpretation. *Psychological Science, 9,* 247–255.

Perruchet, P. (1994). Defining the knowledge units of a synthetic language: Comment on Vokey and Brooks (1992). *Journal of Experimental Psychology: Learning, Memory, and Cognition, 20,* 223–228.

Perruchet, P., & Pacteau, C. (1990). Synthetic grammar learning: Implicit rule abstraction or explicit fragmentary knowledge? *Journal of Experimental Psychology: General, 119,* 264–275.

Posner, M.I., & Keele, S.W. (1968). On the genesis of abstract ideas. *Journal of Experimental Psychology, 77,* 353–363.

Reber, A.S. (1967). Implicit learning of artificial grammars. *Journal of Verbal Learning and Verbal Behavior, 6,* 855–863.

Reber, A.S. (1989). Implicit learning and tacit knowledge. *Journal of Experimental Psychology: General, 118*, 219–235.

Reber, A.S., & Lewis, S. (1977). Implicit learning: An analysis of the form and structure of a body of tacit knowledge. *Cognition, 5*, 333–361.

Redington, M. (1998). *On hybrid models of artificial grammar learning: Commentary on Knowlton and Squire (1996) and Meulemans and Van der Linden (1997).* Unpublished manuscript.

Redington, M., & Chater, N. (1996). Transfer in artificial grammar learning: A reevaluation. *Journal of Experimental Psychology: General, 125*, 123–138.

Redington, M., & Chater, N. (1998). *Computational models of artificial grammar learning.* Unpublished manuscript.

Servan-Schreiber, E., & Anderson, J.R. (1990). Learning artificial grammars with competitive chunking. *Journal of Experimental Psychology: Learning, Memory, and Cognition, 16*, 592–608.

Shanks, D.R. (1997). Representation of categories and concepts in memory. In M.A. Conway (Ed.), *Cognitive models of memory* (pp. 111–146). Hove: UK: Psychology Press.

Shanks, D.R., Johnstone, T., & Staggs, L. (1997). Abstraction processes in artificial grammar learning. *Quarterly Journal of Experimental Psychology, 50A*, 216–252.

Shanks, D.R., & St John, M.F. (1994). Characteristics of dissociable human learning systems. *Behavioral and Brain Sciences, 17*, 367–447.

Squire, L.R., Knowlton, B., & Musen, G. (1993). The structure and organization of memory. *Annual Review of Psychology, 44*, 453–495.

St John, M.F., & Shanks, D.R. (1997). Implicit learning from an information processing standpoint. In D.C. Berry (Ed.), *How implicit is implicit learning?* (pp. 162–194). Oxford: Oxford University Press.

Tulving, E. (1983). *Elements of episodic memory.* Oxford: Oxford University Press.

Turner, C.W., & Fischler, I.S. (1993). Speeded tests of implicit knowledge. *Journal of Experimental Psychology: Learning, Memory, and Cognition, 19*, 1165–1177.

Vokey, J.R., & Brooks, L.R. (1992). Salience of item knowledge in learning artificial grammars. *Journal of Experimental Psychology: Learning, Memory, and Cognition, 18*, 328–344.

Vokey, J.R., & Brooks, L.R. (1994). Fragmentary knowledge and the processing-specific control of structural sensitivity. *Journal of Experimental Psychology: Learning, Memory, and Cognition, 20*, 1504–1510.

Whittlesea, B.W.A. (1997a). Production, evaluation, and preservation of experiences: Constructive processing in remembering and performance tasks. In D.L. Medin (Ed.), *The psychology of learning and motivation* (vol. 37, pp. 211–264). San Diego, CA: Academic Press.

Whittlesea, B.W.A. (1997b). The representation of general and particular knowledge. In K. Lamberts & D. Shanks (Eds.), *Knowledge, concepts and categories* (pp. 335–370). Hove, UK: Psychology Press.

Whittlesea, B.W.A., & Dorken, M.D. (1993). Incidentally, things in general are particularly determined: An episodic-processing account of implicit learning. *Journal of Experimental Psychology: General, 122*, 227–248.

Whittlesea, B.W.A., & Dorken, M.D. (1997). Implicit learning: Indirect, not unconscious. *Psychonomic Bulletin & Review, 4*, 63–67.

Whittlesea, B.W.A., & Williams, L.D. (1998). Why do strangers feel familiar, but friends don't? A discrepancy-attribution account of feelings of familiarity. *Acta Psychologica, 98*, 141–165.

Wright, R.L., & Whittlesea, B.W.A. (1998). Implicit learning of complex structures: Active adaptation and selective processing in acquisition and application. *Memory & Cognition, 26*, 402–420.

CHAPTER FIVE

Knowledge representation and transfer in artificial grammar learning (AGL)

Martin Redington
University College London, UK

Nick Chater
University of Warwick, Coventry, UK

In this chapter we re-evaluate the implications that have been drawn from the artificial grammar learning transfer paradigm and review the evidence on whether the knowledge acquired in artificial grammar learning (AGL) is stored in terms of the original surface form or in an abstract, surface-independent representation.

INTRODUCTION

Research on AGL (Reber, 1967, 1993) has been seen as having potentially far-reaching implications for theories of cognition. These studies have appeared to provide evidence that people are able to learn "implicit" rules, that is, they can learn sets of rules without, in some sense, conscious awareness, and these rules can determine their behaviour. In consequence, AGL research has attracted a great deal of excitement and controversy.

A typical AGL study proceeds as follows: Participants are asked to memorise strings that (unknown to them) have been generated by a finite-state grammar, which dictates the permissible arrangements of letters. After training, participants are told that the first set of stimuli was rule-governed, and are asked to indicate which of a second set of strings obey or violate the rules. Half of these test strings are "grammatical" according to the rules that generated the first set of strings, and half are ungrammatical. In the standard AGL paradigm, with typical materials, participants will get about 65–75% of these classifications correct.

Perhaps the most obvious inference to draw is that people have, to an imperfect degree, learned the underlying rules that governed the strings. And strong claims about the implicit or unconscious character of these putative rules appear warranted, given that participants often declare that they have no idea whatever what rules governed the stimuli. Indeed, if pressed to make suggestions concerning this underlying structure, their suggestions, if any, tend to be partial and vague, and in any case insufficient to account for their performance.

It has, however, become increasingly evident that results of this kind are open to a wide range of interpretations. For example, it could be that people are simply memorising some of the original training items (Brooks & Vokey, 1991), or perhaps that they are learning fragments of these items, such as letter pairs or triples (e.g. Perruchet & Pacteau, 1990; Redington & Chater, 1996). People could be judging the new strings with which they are presented as "conforming to the rules" if they are similar either to specific old strings that they were presented with or if they contain similar frag- ments to those items. Straightforward analysis of typical AGL stimuli has shown that methods of this kind could give rise to high levels of per- formance in classifying new stimuli, and hence could explain human transfer performance. These exemplar- or fragment-based models would also explain immediately why people are able to say nothing about the rules governing the stimuli that they originally learned. They cannot report the rules, not because rule-knowledge is implicit but because their performance is not based on rule-learning at all.

There is, however, a version of the AGL paradigm that does not appear so easily open to alternative explanation by exemplar- and fragment-based accounts. It is the interpretation of these 'transfer" studies with which we are concerned in this chapter.

WHAT IS TRANSFER?

In the transfer paradigm, the surface form of the materials is changed between training and test. For example, the training strings MXVVM and VXMTM might become HJKKH and KJHLH, respectively. The new strings follow the same underlying rules as the original strings, but are expressed in terms of a completely new set of letters. Despite this change in surface form, participants are still able to distinguish test strings that follow the underlying rules from those that violate them at well above chance performance, and above the level of the performance of untrained control subjects.

Transfer has been demonstrated repeatedly (Altmann, Dienes, & Goode, 1995; Brooks & Vokey, 1991; Gomez & Schvaneveldt, 1994; Knowlton & Squire, 1996; Manza & Reber, unpublished manuscript; Mathews, Buss, Stanley, Blanchard-Fields, Cho, & Druhan, 1989; Whittlesea & Dorken,

1993; Shanks, Johnstone, & Staggs, 1997), and appears very robust. As well as transfer across letter sets, transfer has also been demonstrated across modalities (e.g. from sequences of letters to sequences of tones, and vice versa; see Altmann et al., 1995).

Transfer effects tend to be small and with such small effects careful control conditions are required (Redington & Chater, 1996). For example, one useful control is to ask participants who were not exposed to the original training stimuli to attempt to discriminate grammatical from ungrammatical stimuli. It might appear that such participants can only perform by chance guessing, and hence that such a condition is unnecessary but, in fact, such control conditions can yield performance that is consistently slightly above chance. This is possible because some aspects of the structure of the strings can be learned "on-line" as the participant inspects the test strings. After all, half of the strings are generated by the grammar and the other half are only slightly corruptions of grammatical items, and hence a good deal about the grammar can be learned as testing proceeds. Such controls are not always run in transfer studies and the possibility therefore remains that some apparently significant instances of transfer from the original learning items can be explained away as examples of learning during test. None the less, despite this and other methodological issues that can be raised in relation to some of the AGL transfer studies (Redington & Chater, 1996), the weight of evidence seems to strongly suggest that transfer effects are not merely artifacts—it appears that they genuinely reflect the application of some knowledge learned in memorising the training stimuli.

WHY IS TRANSFER IMPORTANT?

As we have indicated, transfer studies have assumed a particular significance in AGL research, in the light of the multiple interpretations available for conventional AGL experiments. We will focus here on two specific theoretical issues for which evidence from transfer has been viewed as important. Both of these claims concern the nature of the knowledge that people are acquiring when learning the training items.

Firstly, the transfer paradigm has been seen as evidence for the claim that participants in AGL studies acquire rule-based knowledge. That is, some theorists (e.g. Knowlton & Squire, 1996) have claimed that transfer could only be explained by assuming that participants learn rules that capture regularities in the items memorised during training. According to this viewpoint, transfer results rule out theories of AGL that propose that participants acquire knowledge of whole instances, or fragments of the training materials, represented in terms of the original surface form of those materials (e.g. Brooks & Vokey, 1991; Perruchet & Pacteau, 1990).

Secondly, transfer has been commonly interpreted as evidence for the claim that the knowledge acquired in AGL is represented not in terms of the original surface form of the training materials but, instead, in terms of an abstract "surface-independent" form (e.g. Mathews, 1990; Knowlton & Squire, 1996). For example, participants might genuinely acquire a representation of the finite-state grammar underlying the training items, with the arcs between the nodes of the grammar marked with abstract symbols that do not denote specific surface features but which can be bound to any surface form. The logic underlying the claim that knowledge is represented in a surface-independent form is that this knowledge can then be applied to stimuli presented in any surface form, as shown in the transfer paradigm.

Thus, the claim is that transfer effects demonstrate that the knowledge learned in encoding the training items is represented in terms of rules, and that it is encoded in a surface-independent format. These claims, and others that follow from them concerning conscious awareness, have given a substantial impetus to the study of transfer in AGL. But, we shall argue, neither of these putative implications of transfer is valid.

WHAT DOES TRANSFER REALLY SHOW?

We will first question the notion that transfer is evidence for rule-based knowledge, and secondly that it is evidence for the acquisition of surface-independent knowledge.

Transfer and rule-based knowledge

The key point here is that surface-independence and rule-based knowledge are orthogonal concepts. Within the AGL literature, discussion has concentrated on three distinct kinds of representation: (1) knowledge of whole exemplars (e.g. Brooks & Vokey, 1991); (2) knowledge of fragments of the training items (e.g. Perruchet & Pacteau, 1990); (3) or rule-based knowledge (e.g. Knowlton & Squire, 1996).

We argue that all three kinds of knowledge can, in principle, be tied to particular surface forms or, alternatively, can discard information about particular surface forms, resulting in a surface-independent representation.

Considering exemplar-based knowledge first, in Brooks and Vokey's (1991) account, participants' knowledge consists of representations of entire training items (such as the string MMTTVVX), with grammaticality judgements being based on the whole item similarity between the test items and the memorised training items. In Brooks and Vokey's account, the representations of these exemplars are expressed in terms of the original surface form, with transfer being accounted for by a process of "abstract analogy" between different surface forms.

In principle, one can conceive of an alternative exemplar-based mechanism, in which participants acquired representations of specific training exemplars but discarded, abstracted away from, or simply forgot, the particular surface features that were present during the training phase. Such a mechanism might acquire representations such as □□◇◇△△▽ (where □, ◇, △, and ▽ are symbols that discard the original surface form [letters] of the item, but retain distinctions between different letters).

If people possessed such a mechanism (and, for the sake of illustration, its contents were accessible to verbal report), we might receive verbal reports like "I can remember the item, but not the actual letters. I know that it had three different letters, each repeated twice, and then a fourth different letter".

Similarly, fragment knowledge, as discussed in the AGL literature, is generally held to be represented in terms of the surface form of the training materials, concerning the occurrence and potentially frequency of occurrence of given fragments (such as VXX) within the training items. However, a mechanism that acquired a similar kind of knowledge but discarded the particular surface form of the relevant features is equally possible, *a priori*. Such a system might learn that the fragment □◇◇ occurred 10 times in the training items, where □ and ◇ have the same meaning as above.

Within the AGL literature, the exact nature of rule-based knowledge is generally left rather vague. Two possible examples of rule-based knowledge are a representation of the finite-state grammar that actually generated the stimuli, and symbolic rules such as "All strings must begin with the letters VX or MX". Either kind of representation could be couched in terms of surface symbols, or in terms of abstract symbols. For example, a surface-independent symbolic rule might be expressed as something like "All strings must begin with one of two specific letters" or "The second letter is always the same".

Within the broad classes of theory defined by the categories of exemplars, fragments, and rules, and the orthogonal categorisation according to whether this knowledge is tied to surface form, or surface-independent, there is still room for a lot of variation and disagreement. For example, if people acquire surface-independent knowledge of exemplars, they might encode these in terms of the repetition patterns, discarding commonalities occurring across strings, so that the training items MMTTVVX and VTXXMV might be encoded as □□◇◇△△▽ and □◇△△▽□. Alternatively, the encoding might respect the identities of the original surface form across training items, so that the items above might be encoded as □□◇◇△△▽ and △◇▽▽□◇.

Additionally, there are accounts that do not fit quite so neatly into the division between exemplars, fragments, and rules, such as Dienes, Altmann, and Gao's (1999) connectionist model of transfer (although this could be argued to acquire knowledge that can be seen as similar in nature to fragments, or rules, according to one's theoretical perspective), as well as "hybrid" accounts that posit more than one form of knowledge (e.g. Knowlton & Squire, 1996; Meulemans & Van Der Linden, 1997).

Overall, though, our claim stands: Evidence that knowledge is surface-independent does not constrain that knowledge also to be rule-based. Exemplar- and fragment-based knowledge can also be represented in abstract terms, divorced from the original surface form of the training materials.

Transfer and surface-independent knowledge

We now turn to consider the implications of transfer for the level of abstraction of information that participants perform during training. In particular, we shall argue that although transfer is compatible with the hypothesis that knowledge is represented independent of surface form, it is not direct evidence for that hypothesis. Rather, there are many accounts in which participants' knowledge is held to be surface-based that can explain the phenomenon of transfer.

Before considering how surface-based knowledge might allow transfer, let us first consider how surface-independent knowledge might support transfer. This could happen in a number of ways.

In one possible account, both training and test items are encoded in a common surface-independent form, and thus the representations of their structure can be compared directly. In its purest form, this account requires that the mapping from surface to abstract form can be computed independently for each item, without possessing any knowledge about the other items. The example given above, where exemplars are encoded in terms of their repetition patterns falls into this category.

In another possible account, people initially acquire surface-independent knowledge and, in the course of testing, learn to map from the surface-independent form to the new surface form, or vice-versa, and thus exploit their knowledge for the purpose of the categorisation task. Note that the mapping between abstract and surface forms at test need not be consistent across items, or even within a particular item—in Roussel and Mathews' account of transfer (cited in Dienes & Berry, 1993), participants' knowledge consists of information concerning whether each letter is the same as, or different from, the preceding letter. All that is required is that the mapping is sufficient to provide some indication of the grammaticality of the test items.

Now consider the case where participants' knowledge is represented purely in terms of the original surface form. Although intuitively such knowledge would appear to be relatively useless for the purposes of transfer, a number of accounts of transfer have argued that participants' knowledge is surface-based.

Brooks and Vokey (1991) argued that knowledge of training exemplars could be applied to transfer test items by a process of "abstract analogy": The test item HHJJKKK is "similar" to the exemplar MMTTVVV, in that they share a common repetition pattern. While the underlying basis of comparison is abstract and unrelated to surface form, Brooks and Vokey are explicitly committed to the view that the knowledge acquired during training is instance-based, and closely tied to the original surface form of the training items. The abstraction that is required to support transfer takes place between surface forms, at test.

Similarly, Redington and Chater (1996) proposed an idealised model of transfer in which participants acquire knowledge of fragments of the training items, expressed in terms of the original surface form. In the transfer paradigm, test items are accepted as grammatical if there is a consistent mapping between old and new surface forms (computed on an item-by-item basis) such that the test item can constructed entirely from the fragments seen during training.

Finally, Dienes et al. (1999) proposed a connectionist account of transfer. The network is trained to produce responses that are specific to a particular surface form. These responses are predictions about which letter will occur next in the string—by comparing the predictions against the actual next letter, the network produces a measure of the extent to which the test item shares a common underlying structure with the training materials. In the context of transfer, the network is effectively "re-trained", but its architecture allows a new input–output mapping to use some of the same weights that were trained initially. With these "core" weights (whose values are frozen) already trained, the learning problem collapses into finding an appropriate mapping from the new input and output units to and from the core weights. This process can be viewed as mapping knowledge that is "bound" to one surface form to the new surface form.

In all three accounts, the knowledge acquired during training is bound to the original surface form of the training items. At test, some form of mapping between the old and new surface form allows this knowledge to be applied to the new materials. Whether, or to what extent, any of these three accounts can explain human performance in the AGL paradigm is open to question. However, they show that theories positing the acquisition of knowledge that is represented in terms of the original surface form are viable, and compatible with the basic fact of transfer of knowledge to a new surface form. This is especially true of the Dienes et al. (1999) and Redington and Chater (1996) work, where computational models were demonstrably able to perform the transfer task, fitting the details of the human with varying degrees of accuracy.

TABLE 5.1.
Actual and possible accounts of transfer in AGL, categorised by the
kind of knowledge (rule, instance, or fragments) and whether that
knowledge is held to be surface-independent or surface-based.

	Surface-independent	*Surface-based*
Rules	Reber (1969)	
Instances		Brooks & Vokey (1991)
Fragments		Redington & Chater (1996)

KNOWLEDGE REPRESENTATION IN AGL

Accepting that transfer is not, of itself, evidence for the acquisition of rule-based or surface-independent knowledge really opens up the field for possible theories of transfer, and AGL in general. If one also accepts that these concepts can be considered somewhat independently, then we can categorise accounts of knowledge representation in AGL into six categories, as shown in Table 5.1.

A note of explanation is required for our classification of the Dienes et al. (1999) connectionist model as "fragment-based", and exactly what we mean by this term. We regard "fragment-based knowledge" as shorthand for learning about simple local, distributional properties of the stimuli, such as bigram statistics—the frequency with which a particular pair of adjacent letters occurred in the training materials. "Localness is logically . . ." is logically independent from the learning of distributional properties but, in practice, most of these accounts propose that what is learnt is the distributional relationships between adjacent or nearby elements of the stimuli (e.g. letters in a string), which tallies with the observation that, with typical AGL training materials, people are more sensitive to violations of local dependencies between letters (e.g. Gomez & Schvaneveldt, 1994). This is the kind of information that the Dienes et al. (1999) connectionist network model acquires (see Chater & Conkey, 1993), and this kind of knowledge is also captured by models that acquire knowledge of fragment occurrence, as in the idealised models proposed by Redington and Chater (1996).

Obviously, the categories in Table 5.1 are somewhat coarse, and there is some scope for debate about their exact boundaries, or which category a particular account belongs in, but generally they reflect the broad theoretical divisions that exist in the literature. Most accounts of implicit learning can be placed into one of these categories. Where hybrid theories propose more than one distinct type of knowledge, those types can themselves each be classified into the categories above. For example, Knowlton and Squire (1996) and Meulemans and Van Der Linden (1997) both propose that that AGL standard and transfer phenomena can be accounted for in terms of the acquisition of both surface-based fragment knowledge, and surface-independent rule-based knowledge.

A division within the literature that is not reflected within the categories above is on the issue of conscious awareness and accessibility of knowledge, which has been a major source of debate within the AGL literature.

We will not focus directly on the question of conscious awareness here because we believe that to a first approximation, how knowledge is represented can be considered independently from whether that representation, or aspects of it, are available to conscious awareness or not (although we concur with Dienes & Perner's 1996 suggestion that some representational forms might be more accessible or transparent to conscious awareness). Indeed, addressing the question of how knowledge about the training items is represented seems to be prior to addressing the question of whether such knowledge is conscious or not. Thus, if knowledge is believed to be represented in terms of rules of a particular kind then we can test, experimentally, whether people are aware of these rules; and if knowledge is represented in terms of fragments, then we can test whether they are aware of such fragments. But it seems to be inappropriate to attempt to address the question of conscious awareness before at least some clarity has been achieved concerning what kind of knowledge may or may not be consciously available.

For the purposes of this chapter, we will also leave aside the question of whether the knowledge acquired in AGL concerns exemplars, or fragments, or is rule-based. Instead we will focus below on the question: Is the knowledge acquired in AGL represented in terms of the original surface form, or in a surface-independent terms?

SURFACE-INDEPENDENT AND SURFACE-BASED REPRESENTATIONS

We have argued that the mere existence of transfer does not immediately imply that the knowledge learned in AGL training is necessarily surface-independent. This raises the question of how we can obtain evidence concerning the level of abstraction of AGL knowledge.

We have previously (Redington & Chater, 1996) discussed this question under the heading of the locus of abstraction in transfer—whether, in the transfer paradigm, there was abstraction away from the original surface form (resulting in a surface-independent representation), or whether (a slightly different kind of) abstraction took place between surface forms at test. Differentiating between these two possibilities is a specific instance of a problem that arises whenever a task requires abstraction of some kind, whether across training instances or away from a particular surface form.

From performance on the task itself, it is not always possible to determine logically whether participants acquired a representation in an appropriately abstract form during training, or whether the necessary abstraction occurred during testing, driven by the demands of the test procedure.

This does not mean that no evidence can be brought to bear. Redington and Chater (1996) proposed that there were three potential lines of evidence for surface-independent representations: (1) verbal report; (2) parsimony; and (3) evidence from indirect tests.

Considering evidence from verbal report first, if it were the case that participants in AGL studies clearly and unambiguously reported knowledge of surface-independent properties of the training stimuli, then this would provide some grounds for believing that participants' knowledge was represented in a surface-independent form. Unfortunately in AGL, as we have already noted, verbal reports are typically not very informative about the extent and nature of participants' knowledge (e.g. Reber & Allen, 1978), and so the evidence from verbal report favours neither a surface-based or surface-independent representation.

Turning to parsimony, all else being equal, it could be argued that accounts positing a surface-independent representation, which allows training and test items to be compared directly, provide a simpler explanation of transfer results than accounts that posit a process of abstraction between surface forms at test. But such an appeal to parsimony is problematic in the light of the consistent experimental findings that, given the same materials, classification performance in the standard (same letter-set) AGL paradigm is reliably higher than in the transfer case (e.g. Altmann et al., 1995; Manza & Reber, 1994)—it appears that participants do retain at least some information about surface form, and can take advantage of this for the classification task. For example, in Manza and Reber's (1994) account of the differential performance between the standard and transfer cases, participants acquire both surface-based knowledge and a subset of surface-independent knowledge. It seems that some surface-based representation will always be required to account for this difference.

Now, parsimony threatens to work against advocates of surface-independent knowledge: Regardless of whether knowledge is represented in surface-based or surface-independent terms, some process of "abstraction" operating either on the acquired representation, or the test item, or both, is required at test to allow the existing knowledge to be applied to the novel surface form. Given that surface-based knowledge has been shown to be sufficient to account for transfer performance, and that some surface-based knowledge is required to account for superior performance when the surface form of the materials is unchanged between training and test, accounts positing a single surface-based representation are arguably simpler than accounts positing multiple representations.

Redington and Chater's (1996) idealised computational models of AGL provide an existence proof for this kind of account, as does the connectionist model of AGL presented by Dienes et al. (1999).

In Redington and Chater's (1996) models, knowledge was represented as knowledge of the fragments (letter pairs and triples) that occurred in the training items, and this knowledge could be applied either directly to the test items (in the standard AGL paradigm) or by a simple process of finding correspondences between each test item and the training items (in the transfer paradigm). These models were able to capture the basic facts of transfer performance, and superior standard (non-transfer) performance, utilising only a single, surface-based representation.

Of course, parsimony might provide an *a priori* reason to favour one account over another, but empirical evidence provides a much more powerful argument. Redington and Chater (1996) suggested that indirect, or incidental, tests of performance, which avoided placing demands on participants that might lead to abstraction during the test phase, could provide evidence for an abstract representation, but failed to identify any converging evidence in the literature. This appears to leave the question of the level of abstraction of knowledge in AGL entirely unresolved.

EMPIRICAL EVIDENCE

There is, however, an early implicit learning study performed by Reber (1969) that does appear to provide strong evidence for the acquisition of surface-independent knowledge.[1] We first describe Reber's study, before considering why it provides a better test of the level of abstraction of AGL knowledge than later transfer studies.

In Reber's (1969) study, in contrast to later transfer studies, there was no test phase where participants classified test items as conforming to or violating the rules underlying the training items. Instead, performance in Reber's study was measured by the number of recall errors that participants made while memorising sets of training items. Each set (of three training items) was presented until the participant successfully recalled all the items on a single trial. The "test phase" of the study consisted of memorisation of a second set of training items. If participants were acquiring knowledge of the underlying structure of the materials during the first phase of the study, then this should help them to memorise items generated by the same

---

[1] Whittlesea and Wright (1997, pp. 190–191) similarly identify Reber's (1969) study as a crucial piece of evidence in favour of the acquisition of surface-independent knowledge, using a similar argument to that outlined here.

grammar in the second phase, providing a "memorisation advantage" for learning these new items.

Reber manipulated the relationship between the training items used in the first and second phases of the study: Whether or not they were generated by the same underlying grammar or not, and whether or not the items were expressed in terms of the same surface form. These factors were varied independently, to produce four experimental groups: same-grammar/same-letters, same-grammar/different-letters, different-grammar/same-letters, and different-grammar/different-letters.

As in previous studies (Miller, 1958; Reber, 1967), participants in the same-grammar group showed a memorisation advantage (made fewer errors when memorising the second set of items) over the different-grammar groups. The crucial result in Reber's (1969) study is that this advantage was maintained even when the surface form of the second set of items was different to that of the first set.

In the same-letter set case, this finding has been explained in terms of an encoding used for the first set of items being available to encode the second set of items, leading to more efficient memorisation (Miller, 1958; Reber, 1967). Reber's (1969) result indicates, as do the transfer results in the context of the classification task, that this encoding can be applied independently of surface form. However, Reber's study differs significantly from the grammaticality judgement studies in that participants in Reber's study knew nothing about the underlying structure of the training items throughout the experiment. Specifically, they did not know that any of the items were generated by a set of rules, or that the second set of items might bear any relationship to the first set.

Participants' naivety as to the letter set change is a critical difference. Accounts of transfer that do not posit a surface-independent representation (e.g. Brooks & Vokey, 1991; Redington & Chater, 1996) propose that a process of abstraction between surface forms takes place at test, and within these accounts this is typically seen as driven by the knowledge that there is a given relationship between training and test items. In the Dienes et al. (1999) model, for example, a set of "core weights" is set during training, but during the classification phase, the values of these core weights are frozen and used to constrain the training of a set of mapping weights (allowing the utilisation of the knowledge embodied in the core weights with the new surface form). In the context of this model, knowledge of the relationship between the training and test items can be seen as the signal to freeze the core weights and start the mapping process. Similarly, in Redington and Chater's (1996) idealised models, a process of mapping occurs at the test phase but there is no process for exploiting knowledge to a different surface form during the training (memorisation) phase. While these accounts are *a priori* compatible with the memorisation advantage in the same-letter set case, they cannot account for the Reber (1969) finding across different letter sets.

Surprisingly, although often cited, the Reber (1969) study has rarely been discussed in detail in the literature. While the reliability of the transfer effect itself has been questioned (Perruchet, 1994), and subsequently proved to be robust, no replications of the Reber (1969) effect have ever been reported.

We recently (Redington & Chater, unpublished data) performed two studies that replicate the underlying logic of the Reber (1969) study. In our first experiment, participants memorised sets of 18 strings in each phase. As in Reber's study, the grammar used to generate the strings and the letter set in which they were instantiated were varied between phases. Within each phase, the strings were presented in groups of three and participants had to correctly recall all three strings in a single trial before proceeding to the next group. The grammars that were used to generate the materials were not exactly the same as those used by Reber (1969) but were similar in nature and complexity (Figure 5.1), and had been constructed to minimise the sharing of repetition patterns between grammars: Of the 43 strings of length 8 or less that each grammar could generate, only 6 shared a common repetition pattern with the strings from the other grammar.

Participants in all four groups showed a statistically reliable improvement, both in terms of the number of presentations that they took to reach criterion for each group of three strings, within each phase of the study, and between the first and second phases. A reliable interaction indicated that the improvement over presentations (groups of three strings) was greater during the first phase of the study.

However, we found no evidence for the effect observer by Reber (1969). In Reber's study, the rank ordering of the performance of the experimental groups in the second phase of the study was as follows:

same-grammar/same-letters > same-grammar/different-letters > different-grammar/different-letters > different-grammar/same-letters

In our study, the rank ordering of the groups was markedly different:

same-grammar/same-letters > different-grammar/different-letters > same-grammar/different-letters > different-grammar/same-letters

The only reliable differences in memorisation advantage between the groups in our study were between the same-grammar/same-letters group and the other groups. Participants who studied items from the same grammar in both phases but instantiated in different letter sets, showed no memorisation advantage relative to the other groups.

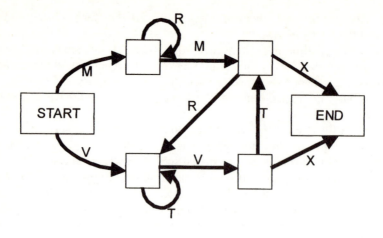

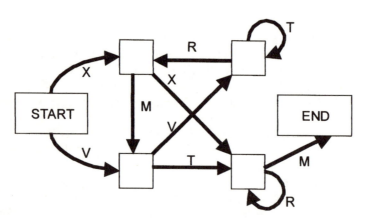

Figure 5.1. The two finite-state grammars in Redington and Chater's unpublished replication of Reber (1969). The strings are generated by beginning at the "start" state and following arrows through the diagram to the "end" state. Traversing an arrow corresponds to generating a symbol.

In a second study, we again presented participants with a memorisation task in two distinct phases, with the underlying grammar and surface form of the training strings varying across phases, as before. The procedure we used in this study was based on that of Miller (1958): Within each phase, the stimuli consisted of a list of nine strings—one set was generated by the grammar used by Miller (1958) and the other set was generated by a grammar of similar complexity. Two different sets of nine strings were chosen from each grammar selected so as to be representative of the grammar, and so that their repetition patterns did not overlap with those of the strings selected from the other grammar. On each trial, all nine strings from the appropriate set were presented, in a random order, and the participants' task was to correctly recall as many of the items as possible. Each phase of the study consisted of ten trials, with the dependent variable being the number of correct responses on each trial.

As before, participants' performance improved reliably over trials and between the first and second phases of the study, with the improvement over trials being greatest during the first phase. The manipulations of grammar and surface form resulted in same rank ordering of the groups as our previous study:

same-grammar/same-letters > different-grammar/different-letters > same-grammar/different-letters > different-grammar/same-letters

Once again, the differences between the same-grammar/same-letters group and the same-grammar/different-letters and different-grammar/same-letters groups were reliable, although the difference between the same-grammar/same-letters group and the different-grammar/different-letters group was not.

Hence, we failed to find any evidence in support of Reber's (1969) effect: There was no memorisation advantage for materials generated using the same grammar when the surface form was altered, relative to materials generated by a different grammar.

Of course, it is possible that the use of different stimuli could explain our failure to replicate Reber's (1969) findings, although other implicit learning effects, such as classification in the standard and transfer AGL tasks, are usually robust in the face of the kind of variation this introduced.

If our results are valid, it seems that the reliability of Reber's (1969) finding is at least open to question and that under "normal" AGL learning conditions, with adult participants, given straightforward memorisation instructions and a moderately complex set of rules governing the materials, the empirical evidence appears to be consistent with the acquisition of a representation that is tied to the original surface form, and does not favour a surface-independent representation.

This conclusion is further reinforced by a more recent transfer study reported by Whittlesea and Wright (1997, Experiment 4). As in a normal transfer study, participants were required to memorise a set of training strings and then, after being informed of the rule-governed nature of the materials, and that the training and test materials shared a common set of underlying rules, they performed a classification test on items that were instantiated either in a different letter set, or as sequences of coloured patches (with each colour corresponding to one of the letters in the original stimuli). Prior to being informed about the nature of the materials and performing the classification task, participants were asked to judge each of a set of test items, instantiated in the same form as the items on the classification task they were about to perform, as being pleasant or dull.

Whittlesea and Wright (1997) chose the pleasantness judgement because of its use as a measure of the mere exposure effect (Zajonc, 1968): Stimuli to which people have been previously exposed are judged as more pleasant than novel stimuli. With standard (non-transfer) AGL materials, Gordon and Holyoak (1983) found that participants were likely to rate grammatical test items as more pleasant than non-grammatical test items.

Just as in the memorisation task used by Reber (1969), the pleasantness judgement task does not require participants to be aware, or informed, that the stimuli are rule-governed, or of the relationship between the training and test stimuli. This decreases the possibility that abstraction to a new surface form is driven by the demands of, and occurs during, the test phase, allowing a reasonable test of the hypothesis that participants' knowledge is represented in surface-independent terms. Participants acquiring surface-independent knowledge should show effects of grammaticality on both the pleasantness and classification tasks under transfer conditions. On the other hand, if people possess only surface-based knowledge then they can use this knowledge to obtain better-than-chance levels of performance in the transfer classification task, by using abstraction at test, but there should be no transfer effects on pleasantness judgements.

The latter pattern of results was observed. Whittlesea and Wright (1997) reported that their participants were able to classify items as grammatical or non-grammatical at above-chance levels when the surface form of the test items was instantiated in a different letter set to that used in training, or as a series of colour patches. However, on the pleasantness task, participants who were presented with sequences of coloured patches at test showed no sensitivity to the grammaticality of the test items, suggesting that they were not exploiting surface-independent knowledge when performing the pleasantness task.

Participants who were presented with strings of letters (instantiated in a different letter set) were reliably more likely to classify grammatical items as more pleasant than non-grammatical items. Whittlesea and Wright (1997) suggest that this does provide evidence that memory is "directly sensitive to the deep structure [surface-independent properties] of the environment" (p. 194). However, it should be noted that the effect is rather small. Only 53% of pleasant or dull classifications corresponded with the items' grammaticality or non-grammaticality (where 50% would be expected by chance). In contrast, their grammaticality judgement score was 60.1%. Additionally, the comparison of participants' performance was against chance rather than, for example, against a control group, leaving open the possibility that at least some of the observed effect was due to participants' pre-existing biases, rather than exposure to the training materials (see Redington & Chater, 1996, for a discussion of this and other possible biases in AGL). Whittlesea and Wright also tested an untrained group, whose pleasantness task performance was also above chance, although not reliably so, but did not compare the performance of the experimental groups against this control.

To summarise, although Reber's (1969) results (which showed a memorisation advantage for participants who had been exposed to stimuli with the same underlying structure but with a different surface form) suggest that people do acquire surface-independent knowledge, we were unable to replicate this finding. Our results indicated that once the surface form of the materials is changed, any memorisation advantage for previous exposure to the grammar disappears. Whittlesea and Wright's (1997) results, using a similarly indirect method to detect the influence of surface-independent knowledge, also show no effect of such knowledge in the case where the surface form of the stimuli was changed from letters to colours, and only a very small (and potentially questionable) effect for letter–letter transfer. All in all, there appears to be little empirical evidence for the acquisition of surface-independent knowledge in adults, in conditions typical of the artificial grammar learning studies: Straightforward memorisation of moderately complex sequential materials.

EVIDENCE FOR THE ACQUISITION OF SURFACE-INDEPENDENT KNOWLEDGE

Although adults might not acquire surface-independent knowledge in "normal" implicit learning conditions, Whittlesea and Dorken (1993) provide some evidence that they can acquire surface-independent representations in some circumstances. Another intriguing line of evidence (Gomez & Gerken, 1999; Marcus Vijayan, Bandi Rao, & Vishton, 1999) suggests that young infants could acquire surface-independent representations, even if adults do not.

In the Whittlesea and Dorken (1993, Experiment 5) study, participants were trained and tested in the standard and transfer AGL paradigms, with a learning phase consisting of exposure to the training materials, making grammaticality judgements about novel strings during the test phase. The important experimental manipulation was in the nature of the training, which was intended to influence the way that participants processed the training items. One group of participants (the incidental repetition group) was told that the training items were distractors in a digit repetition task— they had to repeat a series of letters (i.e. a training item) between presentation and recall of a three-digit number. In the incidental analysis condition, participants' training consisted of a "repetition-detection" task during training: A letter of the training item would be underlined and the task was to indicate whether that letter occurred at any other location in the test item, as quickly as possible. A third group (the memorise group), performed a straightforward memorisation task.

Whittlesea and Dorken found that classification (grammaticality judgement) performance in the standard (non-transfer) conditions was lowest for the incidental repetition and incidental analysis groups, with the memorisation group performing reliably better. In transfer test conditions, the performance of the incidental analysis group, whose training task focused attention on the repetition patterns of the training items, reliably exceeded that of the memorisation task.

The superior transfer performance of the group trained to detect repetition patterns in the training items suggests that, under these training conditions, participants might have acquired surface-independent knowledge during training. It seems unlikely that such a training regime, if it resulted in knowledge that was completely tied to surface form, could lead to improved transfer performance at test. However, the training regime used here is very different to straightforward memorisation: Given that the task directed participants to attend to the repetition patterns of the training items, it is hardly surprising that they acquired some knowledge of these patterns—the implications of this finding for artificial grammar learning occurring under "normal" conditions are limited.

However, recent studies reported by Gomez and Gerken (1999) and Marcus et al. (1999) suggest that even under "passive" learning conditions, human infants can acquire knowledge of surface-independent structure.

The Gomez and Gerken (1999) and Marcus et al. (1999) studies both utilised the Head Turn Preference Procedure (Kemler-Nelson, Jusczyk, Mandel, Turk, & Gerken, 1995). Infants sit on a parent's lap in a three-sided booth. Stimuli are played through speakers on either side of the booth, and the infants' tendency to attend to one side or the other, as indicated by head-turning or looking times, is used as a measure of their ability to distinguish between the stimuli.

This procedure allows an almost exact analogue of the adult artificial grammar learning studies to be performed with infant participants. Saffran, Aslin, and Newport (1996), reported a study on the acquisition of word segmentation, where 8-month-old infants were exposed to a continuous speech stream of four trisyllabic nonsense words presented in random order. Using the head-turn procedure, Saffran et al. showed that the infants could subsequently distinguish between words and part-words or non-words, as indicated by a novelty preference in their looking behaviour when the test stimuli were played.

Gomez and Gerken (1999) and Marcus et al. (1999) performed very similar studies to Saffran's, except that in their studies the surface form of the training materials was switched between the training and test phases of the study. Nevertheless, infants (7-month-olds in the Marcus et al. study, and 11-month-olds in the Gomez & Gerken study) showed some sensitivity to the underlying structure of the training materials. In the Marcus et al. study, infants showed a novelty preference, attending more to stimuli with the same underlying structure as the training materials. In the Gomez and Gerken study, infants preferred to listen to items that shared a repetition pattern with the training materials. The actual direction of the effects is unimportant to the argument presented here—in each case, infants were able to distinguish between items that shared the same underlying structure as the training items and those test items that did not.

Why is this result evidence for the acquisition of a surface-independent representation, when adult studies of transfer are not? Given the age of the infants, no meaningful instructions as to the rule-governed nature of the stimuli and the relationship between the training and test materials could be given. The infant participants were necessarily completely naive, providing an indirect test of the knowledge that they acquired during training.

One caveat to this conclusion is that, in the Marcus et al. (1999) studies, the stimuli were generated from two grammars that generated three-syllable words, all of which had the repetition structure ABB (in one grammar), or ABA (in the other grammar), and the 16 stimuli were each repeated three times in the course of a 2-minute training session. With such a simple structure, in adults at least, it would not be surprising if participants acquired explicit (in the sense of being readily verbalisable) knowledge of this repetition pattern, and exploited this in the test phase, and it seems plausible that a similar process of explicit learning (at some level) could take place in infants. However, the Gomez and Gerken (1999) materials were much more akin to the relatively complex materials used in adult studies, providing a more convincing case for the kind of implicit processing that is seen in adults (although in the case of infants this also seems to encompass surface-independent knowledge).

DISCUSSION

We have seen that the literature of AGL and related paradigms have not yet provided decisive evidence concerning the level of abstraction of information learned during training. Although the existence of transfer in AGL studies has sometimes been interpreted as unequivocal evidence for surface-independent representations, an alternative hypothesis remains open: That "abstraction" away from the surface representation occurs only at test, triggered by the knowledge that there is common structure between the training and test items. Studies in which participants are ignorant of the relationship between training and test items provide a means of distinguishing between these rival hypotheses. Reber (1969) described such a study, which appeared to show evidence for transfer, in a memorisation paradigm where people were unaware that the strings that they were asked to learn were governed by rules, let alone that these rules were in some cases analogous to rules governing previously learned items (the "transfer" condition, in Reber's study). But two attempts to replicate this result led to the opposite conclusion—that there is no evidence for transfer, and hence no evidence for surface-independent learning. Using a different design, Whittlesea and Wright (1997) provided evidence consistent with these results, finding no evidence of transfer for a pleasantness rating task where participants were ignorant of the relationship between training and test items.

However, it appears plausible that when the training task requires participants to attend to the repetition structure of the training materials, as in Whittlesea and Dorken's (1993) study, people will acquire a surface-independent representation. The evidence provided by Gomez and Gerken (1999) and Marcus et al. (1999) suggests that young infants might acquire surface-independent representations, even under passive learning conditions, with speech-like materials.

The debate concerning levels of abstraction in AGL can be viewed as an aspect of a much broader theoretical debate in cognitive science: to what extent is human learning "lazy" or "eager"? (Aha, 1997; Hahn & Chater, 1997, 1998.)

Lazy learning involves storing input material in a relatively unprocessed form; the cognitive work required to transfer this knowledge to some new context (e.g. generalising past experiences to a new situation) is applied only when this work needs to be done. This style of learning is "lazy" because cognitive work is done only when strictly necessary—otherwise, the learning items are simply stored. In cognitive science, lazy learning is exemplified by exemplar models of categorisation (e.g. Medin & Schaffer, 1978; Nosofsky, 1986), memory (Hintzmann, 1986), case-based reasoning (e.g. Kolodner, 1993), and analogy-based models of reading (Glushko, 1979) and morphological processing (Nakisa & Hahn, 1996).

By contrast, eager learning involves actively attempting to extract regularities from new items, as they are encountered. The model of the regularities that has been extracted can then straightforwardly be applied to new items, as they are encountered. Eager learning methods vary between methods that involve the attempt to seek symbolic rules with which to model the incoming data (Lavrac & Dzeroski, 1993; Thagard, 1988), and those that attempt to fit incoming data to some kind of probabilistic model (e.g. a mixture of Gaussians, as in the decision-bound model of categorisation, Ashby, 1992).

It seems likely that the cognitive system uses some mixture of lazy and eager learning processes. For example, given the creativity of language use, it seems at best highly unlikely that the syntactic structure of a language can be learned using purely lazy learning. Instead, it seems possible to learn syntactic rules, which can then be used in ways that can be different from the contexts in which they were learned. But conversely, there is considerable evidence that the surface properties of learned items have a substantial effect on later memory and processing, in studies of categorisation, memory, and reasoning (e.g., Gick & Holyoak, 1980; Hintzmann, 1986; Posner & Keele, 1970).

To the extent that both lazy and eager processes might be operating in the cognitive system, it also seems plausible that both types of processing can be engaged in AGL studies. It might be that the abstractness and unfamiliarity of AGL stimuli, and the regularities defined over them, tends to block the application of eager learning methods. It might be that by using more natural, speech-like materials, as in the infant studies reported earlier, the cognitive system might be able to find abstract regularities during training. Alternatively it could be that learning styles shift during development, so that in the case of repetition structure, infant sensitivity to repetition structure is lost at some point during development.

The difference between the types of material, and experimental task, in which lazy or eager styles of cognitive processing are favoured, is a potentially important direction for future research, and AGL could be a valuable tool for investigating these questions.

ACKNOWLEDGEMENTS

Thanks to David Shanks and Theresa Johnstone for informative discussions on implicit, exemplar, and rule-based learning, and Pierre Perruchet for his comments on the manuscript.

This research was partly supported by ESRC research grant R000236214. Some of the work was performed while the authors were members of the Department of Experimental Psychology, University of Oxford.

REFERENCES

Aha, D.W. (Ed.) (1997). *Lazy learning.* Dordrecht, The Netherlands: Kluwer.

Altmann, G.T.M., Dienes, Z., & Goode, A. (1995). On the modality independence of implicitly learned grammatical knowledge. *Journal of Experimental Psychology: Learning, Memory, and Cognition, 21,* 899–912.

Ashby, F.G. (1992). Multidimensional models of categorization. In F.G. Ashby (Ed.), *Multidimensional models of perception and cognition* (pp. 449–483). Hillsdale, NJ: Lawrence Erlbaum Associates Inc.

Brooks, L.R., & Vokey, J.R. (1991). Abstract analogies and abstracted grammars: Comments on Reber (1989) and Mathews et al. (1989). *Journal of Experimental Psychology: Learning, Memory, and Cognition, 17,* 316–323.

Chater, N., & Conkey, P. (1993). Sequence processing with recurrent neural networks. In M. Oaksford & G.D.A. Brown (Eds.), *Neurodynamics and psychology.* London: Academic Press.

Dienes, Z., Altmann, G.T.M., & Gao, S.J. (1999). Mapping across domains without feedback: A neural network model of transfer of implicit knowledge. *Cognitive Science, 23,* 53–82.

Dienes, Z., & Berry, D. (1993). *Implicit learning: Theoretical and empirical issues.* Hove, UK: Lawrence Erlbaum Associates Ltd.

Dienes, Z., & Perner, J. (1996) Implicit knowledge in people and connectionist networks. In G. Underwood (Ed.), *Implicit cognition* (pp. 227–256). Oxford: Oxford University Press.

Gick, M.L., & Holyoak, K.J. (1980). Analogical problem solving. *Cognitive Psychology, 12,* 306–355.

Glushko, R.J. (1979). The organization and activation of orthographic knowledge in reading aloud. *Journal of Experimental Psychology: Human Perception and Performance, 5,* 674–691.

Gomez, R.L., & Gerken, L.A. (1999). Artificial grammar learning by one-year-olds leads to specific and abstract knowledge. *Cognition, 70,* 109–135.

Gomez, R.L., & Schvaneveldt, R.W. (1994). What is learned from artificial grammars? Transfer tests of simple associations. *Journal of Experimental Psychology: Learning, Memory, and Cognition, 20,* 396–410.

Gordon, P.C., & Holyoak, K.J. (1983). Implicit learning and the generalization of the "mere exposure" effect. *Journal of Personality and Social Psychology, 45,* 492–500.

Hahn, U., & Chater, N. (1997). Concepts and similarity. In K. Lamberts & D. Shanks (Eds.), *Knowledge, concepts and categories* (pp. 43–92). Hove, UK: Psychology Press.

Hahn, U., & Chater, N. (1998). Understanding similarity: A joint project for psychology, case-based reasoning, and law. *Artificial Intelligence Review, 12,* 393–427.

Hintzmann, D.L. (1986). "Schema abstraction" in a multiple trace memory model. *Psychological Review, 93,* 411–428.

Kemler-Nelson, D., Jusczyk, P.W., Mandel, D.R., Turk, A., & Gerken, L.A. (1995). The head-turn preference procedure for testing auditory perception. *Infant Behaviour and Development, 18,* 111–116.

Knowlton, B.J., & Squire, L.R. (1996). Artificial grammar learning depends on implicit acquisition of both abstract and exemplar-specific information. *Journal of Experimental Psychology: Learning, Memory, and Cognition, 22,* 169–181.

Kolodner, J. (1993). *Case-based reasoning.* San Mateo, CA: Morgan Kaufmann.

Lavrac, N., & Dzeroski, S. (1993). *Inductive logic programming: Techniques and applications.* New York: Ellis Horwood.

Marcus, G.F., Vijayan, S., Bandi Rao, S., & Vishton, P.M. (1999). Rule learning by seven-month-old infants. *Science, 283,* 77–80.

Mathews, R.C. (1990). Abstractness of implicit grammar knowledge: Comments on Perruchet & Pacteau's analysis of synthetic grammar learning. *Journal of Experimental Psychology: General, 119,* 412–416.

Mathews, R.C., Buss, R.R., Stanley, W.B., Blanchard-Fields, F., Cho, J.R., & Druhan, B. (1989). Role of implicit and explicit processes in learning from examples: A synergistic effect. *Journal of Experimental Psychology: Learning, Memory, and Cognition, 15,* 1083–1100.

Medin, D.L., & Schaffer, M.M. (1978). Context theory of classification learning. *Psychological Review, 85,* 207–238.

Meulemans, T., & Van der Linden, M. (1997). Associative chunk strength in artificial grammar learning. *Journal of Experimental Psychology: Learning, Memory, and Cognition, 23,* 1007–1028.

Miller, G.A. (1958). Free recall of redundant strings of letters. *Journal of Experimental Psychology*, *56*, 485–491.

Nakisa, R., & Hahn, U. (1996). Where defaults don't help: The case of the German plural system. In *Proceedings of the 18th Annual Conference of the Cognitive Science Society* (pp. 177–182). Mahwah, NJ: Lawrence Erlbaum Associates Inc.

Nosofsky, R.M. (1986). Attention, similarity, and the identification–categorization relationship. *Journal of Experimental Psychology: General*, *15*, 39–57.

Perruchet, P. (1994). Defining the knowledge units of a synthetic language: Comment on Vokey and Brooks (1992). *Journal of Experimental Psychology: Learning, Memory, and Cognition*, *20*, 223–228.

Perruchet, P., & Pacteau, C. (1990). Synthetic grammar learning: Implicit rule abstraction or explicit fragmentary knowledge? *Journal of Experimental Psychology: General*, *119*, 264–275.

Posner, M., & Keele, S. (1970). Retention of abstract ideas. *Journal of Experimental Psychology*, *83*, 304–308.

Reber, A.S. (1967). Implicit learning of artificial grammars. *Journal of Verbal Learning and Verbal Behavior*, *5*, 855–863.

Reber, A.S. (1969). Transfer of syntactic structure in synthetic languages. *Journal of Experimental Psychology*, *81*, 115–119.

Reber, A.S. (1993). *Implicit learning and tacit knowledge: An essay on the cognitive unconscious.* New York: Oxford University Press.

Reber, A.S., & Allen, R. (1978). Analogic and abstraction strategies in synthetic grammar learning: A functional approach. *Cognition*, *6*, 189–221.

Redington, M., & Chater, N. (1996). Transfer in artificial grammar learning: A reevaluation. *Journal of Experimental Psychology: General*, *125*, 123–138.

Saffran, J.R., Aslin, R.N., & Newport, E.L. (1996). Statistical cues in language acquisition: Word segmentation by infants. In G.W. Cottrell (Ed.), *Proceedings of the 18th Annual Conference of the Cognitive Science Society* (pp. 376–380). Mahwah, NJ: Lawrence Erlbaum Associates Inc.

Shanks, D.R., Johnstone, T., & Staggs, L. (1997). Abstraction processes in artificial grammar learning. *Quarterly Journal of Experimental Psychology*, *50A*, 216–252.

Thagard, P. (1988). *Computational philosophy of science.* Cambridge, MA: MIT Press.

Whittlesea, B.W., & Dorken, M.D. (1993). Incidentally, things in general are particularly determined: An episodic-processing account of implicit learning. *Journal of Experimental Psychology: General*, *122*, 227–248.

Whittlesea, B.W.A., & Wright, R.L. (1997). Implicit (and explicit) learning: Acting adaptively without knowing the consequences. *Journal of Experimental Psychology: Learning, Memory, and Cognition*, *23*, 181–200.

Zajonc, R.B. (1968). Attitudinal effects of mere exposure. *Journal of Personality and Social Psychology Monographs*, *9*(2. Pt. 2).

CHAPTER SIX

Artificial grammar learning in amnesia

Thierry Meulemans and Martial Van der Linden
Neuropsychology Unit, University of Liège, Belgium

Amongst the numerous theoretical debates regarding implicit learning, one of the most discussed concerns the implicit nature of the information learned with the implicit learning paradigms. Some authors (e.g. Reber, 1993) argue that the information acquired in implicit learning situations is by nature different from the kind of information acquired in explicit learning tasks (in which, for example, learning is based on hypothesis-testing processes), while others reject the idea of two independent learning processes (Shanks & St John, 1994; Whittlesea & Dorken, 1993). The problem of the implicit versus explicit nature of the information acquired in the implicit learning tasks has been classically investigated in normal subjects by assessing the acquired knowledge through an implicit and an explicit memory task; the arguments in favour of the idea that the knowledge is implicit (or unconscious) rest on the dissociations (or the lack of correlation) observed between performance in the implicit task and performance in the explicit task (e.g. Dienes, Broadbent, & Berry, 1991; Reber & Lewis, 1977). However, the validity of the explicit memory tests used in these studies has been questioned by some authors. One of the criticisms concerns the fact that most of the explicit tests used do not fulfill the sensitivity and information criteria proposed by Shanks and St John (1994). The information criterion implies that the information accessed by the explicit test should be the same as the knowledge used by the subject in the implicit task; the sensitivity criteria means that the explicit test should be sensitive enough to the subject's conscious knowledge. Up to now, in the artificial grammar learning studies, there has been no agreement as to which memory test is better suited to assess the explicit knowledge reached by the subjects during the study phase. While some authors (e.g. Reber, 1989) consider that the subjects' inability to report verbally the rules (or some of the rules) of the grammar is sufficient to show that their knowledge is actually implicit, others argue that more sensitive measures have to be used. Actually, it is difficult to find any clear-cut evidence in favour of one or the other of the two opposite positions in the literature on implicit learning in normal subjects (even if some recent data seem to be promising; see, for example, the study of Dienes, Altmann, Kwan, & Goode, 1995, with the process dissociation procedure); this is notably due to the fact that no task can be considered as being process-pure and, therefore, the interpretation of the results is often ambiguous. For example, Perruchet and Pacteau (1990) have shown that a recognition task could be sensitive to the knowledge acquired by the subjects about the learning items. However, two kinds of mechanisms are thought to underlie recognition processes: (1) a conscious recollection mechanism; and (2) a mechanism based on familiarity, which could, at least partly, be underlain by implicit processes.

The aim of the present chapter is to present the data obtained in amnesic patients in relation to the debate of the implicit versus explicit nature of the knowledge acquired in implicit learning tasks. The study of implicit learning abilities in amnesic patients is considered by many authors as being particularly interesting with regard to this issue: if such patients, who are known to be severely impaired in situations where they have to consciously recollect previously learned information, are able to perform normally in implicit learning tasks, then one could consider that this observation constitutes a strong argument in favour of the very implicit nature of the acquired knowledge.

THE AMNESIC SYNDROME

The amnesic syndrome is classically defined by a deficit in the acquisition of new information (anterograde amnesia) accompanied by a deficit in recall and recognition of information acquired before the lesion was sustained (retrograde amnesia). The importance of the deficit can vary from one patient to another but, even in the most severe cases, intellectual abilities and short-term memory can be preserved. Typically, studies explored amnesics with a variety of aetiologies: Korsakoff patients who have lesions in the midline diencephalon, post-encephalitic patients who have lesions in the medial temporal lobe region and patients suffering from a rupture of an anterior communicating artery aneurysm and who have lesions in the cholinergic basal forebrain (see Mayes, 1988).

Considerable evidence has demonstrated that, despite a severe deficit in explicit memory tasks (such as recall or recognition tasks, which require the conscious recollection of the learning episodes), severe amnesic patients can show preserved or partially preserved learning abilities in a variety of tasks. Firstly, amnesics can acquire perceptual, motor, and even cognitive skills in a normal or almost normal way, although they might have little or no recollection at all of the acquisition episodes (for a review, see Soliveri, Brown, Jahanshahi, & Mardsen, 1992). Secondly, they may also exhibit normal performance on implicit memory tasks, in which no reference is made to the learning experience and subjects' memories are revealed by how they process repeated items. In particular, amnesic patients show normal perceptual priming, even for information that was novel prior to learning (for reviews, see Moscovitch, 1994; Schacter, 1994; Van der Linden, 1994). Some researchers have interpreted this pattern of preserved and impaired memory functions in amnesia by postulating the existence of several distinct memory systems, some of which are affected by the brain damage while some are not. More specifically, amnesics' normal perceptual priming and skill acquisition would be mediated by, respectively, the perceptual representation and procedural memory systems that are intact in amnesia whereas the amnesics' severe deficits in explicit memory tasks would be the consequence of damage affecting the episodic memory system (Schacter & Tulving, 1994; Squire, 1994).

However, conflicting data showing that the ability of amnesic patients to learn new skills is disturbed have also been reported (Cermak, Lewis, Butters, & Goodglass, 1973; Chun & Phelps, 1999; Nissen, Willingham, & Hartman, 1989). This discrepancy between results has been explained by suggesting that amnesics, contrary to normal subjects, could not benefit from episodic (declarative) memory processes for the acquisition of certain procedural tasks (see, for example, Squire & Frambach, 1990). Similarly, some workers had doubts about whether amnesic patients show preserved perceptual priming for all kinds of novel items (see Mayes, 1998). A major interpretative problem relates to how perceptual priming and explicit memory are measured. More specifically, it has been argued that perceptual priming tasks are not pure and that they often depend on both implicit and explicit memory processes. If this problem is to be taken seriously, the priming performance of both normal subjects and amnesics is hard to interpret (see Mayes, 1998, for a discussion of this point).

The integrity of semantic memory in amnesia is even more controversial. According to the Serial Parallel Independent (SPI) model developed by Tulving (1995; see also Tulving & Markowitsch, 1998), information can be encoded into semantic memory independently of episodic memory, but must be encoded into episodic memory through semantic memory. Consequently, this theory predicts that amnesic patients will show flexible, preserved semantic learning even if their episodic memory system is disturbed. More recently, integrating the data obtained by Vargha-Khadem et al. (1997), Tulving and Markowitsch (1998) suggested that semantic memory depends on the peri-hippocampal cortical regions whereas episodic memory depends on the hippocampus (as well as the frontal lobes). In this view, amnesic patients with a limited hippocampal pathology should be able to acquire new factual (semantic) knowledge.

By contrast, Squire and Zola (1998; see also Squire, 1992, 1994) consider the episodic memory and semantic memory as two parallel subsystems of declarative memory, which can be differentiated in terms of the type of information they deal with: personal events versus general facts. More specifically, they consider that episodic memory is a gateway to semantic memory. They also propose that episodic and semantic memory are both dependent on the integrity of the medial temporal lobe and midline diencephalic structures, and that episodic memory depends additionally on the frontal lobes. In this view, both episodic memory and semantic memory should be impaired in amnesic patients with medial temporal lobe/diencephalic lesions. On the other hand, acquisition of new facts should be possible in amnesic patients whose episodic memory deficit is due to frontal dysfunction.

In line with Tulving's (1995) view, there exists some evidence suggesting that amnesic patients are able to acquire substantial factual information either in laboratory learning conditions (e.g. new verbal associations; Hayman, MacDonald, & Tulving, 1993; new concepts, Van der Linden, Meulemans, & Lorrain, 1994; new computer-related vocabulary, Glisky, Schachter, & Tulving, 1986, Van der Linden & Coyette, 1995) or in natural learning conditions (e.g. knowledge of vocabulary and famous people that arose after amnesia; Kitchener, Hodges, & McCarthy, 1998; Van der Linden, Brédart, Depoorter, & Coyette, 1996; Van der Linden et al., 2001; Vargha-Khadem et al., 1997).

However, other studies have also shown that the ability of amnesics to learn new verbal associations, new vocabulary, and knowledge of new famous people is defective (Gabrieli, Cohen, & Corkin, 1983, 1988; Hamman & Squire, 1995; Verfaellie, Croce, & Milberg, 1995). More generally, the data suggesting the integrity of new semantic learning in amnesics have been challenged by Squire and Zola (1998). One of their arguments is that, in most of the reported cases, the amnesic patients show some residual capacities in episodic memory, which "could provide a foundation for the acquisition of factual knowledge". Another difficulty raised by Squire is that it is difficult to know whether results obtained in semantic learning tasks would not have been better if the patient had not suffered from amnesia. Moreover, Squire and Zola argue that the factual knowledge shown by these patients is not always as good as the authors claim. Finally, they suggest that the semantic learning abilities observed in some amnesic patients can be explained by the fact that they did not show a "hippocampal" episodic memory deficit but rather a "retrieval" episodic memory deficit due to frontal lobe pathology. However, the criticisms raised by Squire and Zola appear to be irrelevant with regard to the strictly normal new vocabulary learning abilities we recently observed in a severely amnesic patient (AC; Van der Linden et al., 2001). In particular, according to Squire and Zola's (1998) argument, if new vocabulary learning depends on episodic memory abilities, control subjects' performance in vocabulary-knowledge tasks would logically have been better than that of AC, especially when one considers the severity of AC's amnesia. However, there was no significant difference between AC and the control subjects in the different tasks designed to assess vocabulary knowledge. In addition, it should be noted that AC's severe episodic memory deficit was observed on both recall and recognition tasks, suggesting that his deficit was not strictly limited to "frontal" retrieval processes.

Another interpretation of semantic learning in amnesia has been proposed by McClelland, McNaughton, and O'Reilly (1995; see also Kitchener et al., 1998). According to their computational model of long-term memory, McClelland et al. (1995) suggested that the rapid acquisition of both episodic and semantic information depends on the hippocampus, whose function is rapidly to link or index the sensory traces that compose a specific memory. With re-exposure and rehearsal, the memory is integrated into neocortical representations, which are stored permanently, independently of the hippocampus. When the hippocampal system is damaged, it remains possible to acquire new information, slowly and in an impoverished form, by the accumulation of minimal changes in the neocortical connection weights, resulting in the progressive integration of the information into neocortical representations. However, it appears that this mechanism is not sufficient to explain the semantic learning abilities observed in some amnesic patients (especially AC's abilities). Indeed, one of the characteristics of the knowledge acquired by the neocortical learning mechanism described by McClelland et al. (1995) is its inflexibility. This lack of flexibility is due to the fact that the acquired knowledge is directly located within the neural connections that have been activated during encoding. To access this information it is necessary to reactivate these connections, a process that necessitates not only the presence of cues related to the target information itself but also the presence of the encoding context. In fact, it does not seem that the new vocabulary knowledge acquired by AC is less flexible, or less rich, than that of the control subjects. AC's new vocabulary knowledge was explored by using different tasks, and for none of these tasks was AC's performance worse than that of the control subjects. In conclusion, it appears that, despite a profound episodic memory deficit, some amnesic patients are (normally) able to acquire new semantic knowledge.

In addition to perceptual priming, skill acquisition, and semantic learning tasks, several studies suggested that amnesic patients also perform normally on various implicit learning tasks.

IMPLICIT LEARNING IN AMNESIC PATIENTS: A REVIEW

Implicit learning abilities of amnesic patients have been studied with different experimental paradigms. In the present chapter, we will focus on the two paradigms that have provided the most significant data: (1) the serial reaction time (SRT) task; and (2) the artificial grammar learning task.

Serial reaction time

The SRT paradigm (Nissen & Bullemer, 1987; Nissen et al., 1989; Reber & Squire, 1994) involves the incidental learning of a visuospatial sequence of stimuli in a choice reaction-time task. Nissen and Bullemer (1987, Experiment 4) administered an SRT task to six Korsakoff amnesic patients. After the reaction-time task, the subjects had to say if they noticed a repeating sequence during the task. Results show that sequence-specific learning was similar in Korsakoff patients and in normal subjects, even if only normal subjects noticed the presence of a sequence. The authors concluded that Korsakoff amnesic patients showed normal associative learning abilities, in the absence of any consciousness of what had been learned.

To determine how far Korsakoff patients could maintain their knowledge of the sequence after a delay, Nissen et al. (1989) administered to seven Korsakoff patients, to eight alcoholic control subjects, and to seven elderly subjects, an SRT task involving a delayed retention measure of the acquired knowledge. The task was administered in two sessions separated by a 1-week delay. Apart from the fact that Korsakoff patients were on the whole slower than the other subjects, results showed that, for the three groups, the reaction times were significantly more rapid for the repeating sequence than for the random stimuli during the first session. On the other hand, the three groups showed a similar retention of the sequence-specific knowledge after the 1-week delay. As in the study of Nissen and Bullemer (1987), the results of the Korsakoff patients in the explicit memory test were worse than those of the two other groups. It is interesting to note that, if the reaction-time amelioration for the repeating sequence had been influenced by the explicit knowledge of the sequence, one could have expected that Korsakoff patients would have realised a worse performance in the SRT task than the other subjects, which was not the case.

The results of these two studies (Nissen & Bullemer, 1987; Nissen et al., 1989) suggest that the implicit learning of a sequence does not depend on the neural structures that are impaired in the Korsakoff syndrome. However, one problem with these preliminary studies is that the repeating sequence could be learned through simple associations between pairs of elements in the sequence. One cannot rule out the interpretation that, if the hippocampus (or other neural structures that are impaired in amnesia) is not involved in the learning of simple associations between stimuli, it could be involved in the learning of more complex conditional associations between elements of the sequence. Therefore, as suggested by Curran (1995), it would be interesting to investigate performance of amnesic patients in an SRT task in which the learning of the repeating sequence would involve the formation of higher-level chunks.

In this perspective, Reber and Squire (1994) administered to eight amnesic patients (six with diencephalic lesions and two with hippocampal lesions) an SRT task involving a repeating sequence that could not be learned by forming simple associations between pairs of stimuli. In this study, subjects performed at first four blocks of trials composed of the repeating sequence, followed by the administration of two explicit tests (a verbal recall and a recognition test). Then, subjects had to perform a new block of trials corresponding to the repeating sequence, followed by a last block of random trials. Results showed similar performance levels in amnesic patients and control subjects for the learning of the repeating sequence, as shown by the absence of Block × Group interaction. The presence of a small (non-significant) difference in favour of the normal subjects could reflect the fact that these subjects could benefit from a certain explicit learning of the sequence: indeed, in the verbal recall test, normal subjects were able to recall longer parts of the repeating sequence than amnesic patients; the recognition task, on the contrary, showed no explicit knowledge, neither in amnesic patients nor in normal subjects. So, the main result of this study was that amnesic patients could learn more complex conditional associations between elements of a repeated sequence (but see Shanks & Johnstone, 1997, for an alternative interpretation) than simple pairwise contingencies between two stimuli.

However, this result was questioned by a study conducted by Curran (1997), who administered an SRT task to 10 amnesic patients and 20 matched control subjects. The amnesic patients were administered the task in two sessions: in one session, they learned a first-order predictive (FOP) sequence including pairwise information that was probabilistically predictive and, in the other session, they learned a second-order predictive (SOP) sequence, in which the appearance of a stimulus could never be predicted by the preceding stimulus. Even though both groups exhibited a significant learning of the two sequences (there was no significant interaction with the Group variable), Curran concluded that there was an impairment in the learning of second-order associations in amnesic patients with regard to control subjects, mainly because control subjects learned the SOP sequence better than the FOP sequence, while this advantage for the SOP sequence was not observed in the amnesic patients. While it remains unclear as to why normal subjects learned the SOP sequence better than the FOP sequence, the author concluded that the diencephalic and/or medial temporal regions that are damaged in amnesia actually contribute to implicit learning.

This interpretation has been challenged by Reber and Squire (1998), who showed a crossover interaction between explicit and implicit memory in an SRT task. In their study, Reber and Squire compared the performance of five amnesic patients and that of control subjects in two tasks assessing sequence-specific knowledge: an implicit task (the SRT task), and an explicit task (a recognition task). Before performing the two tasks, control subjects had to memorise the repeating sequence. Their results, showing that the patients performed better than controls on the implicit SRT task but were impaired in the explicit recognition task, suggest that the brain areas damaged in amnesia do not intervene predominantly in the implicit learning of the sequence.

Artificial grammar learning

With the artificial grammar learning paradigm, most of the data obtained with amnesic patients come from studies conducted by Barbara Knowlton, Larry Squire, and collaborators (Knowlton, Ramus, & Squire, 1992; Knowlton & Squire, 1994, 1996). In a first study, Knowlton et al. (1992) administered an artificial grammar learning task to a group of 13 amnesic patients and matched normal subjects. After the learning phase, in which subjects had to memorise a series of grammatical strings of letters, they had to classify new letter strings as grammatical, depending on whether the strings corresponded to the rules of the grammar. Performance levels in the classification task were similar for amnesic patients (63.2% of correct responses) and normal subjects (66.9%). Six weeks later, the same subjects were seen for the second phase of the experiment. Again, they had to learn a series of letter strings (generated by a finite-state grammar that was different from that used during the first session), and the learning phase was followed by a recognition test involving the presentation of 23 grammatical and 23 non-grammatical items. Results in the recognition test showed a significant difference between the two groups, with 62% of correct responses for the amnesic patients and 72.2% of correct responses for normal subjects. These results suggest that the learning of the structure of an artificial grammar could develop normally despite a poor memory for the exemplars themselves. According to the authors, this result is compatible with the existence of two independent memory systems: one system (declarative), which stores in an explicit form the exemplars presented to the subject, and another system (non-declarative), which stores implicitly the information abstracted from the stimuli, for example in the form of rules. Knowlton et al. (1992) suggested that the classification performance in such a task depends principally on implicit memory when the categories are defined by a set of complex rules or by other features which cannot easily be discovered explicitly. On the other hand, explicit memory for the exemplars would intervene especially when the task involves the explicit memorisation of the exemplars and/or when there is an intensive training with the exemplars, or when the features of the stimuli can be easily defined and encoded in explicit memory.

The idea that the acquisition of an artificial grammar could be achieved independently of the contribution of declarative memory was further confirmed by a study of Knowlton and Squire (1994). These authors showed again that amnesic patients can reach performance levels strictly similar to that of normal subjects in a grammaticality judgement task. Their data confirm that a normal performance in this task can be sustained by implicit retrieval mechanisms. With regard to the nature of these mechanisms, Knowlton and Squire showed that, by manipulating independently the variables of similarity (a similar test item being different by only one letter from a learning item) and of associative chunk strength (associative chunk strength is based on the frequency with which bigrams and trigrams making up the test strings appear in the learning strings) between test items and items presented at the learning phase, grammaticality judgements made by amnesic patients were mainly based on the learning of fragments of letter-strings (bigrams and trigrams).

However, one cannot exclude the intervention of a rule abstraction mechanism from the Knowlton and Squire study because their associated strings were also the grammatical ones. Hence, it seems difficult to determine why their participants classified the grammatical strings as grammatical more often than the non-grammatical strings: Was it because of their grammaticality (their adherence to the rules) or because of their greater associative chunk strength? In a more recent paper, Knowlton and Squire (1996; Experiment 1) tried to study independently the role of associative chunk strength and grammaticality in the classification judgements of a group of amnesic patients and a control group. In order to investigate both the chunk-strength and rule-adherence effects, Knowlton and Squire constructed four groups of test items: (1) grammatical with a high-level chunk-strength; (2) grammatical with a low-level chunk-strength; (3) non-grammatical with a high-level chunk-strength; and (4) non-grammatical with a low-level chunk-strength. They administered this task to a group of normal subjects and to 11 amnesic patients. Their results showed that classification judgements depended on both grammaticality and associative chunk strength, and that amnesic patients and controls showed the same pattern of results.

In a second experiment, starting from the hypothesis that the knowledge acquired in the artificial grammar task concerned mainly bigrams and trigrams, Knowlton and Squire administered to their subjects the learning phase followed by a recognition test for the chunks presented in the learning items. They found a dissociation between the performance of the two groups in the recognition task, the mean score of the amnesic patients being only just above chance. According to Knowlton and Squire, this result suggests that the explicit knowledge of the chunks, which has been shown in some studies (e.g. Perruchet & Pacteau, 1990), would be only an epiphenomenon and that the relevant information concerning chunk-strength for the grammaticality judgements is actually implicit.

Finally, in a third experiment, Knowlton and Squire examined the ability of amnesic patients to classify items constructed with another set of letters than those used for the learning phase (transfer test). Results showed a significant transfer of the grammatical knowledge, even though, for amnesic patients as well as for control subjects, performance was better when the same set of letters was used during the study phase and the test phase. According to Knowlton and Squire, the advantage of the no-transfer condition could be due to the influence of chunk strength on grammaticality judgements (the authors suggest that this influence could reflect a perceptual priming effect). Knowlton and Squire interpret these results by suggesting that they reflect both the effect of an abstract knowledge based on rules and the effect of the acquisition of concrete information that is specific to the learning items. The observation that amnesic patients reach performance levels comparable to those of control subjects suggests, according to the authors, that these two forms of knowledge can be acquired implicitly.

However, the Knowlton and Squire study suffers from some methodo-logical weaknesses that call into question the authors' interpretation of their results. Firstly, because of the absence of a control group that was not confronted with the learning items, one cannot be sure that the subjects (and, particularly, the amnesic patients) were not sensitive during the classification task to some characteristics inherent to the test items themselves (apart from their adherence to the rules of the grammar) like, for example, their internal chunk strength (see Meulemans & Van der Linden, 1997). Because of this lack of control, it is difficult to ensure that the effects observed in the classification task are actually due to information learned during the study phase. Secondly, the chunk strength control in the Knowlton and Squire experiments does not seem to have been sufficiently accurate. Indeed, the only measure on which grammatical and non-grammatical items were equalised concerns their global chunk strength (an average measure, based on both bigram and trigram frequency, whatever their position in the test item); the authors did not take into account the chunk strength for the anchor positions (i.e. for chunks located at the beginning and at the end of the letter-strings). Therefore, it is possible that their results might have been partly biased by this lack of control of the chunk strength in the test items.

So, it remained to determine whether amnesic patients are really able to learn the complex information present in the exemplars generated by a finite-state grammar.

In this context, we have conducted a study to investigate the artificial grammar learning abilities in a group of amnesic patients with material in which grammatical and non-grammatical items did not differ as to different chunk strength measures. In other words, with such a material, it is impossible to classify the test items on the basis of a knowledge limited to simple associations between adjacent letters in the learning items. In this task, we also included a new measure of the explicit knowledge acquired by the subjects in the task: a generation task. To determine the sensitivity of this task, and also to ensure that the knowledge demonstrated in this task is actually related to information learned during the study phase (and not to information learned during the classification phase), we conducted a first experiment in which we administered this generation task in different conditions (after the classification phase with and without a study phase, or immediately after the study phase). The comparison of the amnesic patients and the normal subjects was made in a second experiment. If, despite their severe deficit in episodic memory, amnesic patients show performance levels comparable to that of normal subjects, one could conclude that this kind of learning does not depend on the brain regions affected in the amnesic syndrome, and also that the learning of complex knowledge in an artificial grammar task does not depend on the episodic memory processes. Another prediction was that normal subjects would perform better than amnesic patients in the explicit generation task.

Experiment 1

Because of the ambiguity related to the assessment of the explicit knowledge in implicit learning tasks described in the introduction of this chapter, we chose to test another explicit measure: a generation task, in which subjects are asked to generate 10 letter strings they think are grammatical. In a previous study (Meulemans & Van der Linden, 1997), we obtained results suggesting that the information elicited by the generation task was actually due to information learned during the study phase. However, it remained to determine the influence of the classification task on the performance in the generation task, with the classification task taking place between the study phase and the generation task. Therefore, we compared different conditions in order to clarify the link between the performance in the generation task and the information learned during the study phase: (1) the "standard" condition, in which subjects are administered the study phase followed by the classification phase, and finally the generation task; (2) the "no-learning" condition, in which subjects are administered the classification phase followed by the generation task, without any study phase; and (3) the "inverse" condition, in which subjects are administered the study phase followed immediately by the generation task and, finally, the classification phase. If performance in the generation task is due to information learned during the study phase, and if, at the same time, the presentation of the non-grammatical classification items has some kind of detrimental effect on the generation task, there should be a difference between the three conditions, the better performance in the generation task being observed for subjects in the inverse condition and the worse performance by subjects in the no-learning condition. On the other hand, if the classification items have no effect, there should be no difference between the inverse condition and the standard condition. And, finally, there is another possibility, which is based on the idea that the explicit knowledge elicited by the generation task concerns only bigrams and trigrams (chunks; see Meulemans & Van der Linden, 1997). If this is the case, the classification items could have a positive effect on this chunk knowledge because classification items, whether grammatical or not, are all composed of legal chunks. In this perspective, the advantage in the generation task could be in favour of the standard condition.

The task was administered to 60 university undergraduates. Grammatical and non-grammatical test items were similar according to different chunk strength measures, so that it would be impossible to classify these items simply on the basis of a superficial knowledge about bigrams and trigrams (see Peigneux, Meulemans, Van der Linden, Salmon, & Petit, 1999, for a precise description of the material used).

After the study phase, in which subjects had to memorise 51 grammatical strings (generated by the finite-state grammar shown in Figure 6.1), they were administered either the classification phase (standard condition) or the generation task (inverse condition). In the no-learning condition, subjects were administered the classification phase followed by the generation task, without any preliminary study phase. In the classification task, subjects were asked to classify new items (12 grammatical and 12 non-grammatical) as grammatical or not. The series of test items was presented twice in the same predetermined random order.

With regard to the classification task, results indicate that the endorsement-rate difference between grammatical and non-grammatical items was significant only for the standard condition. This shows that

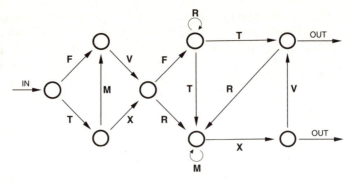

Figure 6.1.   The finite-state grammar used in the experiment described in the text.

subjects who had to classify grammatical and non-grammatical letter-strings either after the generation task or without any preliminary learning phase, could not discriminate between the two types of items.

Results of the generation task show that subjects in the no-learning condition are significantly worse than those in the standard condition with regard to the mean number of grammatical strings generated (0.1 vs. 0.7). The same analysis was conducted on the number of generated strings that correspond either to a learning item or to a classification item. With regard to the generated items corresponding to a learning item, subjects in the no-learning condition produced significantly fewer learning items than subjects in the two other conditions (0.05 vs. 0.42 for the inverse condition and 0.6 for the standard condition). On the other hand, there was no condition effect on the number of generated items corresponding to a classification item. This means that subjects who were administered the generation task after the classification task (the standard and no-learning conditions) did not generate more classification items than those who did the generation task before the classification task (the inverse condition). Another way to analyse the results in the generation task is based on the assumption that the information learned in artificial grammar learning tasks concerns mainly bigrams and trigrams (chunks). Using this perspective, we analysed the generated items with respect to their "chunk strength", that is, the frequency of their chunks in the learning items. Results show that the letter-strings generated by the subjects in the standard and inverse conditions, that is, the conditions in which the study phase was administered, contain significantly more frequent chunks (and fewer novel chunks) than the letter strings generated by the subjects in the no-learning condition, suggesting that subjects had actually learned something from the study phase.

With regard to the generation task, one could also hypothesise that subjects in the standard condition learned both from the study phase and the classification test. This is all the more possible given that the classification items actually contained no illegal chunk; so, the classification task could have reinforced the chunk knowledge of the subjects in the standard condition. On the other hand, if this is true, there could be no difference between the performance of subjects in the inverse condition and in the no-learning condition because, in both these conditions, subjects were confronted with about the same number of grammatical items before being administered the generation task (51 learning items for subjects in the inverse condition, 48 classification items for subjects in the no-learning condition). To investigate this point, we compared the chunk strength of the letter-strings generated by the subjects in the no-learning and inverse conditions. We calculated the chunk strength with reference to the items seen by the subjects before the generation task, that is, for subjects in the no-learning condition, the classification items, and, for subjects in the inverse condition, the learning items. If, in the procedure of the artificial grammar learning task, the knowledge elicited in the generation task depends directly on information learned during the study phase, then subjects in the inverse condition (who were administered a study phase) should show better performance levels in the generation task than subjects in the no-learning condition (who were not administered a study phase). On the other hand, if the subjects' knowledge comes simply from the letter-strings that they have seen just before (whether these items belonged to the study phase or classification task), they should show similar performance levels. In this latter case, the relevance and the validity of the generation task should be questioned. The results of these comparisons (t-tests) are clear-cut: subjects in the inverse condition performed significantly better than subjects in the no-learning condition.

Finally, no correlation was found between the performance in the classification task and the performance in the generation task for both the groups in the standard and the inverse conditions.

To summarise, results of this first experiment showed that the only condition in which subjects were able to classify grammatical and non-grammatical items was the standard condition, that is, the condition in which the classification task followed the study phase. With regard to the generation task, our results show that the best performance levels are reached by subjects in the standard and inverse conditions, while subjects in the no-learning condition performed worse. This suggests that the generation task is actually sensitive to information learned during the study phase, and that this knowledge is not modified by the presentation of the classification items.

Experiment 2

The purpose of this second experiment was to explore the implicit learning abilities in a group of amnesic patients with the same material as in

Experiment 1, that is, a material constructed in such a way that it is impossible to differentiate grammatical and non-grammatical letter-strings on the basis of a simple knowledge of bigrams and trigrams.

Nine amnesic patients (four Korsakoff patients, three head-injury patients, one patient who had suffered a ruptured aneurysm of the anterior communicating artery [ACoA], and one patient who had suffered from anoxia), aged from 33 to 61, were tested, as well as nine normal subjects, matched for age and education.

The procedure was the same as that of the standard condition in Experiment 1: the study phase, followed by the classification task, and finally the generation task.

Results in the classification task showed that the percentage of grammatical strings classified by the amnesic patients as being grammatical was 69.0% (SE_M = 4.8%), and the percentage of non-grammatical strings classified as being grammatical was 61.6% (SE_M = 4.9%); normal subjects classified as grammatical 67.1% (SE_M = 3.4%) of the grammatical items and 57.9% (SE_M = 4.5%) of the non-grammatical items. An ANOVA with Group (amnesic patients versus normal subjects) as the between-subject variable and Grammaticality (grammatical versus non-grammatical) as repeated measure factor showed no Group effect, $F(1, 16)$ = 0.30, MS_e = 228.95, $p > .50$, and a significant effect of Grammaticality, $F(1, 16)$ = 5.31, MS_e = 117.79, $p < .05$, indicating that the subjects could discriminate between grammatical and non-grammatical items, and no Group × Grammaticality interaction, $F(1, 16)$ = 0.07, MS_e = 117.79, $p > .80$, showing that the Grammaticality effect was similar in both groups.

With regard to the generation task, normal subjects produced on average less than one grammatical item; no grammatical item was produced by the patients. For the normal subjects, there was no correlation between the percentage of correct responses in the classification task and the number of grammatical strings written in the generation task ($r = -.17$).

We also analysed the letter-strings produced by the subjects in the generation task with regard to their chunk strength. There was a significant difference between the two groups for all of the chunk-strength measures: amnesic patients always performed worse than normal subjects. Moreover, no correlation was found between these measures and the percentage of correct responses in the classification task.

To summarise, the main result of this second experiment is the absence of Group effect in the grammaticality judgement task, a result showing that amnesic patients were able to classify grammatical and non-grammatical items as well as normal subjects. With regard to the generation task, the better performance of the normal subjects reinforces the interpretation that we suggested of the results of our first experiment: not only is the generation task sensitive to information learned during the study phase, but it can actually be considered as a valid explicit memory task. Indeed, the dissociation between the implicit classification task and the explicit generation task, in addition to the absence of correlation between performance in both tasks, is compatible with the idea that the two tasks tap different kinds of knowledge.

CONCLUSION

The main result of our Experiment 2 is that amnesic patients could perform at the same level as normal subjects in the implicit classification task. This confirms previous results obtained by Knowlton and Squire (1994, 1996), as well as the conclusions of studies that have used the serial reaction time paradigm (e.g. Reber & Squire, 1994): amnesic patients show preserved implicit learning abilities, and these preserved abilities concern not only simple associations between elements but also more complex conditional associations. Another result of our study was that normal subjects performed better than amnesic patients in the generation task. This result is important because it suggests that the generation task constitutes a sensitive measure of the subjects' explicit knowledge in artificial grammar learning tasks.

Knowlton and Squire (1996) suggested that bigram and trigram knowledge underlies the classification performance in artificial grammar learning and, because their amnesic patients could classify grammatical and non-grammatical items normally, they argued that this knowledge could be considered as being implicit. However, with regard to our study, because grammatical and non-grammatical test items did not differ according to their chunk strength characteristics, and because amnesic patients and normal subjects were able to classify these items, their performance in the classification task does not seem to have been determined by a knowledge (whether implicit or explicit) based on chunks.

We suggest that, both in the Knowlton and Squire study and in the present experiment, classification performance was not determined by a knowledge about chunks but rather by the intervention of simple associative mechanisms that permitted the learning of the regularities present in the study material. Our results are compatible with the idea that, in artificial grammar learning tasks, two types of mechanism intervene in parallel (at least in normal subjects): a first mechanism, which is implicit and based on associative processes (like those put forward in connectionist models; e.g. Cleeremans, 1993), underlies the performance in the classification task and is preserved in amnesia; and a second mechanism, resulting from the initial cutting off of the letter strings into bigrams and trigrams, permits the explicit recall of these chunks (in the normal subject). In our study, because of the constraints imposed on the construction of the test material, this mechanism could not play a role in the classification task.

More generally, it now seems reasonable to assert that amnesic patients, despite their profound deficit in episodic memory, show preserved implicit learning abilities. This is consistent with results obtained in studies that have shown that severely amnesic patients are able to acquire new factual (semantic) information after the onset of their amnesia (Vargha-Khadem et al., 1997; Van der Linden et al., 1996, 2001). Other striking evidence suggesting a dissociation between intact implicit (unconscious) learning and defective explicit memory have been obtained in a recent study we conducted in patients with Alzheimer's disease (Meulemans, Dehon, Vinter, Perruchet, & Van der Linden, 1999) by using a method consisting of inducing a behavioural change in the way subjects drew simple geometric figures. This method rests on the "start rotation principle" (SRP), according to which, when subjects have to draw geometric figures (like a circle or a square), they have a strong (but unconscious) tendency to draw clockwise when the starting point is in the inferior part of the figure, and counterclockwise when the starting point is in the superior part of the figure. Vinter and Perruchet (1999) have shown that, through an appropriate training, it is possible to reverse the expression of this principle, with the subjects remaining totally unaware of this change. Vinter and Perruchet argued that one of the advantages of this method is that, contrary to other implicit learning paradigms, it avoids the influence of strategic effects on the subjects' performance because it targets a behaviour that is not the subject of a controlled decision. We administered this task to eight patients with Alzheimer's disease and to eight matched control subjects. Our results showed normal performance levels in Alzheimer's patients, suggesting that implicit learning abilities, assessed by the SRP paradigm, might be preserved in Alzheimer's disease, at least in its mild and moderate stages. This result adds to the studies described above on amnesic patients, most of them confirming that implicit learning abilities are preserved despite a severe impairment of the explicit learning abilities.

REFERENCES

Cermak, L.S., Lewis, S., Butters, N., & Goodglass, H. (1973). Role of verbal mediation in performance of motor tasks by Korsakoff patients. *Perceptual and Motor Skills, 37*, 259–262.

Chun, M.M., & Phelps, E.A. (1999). Memory deficits for implicit contextual information in amnesic subjects with hippocampal damage, *Nature Neuroscience, 2*(9), 844–847.

Cleeremans, A. (1993). *Mechanisms of implicit learning: Connectionist models of sequence processing.* Cambridge, MA: MIT Press.

Curran, T. (1995). On the neural mechanisms of sequence learning. *Psyche, 2*(12) [On-line]. Available http: //psyche.cs.monash.edu.au/volume2-1/psyche-95-2-12-sequence-1-curran.html

Curran, T. (1997). Higher-order associative learning in amnesia: Evidence from the serial reaction time task. *Journal of Cognitive Neuroscience, 9*, 522–533.

Dienes, Z., Altmann, G.T.M., Kwan, L., & Goode, A. (1995). Unconscious knowledge of artificial grammars is applied strategically. *Journal of Experimental Psychology: Learning, Memory, and Cognition, 21*, 1322–1338.

Dienes, Z., Broadbent, D., & Berry, D.C. (1991). Implicit and explicit knowledge bases in artificial grammar learning. *Journal of Experimental Psychology: Learning, Memory, and Cognition, 17*, 875–887.

Gabrieli, J.D.E., Cohen, N.J., & Corkin, S. (1983). Acquisition of semantic and lexical knowledge in amnesia. *Society for Neurosciences Abstracts, 9*, 28.

Gabrieli, J.D.E., Cohen, N.J., & Corkin, S. (1988). The impaired learning of semantic knowledge following bilateral medial temporal-lobe resection. *Brain and Cognition, 7*, 157–177.

Glisky, E.L., Schacter, D.L., & Tulving, E. (1986). Learning and retention of computer-related vocabulary in memory-impaired patients: Method of vanishing cues. *Journal of Clinical and Experimental Neuropsychology, 8*, 292–312.

Hamann, S.B., & Squire, L.R. (1995). On the acquisition of new declarative knowledge in amnesia. *Behavioral Neuroscience, 109*, 1027–1044.

Hayman, C.A.G., MacDonald, C.A., & Tulving, E. (1993). The role of repetition and associative interference in new semantic learning in amnesia: A case experiment. *Journal of Cognitive Neuroscience, 5*, 375–389.

Howell, D.C. (1982). *Statistical methods for psychology*. Boston: PWS-Kent.

Kitchener, E.G., Hodges, J.R., & McCarthy, R. (1998). Acquisition of post-morbid vocabulary and semantic facts in the absence of episodic memory. *Brain, 121*, 1313–1327.

Knowlton, B.J., Ramus, S.J., & Squire, L.R. (1992). Intact artificial grammar learning in amnesia: Dissociation of classification learning and explicit memory for specific instances. *Psychological Science, 3*, 172–179.

Knowlton, B.J., & Squire, L.R. (1994). The information acquired during artificial grammar learning. *Journal of Experimental Psychology: Learning, Memory, and Cognition, 20*, 79–91.

Knowlton, B.J., & Squire, L.R. (1996). Artificial grammar learning depends on implicit acquisition of both abstract and exemplar-specific information. *Journal of Experimental Psychology: Learning, Memory, and Cognition, 22*(4), 169–181.

Mayes, A.R. (1988). *Human organic memory disorders*. Cambridge: Cambridge University Press.

Mayes, A.R. (1998). Neuropsychology of memory and amnesia. In M.A. Ron & A.S. David (Eds.), *Disorders of brain and mind* (pp. 125–146). Cambridge: Cambridge University Press.

McClelland, J.L., McNaughton, B.L., & O'Reilly, R.C. (1995). Why there are complementary learning systems in the hippocampus and neocortex: Insights from the successes and failures of connectionist models of learning and memory. *Psychological Review, 102*(3), 419–457.

Meulemans, T., Dehon, H., Vinter, A., Perruchet, P., & Van der Linden, M. (1999, May). *Exploration des capacités d'apprentissage implicite dans la maladie d'Alzheimer avec le paradigme du Start-Rotation Principle (SRP)* [Exploration of implicit learning abilities in Alzheimer's disease with the Start-Rotation Principle (SRP) paradigm]. Paper presented at the meeting of the Société de Neuropsychologie de Langue Française, Saint-Etienne, France.

Meulemans, T., & Van der Linden, M. (1997). Associative chunk strength in artificial grammar learning. *Journal of Experimental Psychology: Learning, Memory, and Cognition, 23*, 1007–1028.

Moscovitch, M. (1994). Memory and working memory: Evaluation of a component process model and comparisons with other models. In D.L. Schacter & E. Tulving (Eds.), *Memory systems 1994*. Cambridge, MA: Bradford Books/MIT Press.

Nissen, M.J., & Bullemer, P. (1987). Attentional requirements of learning: Evidence from performance measures. *Cognitive Psychology, 19*, 1–32.

Nissen, M.J., Willingham, D., & Hartman, M. (1989). Explicit and implicit remembering: When is learning preserved in amnesia? *Neuropsychologia, 27*, 341–352.

Peigneux, P., Meulemans, T., Van der Linden, M., Salmon, E., & Petit, H. (1999). Exploration of implicit artificial grammar learning in Parkinson's disease. *Acta Neurologica Belgica, 99*(2), 107–117.

Perruchet, P., & Pacteau, C. (1990). Synthetic grammar learning: Implicit rule abstraction or explicit fragmentary knowledge? *Journal of Experimental Psychology: General, 119*, 264–275.

Reber, A.S. (1989). Implicit learning and tacit knowledge. *Journal of Experimental Psychology: General, 118*, 219–235.

Reber, A.S. (1993). *Implicit learning and tacit knowledge: An essay on the cognitive unconscious.* New York: Oxford University Press.

Reber, A.S., & Lewis, S. (1977). Implicit learning: An analysis of the form and structure of a body of tacit knowledge. *Cognition, 5*, 333–361.

Reber, P.J., & Squire, L.R. (1994). Parallel brain systems for learning with and without awareness. *Learning & Memory, 1*, 217–229.

Reber, P.J., & Squire, L.R. (1998). Encapsulation of implicit and explicit memory in sequence learning. *Journal of Cognitive Neuroscience, 10*, 248–263.

Schacter, D.L. (1994). Priming and multiple memory systems: Perceptual mechanisms of implicit memory. In D.L. Schacter & E. Tulving (Eds.), *Memory Systems 1994* (pp. 233–268). Cambridge, MA: Bradford Books/MIT Press.

Schacter, D.L., & Tulving, E. (1994). What are the memory systems of 1994? In D.L. Schacter & E. Tulving (Eds.), *Memory systems 1994*. Cambridge: Bradford Books/MIT Press.

Shanks, D.R., & Johnstone, T. (1997). Implicit knowledge in sequential learning tasks. In M.I. Stadler & P.A. French (Eds.), *Handbook of implicit learning* (pp. 533–572). Thousand Oaks, CA: Sage Publications.

Shanks, D.R., & St. John, M.F. (1994). Characteristics of dissociable human learning systems. *Behavioral and Brain Sciences, 17*, 367–447.

Soliveri, P., Brown, R.G., Jahanshahi, M., & Marsden, C.D. (1992). Procedural memory and neurological disease. *European Journal of Cognitive Psychology, 4*, 161–193.

Squire, L.R. (1992). Memory and the hippocampus: A synthesis from findings with rats, monkeys, and humans. *Psychological Review, 2*, 195–231.

Squire, L.R. (1994). Declarative and nondeclarative memory: multiple brain systems supporting learning and memory. In D.L. Schacter & E. Tulving (Eds.), *Memory systems.* Cambridge, MA: Bradford Books/MIT Press.

Squire, L.R., & Frambach, M. (1990). Cognitive skill learning in amnesia. *Psychobiology, 18*, 109–117.

Squire, L.R., & Zola, S.M. (1998). Episodic memory, semantic memory, and amnesia. *Hippocampus, 8*, 205–211.

Tulving, E. (1995). Organization of memory: Quo vadis? In M.S. Gazzaniga (Ed.), *The cognitive neurosciences* (pp. 839–847). Cambridge, MA: MIT Press.

Tulving, E., & Markowitsch, H.J. (1998). Episodic memory and declarative memory: Role of the hippocampus. *Hippocampus, 8*, 198–204.

Van der Linden, M. (1994). Neuropsychologie de la mémoire [Neuropsychology of memory]. In X. Seron & M. Jeannerod (Eds.), *Neuropsychologie humaine* (pp. 282–316). Liège, Belgium: Mardaga.

Van der Linden, M., Brédart, S., Depoorter, N., & Coyette, F. (1996). Semantic memory and amnesia: A case study. *Cognitive Neuropsychology, 13*(3), 391–413.

Van der Linden, M., Cornil, V., Meulemans, T., Ivanoiu, A., Salmon, E., & Coyette, F. (2001). Acquisition of a novel vocabulary in an amnesic patient. *Neurocase, 7,* 283–293.

Van der Linden, M., & Coyette, F. (1995). Acquisition of word processing knowledge in an amnesic patient: Implications for theory and rehabilitation. In R. Campbell & M. Conway (Eds.), *Broken memories: Neuropsychological case studies* (pp. 54–80). Oxford: Blackwell.

Van der Linden, M., Meulemans, T., & Lorrain, D. (1994). Acquisition of new concepts by two amnesic patients. *Cortex, 30,* 305–317.

Vargha-Khadem, F., Gadian, D.G., Watkins, K.E., Connelly, A., Van Paesschen, W., & Mishkin, M. (1997). Differential effects of early hippocampal pathology on episodic and semantic memory. *Science, 277,* 376–380.

Verfaellie, M., Croce, P., & Milberg, W.P. (1995). The role of episodic memory in semantic learning: An examination of vocabulary acquisition in a patient with amnesia due to encephalitis. *Neurocase, 1,* 291–304.

Vinter, A, & Perruchet, P. (1999). Evidencing unconscious influences: The neutral parameter procedure. *Quarterly Journal of Experimental Psychology, 52A*(4), 857–875.

Whittlesea, B.W.A., & Dorken, M.D. (1993). Incidentally, things in general are particularly determined: An episodic-processing account of implicit learning. *Journal of Experimental Psychology: General, 122,* 227–248.

Author index

Subject index